Lessons from a Diplomatic Life

走馬觀花

Lessons from a Diplomatic Life

Watching Flowers from Horseback

Marshall P. Adair

ROWMAN & LITTLEFIELD PUBLISHERS, INC.
Lanham • Boulder • New York • Toronto • Plymouth, UK

Published by Rowman & Littlefield Publishers, Inc.
A wholly owned subsidiary of The Rowman & Littlefield Publishing Group, Inc.
4501 Forbes Boulevard, Suite 200, Lanham, Maryland 20706
www.rowman.com

10 Thornbury Road, Plymouth PL6 7PP, United Kingdom

British Library Cataloguing in Publication Information Available

Library of Congress Cataloging-in-Publication Data

Adair, Marshall Porter, 1948-
Lessons from a diplomatic life : watching flowers from horseback / Marshall Porter Adair.
p. cm.
Includes bibliographical references and index.
ISBN 978-1-4422-2080-5 (cloth : alk. paper) -- ISBN 978-1-4422-2081-2 (electronic)
1. Diplomats--United States--Biography. 2. United States. Foreign Service--Biography. 3. United
States--Foreign relations. I. Adair, Marshall Porter, 1948- II. Title.
E840.8.A33 2012
327.730092--dc23

2012045158

The design in the center of the front cover is a "mola", made by the women of the Kuna
people on the San Blas islands off the north coast of Panama. This particular design is a
copy of the Great Seal of the United States, which was made for and presented to Ambassador Charles W. Adair, Jr. in the late 1960's. The author spent a month in a Kuna village
in 1966.

The paper used in this publication meets the minimum requirements of American National
Standard for Information Sciences Permanence of Paper for Printed Library Materials,
ANSI/NISO Z39.48-1992.

Printed in the United States of America

Dedicated to
Zen Master Nan Huai-Chin
1918-2012

Contents

Preface

Watching Flowers from Horseback

This book is a retrospective—albeit incomplete—on fifty-five years of life and work in the U.S. Foreign Service. The sub-title is based on a Chinese literary expression that translates literally as "Ride-Horse-Watch-Flowers" (走馬觀花). It is an idiom that generally means "to make a hasty judgment." It is also a kind of warning that observing phenomena from a distance while passing through can lead one to superficial or incorrect judgments. From horseback one can't see the individual flowers well, smell their fragrance, or understand how they are put together. One can't really see and understand an object unless one slows down and gets up close.

It is an appropriate reminder for diplomats. We spend our lives traveling through the world observing other nations and trying to understand and appreciate the cultivation of their cultures. We watch to see what might benefit or threaten our own culture, and we then make recommendations to our government about how our nation should conduct its relations with those other nations. Depending on our government's instructions, we then exchange flowers and cultivation techniques—and we may even interfere in the cultivation of others.

The understanding that diplomats develop and the recommendations they make are critical to actions their governments decide to take, so the depth of that understanding and the accuracy of those recommendations are important. It is a challenge to the individuals who serve and the government that prepares them for that service.

Of course, there can also be some advantages to observing from horseback. The height and the distance give one perspective. One can see a broader field of flowers and see how they fit with the surrounding landscape—and one can avoid the discomfort or danger of getting up close (allergies, bugs, predators). The people who serve in the American Foreign Service usually don't just ride through. We dismount and we stay for a while—usually longer than our fellow citizens from the private sector or other parts of the government. We learn more about those cultures by virtue of our presence than do many of our compatriots; but we also have to remember that we can't eliminate the distance. We stay for years rather than for decades. We are government officials protected from many of the inconveniences and dangers commonplace to permanent residents of those cultures. Sometimes we are intentionally kept isolated by our hosts from those cultures—and occasionally we isolate ourselves. We must put together the best possible picture and provide the best possible analysis, but we must recognize that it will always be incomplete.

***

My father, Charles Wallace Adair Jr., was born in the year of the "Great War"—1914—and grew up in the small midwestern town of Xenia, Ohio. His parents impressed upon all five of their sons the importance of serving both community and nation. Four of them did military service in the European or Pacific theaters during World War II and then returned to live and work in Ohio. My father joined the U.S. Foreign Service (which almost no one else in Xenia had heard of) before World War II, and he stuck with it for thirty-five years. He and my mother, Caroline Lee Marshall, who joined him for twenty-five of those years, believed the United States was the greatest force for good in the world, and they proudly dedicated their lives to serving it.

Raised in a diplomatic environment, I became accustomed to living in different cultures—and to being always a foreigner. I inherited my father's pride of country, but in a different time and from a different perspective. Growing up in European and Latin American cultures, my pride was tempered by the perspectives of my friends in those cultures, and eventually by the concern that my country might do as much harm as good. Driven by the latter, I experimented briefly with international service at the United Nations, but I soon concluded that the U.S. government was still the best master to serve to make a difference. I, too, spent thirty-five years in the Foreign Service, twenty-five of them with my wife, Ginger. She had yet another perspective on the world, having been born and raised in Taiwan.

A year before I retired from the Foreign Service, I was very surprised to discover that my mother's father had also served this country as a diplomat—during and after World War I. I had barely known my grandfather, since he died when I was very young, and neither of my parents had ever mentioned that service to me. It is possible that they never knew, since it happened before my mother was born. A banker by profession, during the war Hugh Dow Marshall became associated with the Department of State's Far East Bureau, and he took part in the Paris Peace Conference addressing financial issues related to China. In the same time frame, his future wife, Adelaide Morrison Porter, left her father's farm in Black Mountain, North Carolina, and made her way to France, where she served as a nurse until the war ended.

So, my family has now given three generations of service to this country beyond its borders. We have encouraged our son, Charles, to serve; and Ginger has advocated the Foreign Service. Remembering my own ambivalence about growing up in a diplomatic environment, I have avoided actively proselytizing my son—though I think he would be very good at my profession. So far, Charles seems to be shifting the focus back home, studying economics and environmental policy at the College of William and Mary and Duke University and putting that education to work in North Carolina, not far from the town that his great-grandmother left during World War I.

***

This book is about my experience in government service overseas. I was encouraged to write it first because my father did not record his experience, and I wished that he had. He served during a critically formative period in our nation's history. Working in Asia, Latin America, and Europe, and laboring on the foundations of multilateral and international organizations like NATO, GATT, and the OECD, he had ample opportunity to appreciate both wisdom gained and wisdom ignored by our species.

He was twice an ambassador and rose to the personal rank of minister, the Foreign Service's second-highest career level. His career was very successful, and he was greatly admired. He didn't keep a diary, because he feared it might fall into the wrong hands. He limited the knowledge he shared with his wife and children, thinking that if *we* fell into the wrong hands, the less we knew the safer we would be. During the Cold War, the first concern was probably justified. Toward the end of his career, when he was ambassador to Uruguay during the Tupamaro urban guerilla campaign, the latter concern may also have been justified. However, not long before he died, he confided to Ginger that one of his regrets was not having kept a record or shared more of his work with his family. While I spent much of my life challenging the wisdom he offered to me, I did not challenge that particular lesson. I have shared more of my professional life with my family than he did with me, but still not enough. This book attempts to rectify that.

I would not actually have written it, however, without another source of encouragement. After spending several years in Hong Kong and Beijing,

Ginger and I had the good fortune to meet, in the United States, an extraordinary scholar of Chinese history, philosophy, and politics, who was also a Zen master. Born early in the twentieth century in Zhejiang Province, Nan Huai-Chin received an extensive classical Chinese education. As a young general in Chiang Kai-shek's army, he was involved with the effort in Sichuan Province to oppose the Japanese invasion; he then studied with Buddhist and Taoist masters in China and Tibet. At the end of China's civil war he moved to Taiwan, where he taught at several universities, established a cultural institute, and began publishing his own books, which have now sold a couple million volumes. He moved back to China at the beginning of this century, and established the Taihu Centre for Great Learning west of Shanghai. It is dedicated to reintroducing to the Chinese people the knowledge and wisdom developed over the course of China's five-thousand-year history, and to stimulating an exchange and synergy with other current and past world cultures.

Over the years we have visited him regularly in Hong Kong and Shanghai, where he has guided us in spiritual cultivation and helped me better understand the historical and intellectual underpinnings of Chinese policies. As I prepared to retire from the Foreign Service, he encouraged me to write an account of what I had seen and experienced in the course of fifty years of diplomatic life, expressing the hope that it might help promote understanding between Western and Eastern cultures in the years ahead. I hope that in some small way this book may do that.

***

Diplomacy in general, and American diplomacy in particular, is not well understood within the borders of the United States of America. In my experience traveling around the United States, many (perhaps most) Americans don't even know that the United States has a professional diplomatic service. Headquartered in the Department of State, one of the smallest federal departments, the U.S. Foreign Service is one of the smallest professional services in the U.S. government, employing less than ten thousand Americans.

Watching my parents and others while growing up, I saw what I thought were many flaws and weaknesses in the Foreign Service. Foreign Service officers seemed to be so careful about what they said—even careful about what they thought! While committed to tolerance of other cultures, they also seemed to be extraordinarily bound by conventional wisdom. Thirty-five years of work as a Foreign Service officer myself confirmed some of those youthful observations. However, I came to believe that what Winston Churchill said about democracy—that it was the worst form of government except for all the others—could also be applied to the Foreign Service as compared with other federal government services.

Today, I am convinced that of all the agencies and services of the government dealing with foreign affairs—including the military—none is more qualified, competent, dedicated, or effective than the State Department's Foreign Service. With the possible exception of the CIA, none subject their people more regularly over the course of a career to more risks in unfamiliar environments—including the military. Foreign Service personnel don't just go overseas to dangerous places for six months at a time. They go for two to four years at a time. They go with their families, who share the benefits and the hardships. They do not live on bases like their military counterparts, and they live only rarely in protected compounds. They mostly live in ordinary houses in ordinary neighborhoods. They are advised on how to take precautions, but more often than not, they live and serve beyond the U.S. government's umbrella of protection.

***

Henry Kissinger, the most high-profile and flamboyant American diplomat of our time, wrote an impressive book that describes the high-stakes, strategic diplomacy of nation-states. However, most Americans forget that diplomacy is not just the strategic maneuvering of presidents, secretaries of state, or even ambassadors. It is also work that is being carried on by far less high-profile and less exciting people operating beneath the media radar screen, working on issues that usually don't get the attention of the average citizen or even the average student.

Sometimes those issues are hardly of interest to anyone—because they have not yet become problems. There is a very important element of diplomacy between nations that is directed at preventing situations from becoming problems that might threaten us in the future. Usually, it is directed overseas. For as long as I have been in the Foreign Service, American ambassadors have been beseeching Washington (both the executive and legislative branches) to provide more resources for economic development, cultural exchanges, or other things not on the immediate priority lists of American politicians or taxpayers. It is also directed at ourselves, trying to prevent different elements of our own nation from doing things in pursuit of one interest that may damage other more important interests down the road. Our export controls on advanced technology and weapons systems are one well-known example—trying to curb the profit imperative of the American defense industry is not easy. Nor is it easy to discipline our proclivity to pontificate on issues important to other domestic interest groups—or our principled interest in the protection of human rights which, admirable as it is, can sometimes cause us and even those we are trying to help more harm than good.

American diplomats are charged with building relationships of trust and understanding with officials and citizens of other nations that can help us to better understand the factors at work in other nations, to prevent future misunderstandings, or to make us more effective in finding mutual solutions to problems when they do arise. This effort is not restricted to the men and women earning salaries paid by American taxpayers. Their families are important players as well.

When I was a child, it often seemed to me that my mother was busier than my father. During the day she was constantly calling on the spouses of other diplomats or government officials and participating in a variety of social and educational events—as well as tending to the business of running a home and educating her children in a foreign environment. She knew the families of the people my father worked with, and she added a perspective that he might not otherwise have achieved. He relied heavily on her. My father used to remind me and my two younger sisters that we, too, were in those countries as representatives of America, and that people would judge our country by our behavior. That is a pretty heavy message for a six-year-old.

When I was stationed in Asia, Ginger was able to establish more comfortable, lower-profile relationships during sensitive times than was I. She was much better than I at reading the indirect messages that we would get from the vast array of officials on whom our affairs depended, and I would seek her perspective on initiatives that I wanted to undertake. Even our five-year-old son Charles contributed, opening doors and taking us into places and circumstances that we would not have thought of otherwise.

***

My eighty-year-old neighbor in New Hampshire, Bob Peckett, is fond of saying, "If I don't learn something new every day, I'm just not listening." One of the best things about a career in the Foreign Service is being thrust every day into situations where we can't help but learn more about the human condition and the multiplicity of ways that people and cultures deal with it. One of the most frustrating things about a career in the Foreign Service is being reminded that so many Americans see little relevance to their own lives in that exposure.

While graced with a homeland that is relatively rich and secure, we twenty-first-century Americans are not alone in this world. Compared to many other nations, we are very young—adolescent at most. We have much to learn from people and cultures that have grown and flourished—or just survived—in circumstances different from our own. We will likely have to cope with similar circumstances ourselves in the future.

If we see ourselves primarily as benefactors or purveyors of political and economic wisdom, we imperil ourselves and others. The experience or values of other cultures may not appear relevant to today's concerns in New Hampshire, Alabama, Idaho, or Ohio, but we ignore them at our peril. The world changes faster than most of us are prepared to believe. Few thought in the 1970s that within a few decades the Soviet Union would collapse, that the United States would essentially change places with it in Afghanistan, or that "Communist" China would become an economic superpower.

***

In writing this account of my overseas experiences, I have chosen to make an important compromise. The most interesting aspect of most human activity is the individual person. In diplomacy, this is certainly true. Insights into personalities who have shaped major events are both fascinating and helpful. Unfortunately, in many of the places where I have served, being mentioned by name in a foreign publication, positively or negatively, can have serious consequences, not just for the individuals but for their families and others. Therefore, with only a few exceptions (mostly Americans, who are still relatively safe from persecution), I have chosen not to identify people by name.

***

I am deeply grateful for the help, advice, and patient support of many friends and family members in this endeavor. In particular, my wife, Ginger, who shared most of the experiences described here, played as critical a role in conceiving and finishing this book as she did throughout our time in the Foreign Service together.

***

The opinions and characterizations in this book are my own. They do not necessarily represent official positions of the U.S. government.

Chapter One

First Assignment: Paris (August 1972–June 1974)

"How would you like to go to Paris?"

When new recruits to the U.S. Foreign Service take the oath of allegiance to serve their country and then receive their presidential appointments, they sign up to a basic agreement that they will serve anywhere in the world, according to the "needs of the Service." That means wherever the Department of State determines their presence is necessary for the conduct of the nation's diplomacy. In 1972, the twenty or so members of my entering class awaited with considerable trepidation the unveiling of the list of posts to which they could be sent for the next two or three years of their lives. We ranged in age from twenty-one to our mid-thirties. Some were married: some were single. Some had already traveled extensively, and some had barely left home. Most were ready for adventure—and most would have considered Paris the ultimate adventure. When the list came, the posts ranged from Fort Lamy, a former French Foreign Legion post in the Sahel just south of the Sahara desert, to Edinburgh, Scotland—and Paris.

Candidates for the Foreign Service must pass written and oral examinations, undergo a security background check, and pass a physical examination to ensure availability for worldwide service. They are assigned to a substantive "cone" based on the results of their exams and their previous experience. In the early 1970s those cones included political, economic, consular, and administrative. Once those processes have been completed the candidates go onto a waiting list until the Department of State has sufficient positions and funding to bring them on duty. In principle, once on that waiting list the individual has made it. However, Washington's budgetary politics can drag things out, and some never make it. In my case, I was accepted into the economic cone and then waited for over a year before being assigned to an entering class in May 1972.

In 1972 virtually all Foreign Service officers were sent overseas for their first assignment. However, before that, they would spend two to three months together at the Foreign Service Institute (FSI), being introduced to the basics of government service and the mysteries of the Department of State through FSI's A-100 course. This included taking classes in cross-cultural communication and consular law, being tested for language proficiency, and so forth. In our case, we were about halfway through this process before we began to focus on our individual assignments.

We were told we would be presented with a list of overseas positions available to newly commissioned officers and given the opportunity to offer our preferences. These preferences would be "considered" in meeting the "needs of the Service." This evoked considerable excitement and apprehension, and there was a good deal of joking about who would be consigned to the outer limits of nowhere. It wasn't a joke for me, though. Being single and one of the youngest members of our twenty-four-member class, the outer limits were exactly where I wanted to go. I thought that Fort Lamy would be a great adventure.

So, when the director of our course so generously offered me one of the Foreign Service's plum positions for a new officer, he presented it more as a rhetorical question than one requiring an answer.

"How would you like to go to Paris?"

"No. Thank you, but I've already been there."

I imagine that if any of my classmates had been in the room with me at that time that would have confirmed for them what they were growing to suspect: I was too young; I was too naive—and now, I was quite possibly insane. But I was serious. I had been there, and—I thought—done that. I was thirteen when my father, a Foreign Service officer, was assigned to the Organisation for Economic Co-operation and Development (OECD), whose headquarters were in Paris's swank sixteenth arrondissement. I spent my early adolescent years in the city and the culture that made sex into a cultural, social, and even political art form, and I adored it (all of the above). No city in the world could ever surpass the impact Paris made on me at the most impressionable point in my life (second most impressionable, if you include birth). However, in 1972 I had steeled myself for the most backward, out-of-the-way, threatening place on earth, and I was not prepared to allow anyone to entice me out of it. The director was more than a little surprised. He explained that they needed someone right away, and that I was the only person in the class who fit the needs at that time (French language and economics). Then he suggested gently that I think about it a little.

As I left his office, I realized I had just contravened both of two principles which I had envisaged would guide this experimental foray into the institution to which my father had committed himself and his family for the previous thirty-five years. First, my father had often said to me that he believed we should take whatever came to us, Foreign Service assignments included, and make the best of it. This was not just to be stoic, though that was pretty high on his value scale, but because he believed there are reasons for everything that comes our way. Most of us are not smart enough or wise enough to recognize those reasons, and we should be flexible enough to adjust to what we are thrown into. My father was an elegant, gracious, honorable, and very successful American diplomat. I admired and respected him—and fought tooth and nail with him for at least half of the first twenty-two years of my life over every conceivable issue from table manners to the Vietnam War. However, this particular bit of shared experience and advice made a great deal of sense to me.

Second, I had decided to join the Foreign Service at least partly to understand better what my father had been doing all those years that had caused me so much childhood and adolescent angst—because he rarely talked about it. As I walked down the hall, I recognized the irony of trying to continue what had become a nomadic habit of leaving behind everything familiar— when I had just been offered the chance to see firsthand what my father had been doing in a place where he did it—and that place happened to be one of the most beautiful and exciting places in the world. I turned around, went back, and told the director that I would take the assignment.

***

France has an important place in the minds and hearts of Americans. Our two countries have been inexorably bound together since at least the eighteenth century, when the American Revolution created the United States and the French Revolution redefined France. While most of the European inhabitants of the colonies that sought independence from Great Britain were British, if France had not sided with the colonists in the Revolutionary War, the United States probably would not have won that independence—or at least not then. The English philosopher John Locke may have been the grandfather of the Declaration of Independence, but it was the French Baron de Montesquieu's ideas about separation of powers that provided the intellectual framework for the constitution that has now held this historic experiment with democracy together for more than two hundred years.

According to the World Tourism Organization, France is visited by more tourists than any other country in the world. A high percentage of those tourists are American. Many Americans, while never as internationally focused as Europeans, still tend to think first of France when looking beyond our borders. We are more familiar with the Eiffel Tower than with the Great

Wall of China or even London Bridge. Most Americans butcher the French language if we ever develop sufficient interest and courage to speak it, but we think the sound of English spoken with a strong French accent is charming, particularly if spoken by the opposite sex. Most of us shudder at the mention of the guillotine, think Napoleon was the greatest general who ever lived, admire French cuisine, believe French wine sets the standard (whether we drink it or not), and know who Marie Antoinette was, even if we can't name her husband.

As in every close relationship, there are both positive and negative elements. Many thousands of young American soldiers died on the battlefields of France to preserve or restore French independence during the two world wars of the twentieth century. Their fellow citizens and their counterparts in France remember and honor that sacrifice, but as with siblings different opinions and perspectives create frictions, frustrations, and conflicts. We admire each other and we also infuriate each other. The French often see Americans as boorish and offensive. Americans are annoyed by what they perceive as French arrogance, and we are particularly offended when France challenges America publicly—as it did recently in the months leading up to the Iraq War. While the United States has been honored in France for its World War II sacrifices and its contributions to European reconstruction, it was also seen as an interfering bully because of its postwar anticolonialist stance. This contributed to France's loss of many of its colonial territories. Many French believed they not only lost colonies, but half of their native soil, having convinced themselves and taught their children that Algeria was an integral part of French territory.

The French government's decision to grant Algeria independence in the early 1960s, though brought about by a national referendum, touched off violent resistance within France, including an attempted coup d'état and widespread terrorist bombings of public places. This came particularly from the *pieds noirs* ("black feet"), who had made their homes in Algeria and lost everything. As a young teenager in Paris at the time, I remember one morning being told to walk a different route to the school bus stop, because the night before a building around the corner on the Avenue d'Eylau had been bombed by the Organisation de l'armée secrète (the OAS, a militant French military organization). When we returned in the afternoon we were allowed to walk past it. The front door was damaged, and there was still glass strewn across the street. It was nothing compared to the terrorist bombings of today that destroy entire buildings, but it impressed us. We were told that no one had been hurt, but I don't know if that was true. *Plastique*, the term for plastic explosives, became an important part of our vocabulary.

In those years, I also got my first taste of anti-Americanism, probably directly related to that resentment. As a young child in Belgium I had become used to the exasperation of Europeans who were not accustomed to or who disapproved of congenitally less disciplined and less respectful American children. But that was usually expressed with a short burst of invective and then dismissal. It was directed at behavior rather than at being. My first exposure to something more was when I ventured alone at age thirteen into a Parisian barbershop. I was certainly not misbehaving. I was nervous, quieter than usual, and I thought very respectful. When I was seated in the chair and immobilized with the sheet that barbers wrap around you, the barber, who seemed to be my father's age, asked me where I was from. As I remember, he gave me a choice of being English or American. I proudly replied that I was American, fully expecting the friendly, even effusive, response that I was used to from shopkeepers, teachers, Metro workers, and the like. Instead, I received a heated, and for me a little scary, tirade about American wealth, arrogance, and interference. I was proud to be an American. I clung to that pride, perhaps a little desperately, to sustain me when I felt I did not fit in or couldn't identify my friends. Generally, it seemed to work. When I was not a member of the family or an accepted member of the community, when I did not have the language or skill at the local sports, announcing that I was American somehow supplied a certain value in itself. However, it had the opposite effect in that barbershop. I was a captive, constrained by a sheet around my body and a cloth wrapped tightly around my neck, and being admonished by a large adult barber wielding sharp scissors (thankfully not a razor), loudly and in front of all the other clientele. My memory now is that the barbershop was full of people all staring at me like an alien—though it is just as likely there were no more than three or four. I didn't only feel embarrassed. The core of my already shaky identity was being dismantled articulately and ruthlessly. How on earth could I have missed that I and all other Americans were so clumsy and inconsiderate—or at least that others thought so? Why was being wealthy and giving that money away a bad thing? (I'm pretty sure that the Marshall Plan was included in the harangue.) Did everyone feel that way beneath the bright *"Bonjour, jeune homme!"* with which I was usually greeted? That was the longest haircut of my entire life, and one of the few in which I never even considered what I looked like when I left. When it was all over, the barber assured me that his comments were not personal, and that I seemed like a nice young man—in spite of being American—and he hoped I would come back. I paid for my haircut, walked slowly out the door as if I were surrounded by growling dogs that should not be provoked—and then fled. I never went back. I think I avoided the street for months afterward.

In the 1960s French appreciation for American support for France's Indochina War had gradually metamorphosed into strong French opposition to America's Vietnam War. In the same time frame the French Communist Party was on a roll and appeared to be supported by 25 percent of the French electorate. The conservative president, Charles de Gaulle, had challenged the very concept of a bipolar world by presenting France as an alternative to the two superpowers and making direct overtures to the USSR. He had pulled France out of NATO, shaking the foundations of America's Cold War thinking and commitments.

By the early 1970s the relationship had settled down again. France had gone through its own identity crisis. President de Gaulle had been forced from power by domestic opposition and replaced by the less flamboyant Georges Pompidou. Trans-Atlantic trade was booming, and Paris's independent stance, while still irritating to the United States, had made the city an attractive and effective site for sensitive East-West diplomacy, including the U.S.-Vietnam peace talks and secret and not-so-secret initiatives in U.S.-China relations. French–American competition became more economic than strategic—though it still had some interesting and sometimes baffling strategic dimensions.

Sometimes, we Americans see our disagreements with France or France's disagreements with us as pure arrogance or pride—France's arrogance, of course, not ours. Pride, in fact, is very important in France, and the French have much to be proud about. French pride is closely associated with a sense of personal and national honor. The French author Alexandre Dumas (*The Three Musketeers*) beautifully portrayed both the nobility of that honor and also how it can occasionally slip into bravado and even absurdity. During that first tour in Paris, I thought I was observing the latter. In reality it turned out to be quite different.

In the fall of 1973, oil-exporting nations announced a huge increase in the price of oil and then an oil embargo to punish the United States (primarily) and European nations (secondarily) for supporting Israel in the Yom Kippur War. Most of the targeted countries quickly implemented austerity measures to cope with the crisis. The U.S. government rationed petroleum distribution to the states and called on businesses and citizens to restrict energy consumption. Americans and Europeans all tightened their belts—all except the French. While other countries were dimming their lights—and the United States extended daylight savings time to a full year—France deliberately kept the "City of Lights" blazing and declared it would not be put on the defensive by such threats. Many Americans in Paris thought the French government was simply crazy. In fact, France and other European countries moved quickly to distance themselves from support to Israel and succeeded in getting the oil embargo lifted several months before it ended for the United States. France's bravado was carefully calculated. It also had a safety net, with substantial nuclear energy capacity already online and the knowledge that capacity would double over the next year.

***

The American Embassy in Paris is one of the largest American embassies in the world, and since American embassies tend to be larger than those of any other country it is one of the largest embassies in the world—period. Perhaps no other diplomatic mission in the world is represented by so many different government agencies: State, Defense, Commerce, Agriculture, Justice, Treasury, the Battle Monuments Commission, and so on. Today the embassy's website states that there are over fifty federal agencies and departments represented there. It is an overseas bureaucracy—and often acts like it.

When I arrived at Orly Airport (before Charles de Gaulle Airport was built), I was met by the person I was replacing at the embassy. This in itself was unusual. The Foreign Service is notoriously understaffed, and people almost never overlap, regardless of how useful passing the baton of experience might be. This was the only time in my career that it happened. On the way in from the airport I asked when I should get to the embassy in the morning. He responded that the embassy hours were 8 to 6, no more of those "cushy 9 to 5 State Department hours." I thought that was sort of a weird thing to say, and the thought of working long hours didn't really appeal to me. As things turned out, I ended up working more like 7 to 7.

When I was back in Washington, I had wondered why on earth the U.S. government needed to employ so many people in Paris. From my studies and my observations growing up in a diplomatic environment, our diplomatic missions had essentially two functions: to understand the host country and convey that understanding to policy makers in Washington, and to communicate with the host government (to promote and defend U.S. interests). Committing trained diplomats to places like Cambodia, Saudi Arabia, Tanzania, and Brazil made eminent sense. These were places far from Washington, with which Americans were not very familiar and with whom we had relatively little communication. The Cold War and the globalization of U.S. interests meant that we needed to be constantly aware of developments all over the world. But France was almost next door, and though the French spoke a different language, their culture was not that different from ours (so I thought). We could see what was going on in France by reading the newspapers and watching television. Thousands of American businesses were active in France on a daily basis, and millions of American tourists visited there every year. If we had serious issues with the government, we could pick up a telephone in Washington and call (even in the dark ages of the 1970s). Why did we need so many diplomats?

***

American Foreign Service officers are sent overseas for their first several assignments for essentially two reasons (not necessarily in this order): most American diplomatic training is done on the job; and that is where the greatest need for warm bodies is. "First tour" jobs in small embassies tend to offer more opportunities for responsibility from the moment one arrives at post. Because the missions are small, each person is an integral member of the team, and the team depends on his or her performance for its success—for better or for worse. In larger missions the newcomers tend to be small cogs in large machines. These are bureaucracies, and the involvement of "junior officers" is often minimal. That said, the large posts can also provide training and exposure that the smaller posts don't. I was chosen to go Paris partly because I was classified as an economic officer, but I was sent to what was called a "rotational assignment." That meant that I was supposed to spend time in different parts of the embassy: six months in economic work, six months in political work, six months in consular work, and so on. I was to get intensified exposure to the different disciplines of diplomatic work.

My first seat was in the commercial section. It was one part of the embassy's broader economic component, which included people who worked on trade policy, export promotion, financial matters, agriculture, civil aviation, maritime issues, and a host of other "economic" subjects. The people staffing these sections were sent not just from the State Department, but also from Commerce, Treasury, Agriculture, and other Washington agencies. It was all headed by an "economic minister," who was a Foreign Service officer senior in rank to most ambassadors that we send around the world.

The commercial section was dedicated to helping American companies and promoting American exports. Again, I questioned why the U.S. government should be devoting public resources—taxpayer money—to assisting the private sector, which seemed to be doing very well on its own. My first assignment was to call French companies who were behind on their payments to American exporters. I was uncomfortable and a little embarrassed by the task, but I did it—and I could not have been more surprised by the results. The companies I called were not just cordial but deferential and friendly. While the press, the politicians, and many of the government officials were critical, terse, and sometimes almost hostile, the French business community was a reservoir of goodwill. Of course, they were making money from the relationship, but they also seemed to enjoy being with Americans. I had many interesting conversations and even a weekend invitation to a country estate—which I unfortunately had to decline at the last minute.

***

When after a month I was shifted to the economic policy section, my work actually became less diplomatic and more cerebral. I was reading newspapers and reporting on issues of the moment, like the growing testiness in French–American civil aviation relations as France and Britain got ready to launch the world's first supersonic jet airliner the Concorde. American aerospace companies had decided that a supersonic airliner would not be economical, and they had scrapped their programs in favor of new wide-bodied aircraft. At the same time, American airline companies were worried that a European monopoly on the supersonic alternative would put Americans at a disadvantage. They complained that the European companies could only make it work because they received government subsidies, and they sought to have supersonic flights into the United States restricted on the grounds that the new planes produced too much noise pollution. Both sides were crying foul, and governments on both sides of the Atlantic were involved. It was quite fascinating, but I had virtually no contact with my French counterparts.

I was observing and analyzing for others, which seemed appropriate since I had no real experience myself. During this time, I was asked by the ambassador's special assistant, an experienced political officer, to write a speech for the ambassador on U.S. trade and investment policy that he would give to the American Chamber of Commerce in France, which was quite large and influential. I was a little uncomfortable with the task, since I thought the ambassador knew a lot more about the subject than I. However, I dutifully did my research and tried to tie it into the issues that I thought American companies were facing there. I gave it to the ambassador's special assistant a week before the speech and asked him to let me know what changes he would like me to make. I assumed there would be quite a few. When I heard nothing from him, and the day of the speech passed, I assumed that he or the ambassador had rewritten the speech. When I next saw him, I asked him how the speech had gone. He replied it was fine. He had given it to the ambassador in the car going over to the meeting; the ambassador had asked him if he needed to review it first; and he had told him no, it was fine. I was horrified. Had I known that the ambassador would simply read it to that group, sight unseen, I never would have been able to finish it! My colleague was quite amused.

***

Then, I got my first view of how the Foreign Service is so different from the other U.S. government services, and I was moved back into the actual work of diplomacy. One of the agencies represented at the embassy in Paris was the Civil Aeronautics Board (CAB). It staffed a position called the Civil Aviation attaché—a senior position, filled by an individual whose civilian rank, GS-14 (equivalent to a senior army colonel), was one that normally takes twenty to twenty-five years of service to reach. When I arrived in the economic section, the attaché position had actually been empty for almost six months. The individual had become ill, and the CAB had not yet been able to replace him. My supervisor in the economic policy section, who had to cover the absent attaché's responsibilities, recommended to the embassy's economic minister that he put me, the lowest-ranking American in the entire embassy, into that position—and out of desperation he did it. In this case it was a temporary assignment, and technically many government agencies are able to shift personnel on a temporary basis. However, the Foreign Service has traditionally been far more flexible than other services. It can send junior personnel to positions above their grade and place senior personnel in positions below their grade (though this happens more rarely) anywhere in the world. It has to be flexible, because it must respond to constantly changing demands with chronic understaffing.

I certainly benefited. While I was still questioning the theoretical justification for such a large embassy, being underemployed or bored was definitely out of the question. Told to occupy the attaché's office the next day, I entered in predawn darkness and wondered what the enormous piece of furniture in the middle of the room was. After finding the light switch, I discovered it was an ordinary desk (well, a very nice desk) with three feet of papers (approximately forty-five cubic feet) stacked neatly on top to welcome me. The first several weeks were harrowing, as I tried to move that mountain of paper and learn the technical and bureaucratic jargon that went with it. After that things got smoother, though I tugged inordinately often on the sleeves of my many bosses for direction, correction, and even some protection.

That job sent me out to interact with some of the French regulatory agencies as well as the foreign ministry. It put me in regular contact with the American airlines and other companies that did business in the aviation field and with French companies as well. It gave me access to many of the most senior people in the embassy, though it didn't necessarily give me all the resources necessary to do the job.

***

I was not the only junior officer at the embassy. There were at least five or six of us from the Department of State and ten or more from other agencies. One of the disadvantages that we had was that we were not on the diplomatic list. This is the list of people who are formally accredited to the host country government as official representatives of their home governments. Each mission notifies the host government of its official personnel, and if accepted they are put on the diplomatic list. These people are then accorded full diplomatic privileges and protections, intended to protect the diplomat from government interference or detainment, and to provide smooth access to places and people necessary for carrying out official duties.

The U.S. Embassy management explained to us that it was under pressure from the French government to keep the list of official diplomats to a minimum. One of the reasons given was that the French wanted to keep Soviet diplomatic personnel to a manageable number—and how could they do that if the American Embassy kept expanding? Embassy management argued to the junior officers that in reality we had all the protection and access we needed.

We junior officers didn't think so, and I still remember with crystal clarity the time that I was instructed by Washington to make a demarche to the ministry of foreign affairs on behalf of an American airline whose urgent request for special flight clearance had been delayed. A more senior colleague from the economic section accompanied me as it was my first venture into that territory, but I was responsible for the demarche. When we entered the office in question the foreign ministry official pointedly pulled out his copy of the diplomatic list and asked where Mr. Adair was. I felt both chagrined vis-à-vis the ministry and vindicated with regard to embassy management. The ministry official made his point—among other things, that I would not have been given the appointment but for the other officer, who was on the list—then graciously listened, and the airline was able to make its flight.

***

The enormous Paris embassy gave me my first encounter with obtuse government bureaucracy and with the sometimes brilliant individuals who—for the best of reasons and the worst of reasons—promote and defend it. To my discredit, in thirty-five years of government service I never managed to make peace with it.

To be fair to that system and to the individuals who staff it, there are reasons other than bureaucratic inertia that newly minted officers are sometimes not given the same status as their more experienced peers. We don't always exhibit the optimal judgment, as I demonstrated on another occasion slightly outside the parameter of my official duties. In addition to the embassy in Paris, in the 1970s we had several consulates in major French cities. They were essentially extensions of the embassy, providing an official American presence, interacting with the local officials and population, and helping American citizens and businesses. On one occasion, the American consul in Strasbourg, an experienced Foreign Service officer, needed to come up to Paris for a long weekend to take part in some events there. He did not want to leave the consulate alone for that long a period of time, and I was asked to go down and sit in for him for a few days in case something came up. Strasbourg is a wonderful city, and it was great fun for me. However, one evening I came back to the consul's residence and discovered the door to his bedroom locked from the inside. I had not locked it and concluded there must be an intruder. So, I called the police and explained my concern. They sent the fire department, which arrived with sirens blazing, put up a ladder to the bedroom window, and opened the door—which had blown shut and was simply stuck. I was mortified and apologetic. They were polite but not amused.

***

After that first six months in the economic section, I was sent to do my time in the consular section. Traditionally, all Foreign Service officers must have one tour of duty in consular work. This involves providing services to Americans living or traveling overseas and responding to host-country nationals and third-country nationals who wish to travel to the United States. I spent six months interviewing prospective visitors to the United States during the week, and then helping Americans who got into trouble in the evenings or on weekends.

All Foreign Service officers are supposed to do visa work. They are required to know consular and immigration law, and they are charged with the responsibility of applying that law. My consular work was primarily in nonimmigrant visas—that is, working with people who were applying to visit the United States, not to become permanent residents. U.S. immigration law requires that the visa officer certify the applicant has all the required documentation from U.S. agencies to work in the United States, or be convinced that the applicant has no intention of remaining in the United States for more than a short visit. It is extremely difficult work, and looking back on my career, I believe it was the most personally stressful work that I had. First, the volume of applicants was very high, and we were interviewing five to ten individuals per hour for six to eight hours a day. We had a highly competent French staff, who screened the applications and forwarded to us only the individuals who appeared questionable. At the end of the day, we would review the other applications that the French staff had processed and sign them as well. In peak season four or five of us were actually issuing over a thousand visas a day.

Many of the applicants we interviewed were deemed not to be bona fide nonimmigrants, and we had to turn them down. This was hard for us, and of course much harder for them. In some cases we were dashing the hopes of young people who wanted to visit the United States just for a month and hoped to defray expenses by babysitting for families who offered to pay their board. Today that is legal, but then it was not. In some cases the issues were much more serious. At that time there were many Iranians seeking to escape the oppression of the shah's regime. They were often educated and talented people who could not return to Iran and sought to make a new home in the United States. Many would have been wonderful additions to our nation, but the option of an immigrant visa was not practicably available to them. I would go home every night exhausted, because I found it so difficult to divorce myself from the emotions in play.

There were lighter moments, though. One day a group of about fifty gypsies came in, applying for tourist visas to visit the United States—with their caravans and animals. They were able to demonstrate that they could support themselves while in the United States without becoming wards of the state by producing bags of gold, which they plunked down on the visa counter. However, they were not able to demonstrate that they had a home which they had no intention of abandoning—because their homes moved with them. We turned them down, and they departed. For weeks afterward several of us would tease our very competent but rather high-strung supervisor that if she demanded too much of us we would call the gypsies back and issue them visas, caravans and all. Later, we learned the group had made it all the way to Canada and presented themselves at one of the U.S. consulates there—where they were turned down again.

The people who make consular work their career are truly unsung heroes. Their work is stressful. It is rarely glamorous. They deal with real problems of real people, and help many of those people one by one. They visit prisons where individual Americans are incarcerated, rightly or wrongly, and where those visits may be their compatriots' only ray of hope. They comfort strangers who have suddenly lost loved ones, or who themselves may be dying alone, far from home. I had to visit an elderly American tourist one night in her hotel room to inform her that her son—and last immediate relative—had been killed suddenly in an accident. They carry the power to change lives by issuing or denying visas to the United States for study, to reunite families, or to obtain priceless medical care. The law gives these individual officers both power and responsibility. No one, not even the ambassador, can order them to issue or deny a visa. While they can later be held responsible for mistakes, at the time of decision only they can determine just how much interpretation of the law is needed or allowed in the individual case. It is sometimes a terrible trade-off between human compassion and bureaucratic self-protection. Today, the equation is even more difficult, because it includes the constant threat of international terrorism and potential danger to the nation.

After the consular section, I returned to the economic section as staff aide to the economic minister. He supervised an extraordinarily diverse set of people representing powerful Washington agencies. Some believed a staff aide might be able to take some of the more mundane chores off his shoulders and allow him to focus his experience and intellect more on policy and the intricate diplomacy he was so good at. I did the best I could. He could solve problems in minutes that would take me hours or days, but it still helped reduce his burden. It also taught me a great deal about the diversity of American economic agencies and how our embassies coordinate and focus them overseas. However, I was frustrated by the size of the operation there and impatient to have more responsibility of my own.

***

There is one very important advantage to being a junior person in a very large embassy, which is that after regular working hours your time is mostly your own (at least what is left of it). That is not true for the more senior people in the embassy, who often have a heavy schedule of evening and weekend events that are pretty much obligatory. I had very little of that and so had plenty of time to enjoy Paris—and there was a great deal to enjoy.

Many changes had occurred since I had last lived there. The City of Lights that I had lived in twelve years earlier had been black and white. The buildings were black from centuries of soot. While this had made them look older, the contrast with all the lights at night had also been rather elegant. In the intervening years the entire city had been sandblasted clean, and the change was stunning. Twelve years earlier, the cars had been black and square and even had running boards. That is, except for a few American cars like the one my father brought with him—a white Pontiac Catalina with fins that dwarfed anything else on the road. It sailed through the streets of Paris like a whale scattering the smaller creatures to the sides, and sometimes had to beach itself on the sidewalks so as not to block the streets when parked. I remember my father was stopped once for speeding driving near the city of Dijon. The policeman was driving a tiny Renault that looked like it could fit in the Pontiac's trunk, and I think he had deliberately ignored the diplomatic plates just so he could inspect the white whale up close. There were lots more cars in Paris of the 1970s as well. A highway had been built down along the Seine, below the level of sight of anyone not actually down by the river or in one of the buildings overlooking it. Huge underground parking lots had been carved out of the ground beneath the old buildings and cathedrals to accommodate all the new vehicles. Paris had a skyscraper—one. The Tour Montparnasse caused such an outcry when it was completed in 1972 that all future skyscrapers in the city were essentially consigned to the suburbs. One of those suburbs had become a small city itself, La Défense, and could be seen from many vantage points in Paris looming up over the horizon like an invading army from outer space. The Métro (subway)—which had given me my first taste of independence when I was twelve years old—was more crowded. It also ran on rubber tires instead of steel wheels, but it went to the same places—and it still smelled the same.

Today, after having visited most of the world's major cities one way or another, I still think that Paris is—hands down—the planet's most beautiful city. Cape Town, Hong Kong, and Vancouver have spectacular natural settings. Paris's setting is softer, but it has created its own vistas with architecture enhancing its hills and river. Paris has rooftops that you can look out on from apartments, restaurants, offices, and even parks. This immediately sets it apart from and above most modern European and American cities, which use their rooftops as parking lots for machinery and are better kept out of sight. Venice is enchanting, but it doesn't have the expanse and variety of Paris. Rome and Beijing are both older, but while Rome made its older sections museum pieces and Beijing destroyed much of its heritage, Paris incorporated its history into everyday life. Nowhere but Venice has the quality of light that Paris has. In the daytime the sun filters through the trees onto the sidewalks and café tables, and past balconies into interior spaces that all seem focused outward. At night the streetlights sparkle like jewels—particularly when it rains and the city is wet—and even the cars careening down the Champs-Élysées look like decorations. And it is all accessible. If there were nothing else to do in Paris, one could spend months or even years just walking through the streets and looking.

Above all, it is eminently livable. The climate itself is sensuous. Each season is just sharp enough to be stimulating without being oppressive or intimidating. Every part of the city is a neighborhood, even where the government offices are located. Every neighborhood has its own character, but they are also easily connected to every other neighborhood, because it is so easy to get around. The public transportation is omnipresent and affordable—and there is always walking. No matter where you are, there is always a bakery within walking distance (and smelling distance), and the same goes for cafés, restaurants, and markets with fresh produce. Visual arts, performing arts, ancient bookstores and new; museums, theaters, art galleries, street art, and street performances—there is just about any kind of culture or entertainment that one can think of. And it is not just in French, though that of course is part of the attraction. It's available in English, and in European, Asian, Middle Eastern, and North African languages.

***

In some respects, it's a shame that one had to work at all, but Paris can be hideously expensive. This was particularly true for a junior American government employee who had rented an apartment right at the limit of his affordability. My apartment was too expensive because I had become seriously spoiled during my first three months in Paris. At that time the embassy provided a housing allowance that would accommodate a modest small apartment in a good though not luxurious neighborhood. It also provided a temporary housing allowance to cover the period when one looked for an apartment. That was more generous and was available for up to a maximum of three months. Shortly after I arrived, a colleague told me about an American who was looking to rent his apartment on the Île Saint-Louis for three months when he returned to the United States to work in the presidential campaign. The Île Saint-Louis is the small island in the Seine just upriver from the Île de la Cité, on which Notre Dame Cathedral is located. It is one of the most exclusive communities in Paris. The then president of France, Georges Pompidou, had an apartment there, as did the artist Marc Chagall, among others. For three months I enjoyed a small apartment with a large terrace on the top floor of an old building overlooking the Seine, just opposite one of the most exclusive restaurants in Paris, La Tour d'Argent. Spoiled is too mild a characterization of what this experience did to me and my aspirations and expectations for the next few years. When my absent landlord returned from his unsuccessful effort to elect George McGovern, I desperately looked for another apartment on the island. I found one that was just barely affordable if I exercised tremendous discipline in my personal life.

Unfortunately, my personal discipline was no match for the forces of history. In 1973 the inflationary impact of the Vietnam War and President Nixon's 1971 decision to cancel the U.S. dollar's convertibility to gold caught up with Americans living overseas. In the first six months of that year, the dollar depreciated by almost 20 percent against the French franc. While that was wonderful for American exports, it was devastating to my available income. I suddenly discovered that not only could I not pay for my apartment, but I had to cut back seriously on eating. So, I found a newly arrived American businessman wealthier than I, turned the apartment over to him, and spent another few months house-sitting until I could find something more modest.

***

French cuisine is not just expensive fancy restaurants with multiple courses and multiple wines. It is a central theme in an intricate cultural tapestry, and this makes it and France wonderfully different from the United States. After four hundred years on the North American continent, the Europeans, Africans, and Asians who created the United States of America still don't seem to place a high value on culture—at least not national culture (in spite of the admirable job that the U.S. Information Agency was doing promoting American visual and performing arts at the American Cultural Center in Paris). While we do have some notable regional culinary specialties like North Carolina BBQ, Louisiana Cajun, and New England clam chowder, we have few traditions that embrace, preserve, and enhance our regional creativeness in a national package as has been done in France. The French take an interest in where dishes come from, and they have combined all of their differences in a cuisine that harmonizes those qualities rather than homogenizing them.

Another notable difference between French and American culinary values is the importance that the French place on freshness. Most French meals do not start with food taken from the refrigerator or freezer. They don't even start with the market, butcher, or baker. They start on the land in particular places in particular regions. People like to know where their wines, cheeses, pâtés, mushrooms, and even their flours come from. Meat, seafood, and vegetables all taste better fresh, and popular French culture makes the whole process of finding, selecting, and purchasing these products, if not strictly entertainment, then at least a meaningful exercise. We Americans may occasionally linger at the supermarket, but on the whole we try to get our grocery shopping done as quickly as possible, and if we do it more than once a week it is probably for lack of planning rather than for enjoyment. I never believed that refrigerating or even freezing meat changed its taste. When I lived in Paris at age thirteen, I remember my parents expressing some bewilderment at the need to shop every day instead of simply keeping two weeks' supply of meat in the freezer. At that time it was even a little unusual to have a refrigerator in Paris. Our kitchen had a cupboard, the back of which was a screen that opened to the outside to keep things like dairy products cool.

The most obvious example of the premium put on freshness is the culture of bread in France. Real bread is not something you get once a week wrapped in plastic; it is purchased freshly made every day. Sometimes it is purchased before each meal. Every neighborhood has a bakery, sometimes several, and rarely does one walk in Paris without smelling freshly baked bread at some point. The traditional French baguette's ingredients are even nationally regulated, and preservatives are prohibited.

Some of us at the embassy took a course in wine tasting—ironically, from an Englishman—that taught us to notice different kinds of acidity in wines, how to taste things on different parts of the tongue, how aroma/fragrance affects taste and appetite, and how different kinds of wines complement different kinds of foods. This has now caught on big in America. However, there is much more, such as how to make sauces that enhance rather than overpower the food, how to build meals with complementary foods, how to space and pace them with different courses, and so on.

When I was in Paris in the early 1960s, the movie *West Side Story* was playing on the Champs-Élysées. It made a big impression on Paris and a big impression on me. There is a scene where the Sharks, members of a Latino gang, and their girlfriends do a lively number called "I Like to Be in America." It's a sexy competition, where the men criticize all aspects of American life and the women extol it. Ten years later I watched a similar dance (though rather less sexy) as the French and American governments went through one of our endless cycles of mutual recriminations about trade in agricultural products. We complained that the French government was obstructing imports of low-priced American grain to Europe. The French complained that the United States applied nontariff restrictions to things like cheeses made from unpasteurized milk. We argued that France's agricultural system was inefficient, because it supported small farms with subsidies and trade protection, and that this discriminated against large American agribusinesses who could produce wheat, corn, and beef more efficiently and with less cost to consumers. Both sides were partially right. What we tried to deny in this, however, as the Sharks did in *West Side Story*, was that the French had created something that we wanted and needed—but didn't really understand. They had created a cultural treasure. It was not just the cuisine but the approach to life, which was most obvious and accessible in the culture of food.

***

Over time—a lot of time—the French have taught themselves to *notice* things. This is not just true with food but with many aspects of life. French culture has concentrated both on the details of life and on how those details combine to give life a meaning for both individuals and society. France taught much of the world to smell—not just wines and cheeses but perfume, which the French made into a science as well as a business. French painters like Renoir and Monet pioneered the impressionist movement and made us more aware of the power that patterns of light have on emotions. French architects created buildings that combine detail and simplicity, majesty and balance; and French city planners helped put them together in cities with broad avenues that are both spectacular and livable.

In the seventeenth century these qualities were employed to build physical structures like the Palace of Versailles and to enhance the imposition of court etiquette specifically to support the efforts of Louis XIV and before him Cardinal Richelieu to harness human desires and ambitions and build a centralized state, putting an end to centuries of regional strife. They strengthen their sense of national identity with what appears to us to be an inordinate attention to the details, rules, and vocabulary of their language; and they even have a prominent government institution, the Académie Française (also created by Cardinal Richelieu), to oversee it. And, of course, they pay attention to love.

Nothing is more powerful than the physical and compassionate energies generated by communication between the sexes. Many societies have tried to control it through suppression. France has extolled it with *"Vive la différence."* Sexual attraction and courtship are art forms. Marriage is an honored institution, strongly supported by both the government and religion, but for centuries there has also been a social system for accepting and managing extramarital affairs that to a large degree has succeeded in protecting both the institution of marriage and sexual freedom. When I was in Paris in the early 1970s, it was working well. Even the president of the republic had a mistress. It was accepted and kept within bounds.

The extraordinary appreciation for life in so many of its aspects would not be possible without extraordinary discipline, whether it is exercised individually or socially. You can't taste all the nuances of a good wine unless you take the time to train yourself, and you can't do it fully without restraint, either. I was surprised by the natural restraint that I saw. When I was in Paris, a movie came out called *La Grande Bouffe* ("Blow-Out"). It is about four friends who lock themselves in a villa and eat themselves to death, and it is essentially a satire on aspects of the French obsession with eating. At the time, I knew a bunch of young Americans who were studying at the Cordon Bleu cooking school in Paris. The movie became an icon for them, and they threw cooking/eating orgies on a regular basis that were extraordinarily decadent. But that kind of thing is not sustainable, as the protagonists in *La Grande Bouffe* demonstrated, and most of the French didn't feel the need to go that route. The appreciation for life includes appreciation for balance and sustainability.

Paris is well known for its acceptance, and even promotion, of fringe behavior, whether it be personal, political, or artistic. It has been a sanctuary for political revolutionaries like the Chinese communists Zhou Enlai and Deng Xiaoping. It has been a stage for philosophical heretics like Sartre and Descartes. It is a playground for rich hedonists from North America to Asia and Africa, and it has allowed the flaunting of sexual promiscuity of all kinds. It has been a fertile environment for ground-breaking artists like Frédéric Chopin, George Sand, Pablo Picasso, Henry Miller, and Ernest Hemingway—and for many more who did not succeed. But much of this has survived over the centuries only because the host society was strong enough and sure enough of its own identity to avoid being compromised by these currents on too large a scale. It instilled in most of its population essentially conservative personal and social disciplines that made possible the tolerance of outrageous thought and behavior in others.

As a teenager in Paris I found the traditional French attitudes frustrating and limiting. As a young adult in Paris I was more interested in excess than in discipline; more interested in the experimental and revolutionary French character than in the conservative and traditional one. I found the young students' challenges to virtually everything refreshing, and I had difficulty understanding how many of them could then metamorphose into young bureaucrats with Cartesian adherence to set forms of bureaucratic behavior and political thinking.

***

Spending two years at the American Embassy in Paris gave me an answer to my question about whether we really needed an embassy in Paris: it was essentially that our relationship could not—or should not—be conducted by proxy or by technology.

Government officials posted overseas see things differently than do journalists, who also seek and report information on the host country. Officials are sent to build state-to-state relationships and to promote U.S. national interests—as defined by the U.S. administration that is in power at the time. Both government officials and journalists are charged with reporting the actual situation on the ground—and with challenging popular assumptions if what they see is different from what is expected back home. However, they have different capabilities that are tuned to their respective consumers. The officials report to a limited audience that is concerned foremost with issues that impact the nation. Journalists report, via their editors, to an almost unlimited audience, that is, to members of the general public who are concerned less with issues that affect the nation than with those that impact themselves—and that impact includes pure entertainment.

Officials have the advantage of being able to protect the identities of their interlocutors and even to keep their views—personal or official—out of the public eye. This can be particularly important for foreign government officials who are willing to explain underlying and less obvious factors behind government policies, or who are willing to present personal opinions at variance with those of their government. This advantage is of course undermined—as are the individuals who have been considerate and courageous enough to share their opinions with us—when official U.S. reports are exposed to public view, such as has happened recently with WikiLeaks. While officials can be constrained by their supervisors' desire to protect a particular policy, the Department of State also maintains a "dissent channel" that allows any individual in the embassy to present a different view to Washington without the stamp of approval of the ambassador.

We also need to establish personal relationships with our counterparts in foreign governments. We are human and need those relationships for perspective, though it is not always easy to develop them. There has to be exchange, sharing, and mutual appreciation for opinions, values, and the cultural soil from which they grow. Personal exchanges about official disagreements over policies like agricultural or civil aviation regulations and subsidies and what they mean for the respective economies and societies can mitigate the broader antagonisms that they generate.

Of course, this official presence needs to be provided by people who are able and willing to make communication with the local culture and people a primary objective. Language is a critical part of this. Many people at the American Embassy in Paris could only speak rudimentary French, and some spoke none at all. This was less true of those sent from the State Department, but not even all the Foreign Service officers were fluent. We still believe that we can rely on our French counterparts to speak English or on our French employees to interpret for us. That is wrong. We need to be able to communicate with our counterparts on their turf and their terms and do it as equals. We also need to be able to go beyond the official world to understand the environment with which we are dealing.

I left Paris both intellectually and emotionally impressed by French culture, though I still felt more affinity with its revolutionary spirit than with its establishment. At that time in my life, it was easier and more fun to challenge the rules than to conform to them. I particularly had difficulty accepting the importance assigned by French culture to both public and private responsibilities for managing community life, including the material manifestations of it like food, dress, and lifestyle. American tradition extols freedom above all else. We are terribly attracted to the beauty, sophistication, and sensuality of French culture, but it is hard for us to create it ourselves. Perhaps that is because we lack the discipline—or the support of a disciplined cultural and social environment.

Several of my French friends had gently sought to edge me toward an understanding of the need for balance between freedom and creativity on the one hand, and established parameters of social discipline on the other. They had accepted the premise that the former could not exist without the latter— at least not for any extended period of time. While they might cheer on the socialists and even the communists, and while they might participate in public demonstrations, they would often back off if elements of the cultural value system were threatened. After making their point on the streets, they might very easily vote for the conservative candidate against whom they had been demonstrating. In the end they would opt for maintaining those parameters of social discipline. I was not yet prepared to accept that bottom line.

So I headed for my second post—in Africa—still looking for the adventure that had eluded me when I was offered that to-die-for Paris assignment. Only after that next assignment—in an environment that had almost none of the social and cultural structures I found so restrictive—would I begin to accept what my French friends had been trying to teach me.

Chapter Two

Edge of Darkness: Lubumbashi (September 1974–July 1976)

My African assignment began when I received a letter from the person in Washington who was my "career counselor." I was in my office at the U.S. Embassy in Paris when I opened the letter, which read,

> Dear Marshall,
> I have proposed you for the position of Economic-Commercial Officer in Lubumbashi, Zaire. I hope the panel accepts this recommendation, because I believe it would be good for your career.
> Sincerely . . .

In theory, this individual in the State Department's office of personnel was responsible for marrying the Service's immediate need to fill its positions worldwide with its longer-term need to develop the diplomatic and foreign policy skills of its personnel. The term *counselor* suggested that communication and guidance of the personnel being assigned was part of the job. The 1970s was a transition period of sorts for the Foreign Service. In the 1940s, 1950s, and 1960s, Foreign Service officers had very little input (at least not formally) in their assignments. The process was based almost exclusively on the "needs of the Service." Foreign Service officers still maintain the commitment made when they join to serve anywhere in the world that the Service needs them, but today substantially more effort is made to elicit the preferences of the individuals before assignments are finalized. In the early 1970s the names had been changed, but to a large degree the system was still functioning as before. This was the first time that I had heard from my counselor—even the first time I had seen his name. Also, given that I was informed by a letter that had probably taken two weeks to get to me, I had most probably already been assigned by the time I received news of the "recommendation."

However, none of that made any difference to me. I could not have been more thrilled—particularly since I had never heard of Lubumbashi. Zaire sounded familiar. I thought it was probably in Africa, but I would not have bet on it. So I raced downstairs to the embassy library, a beautiful, high-ceilinged room on the first floor (European) across from the ambassador's office. I pulled out a large atlas and laid it on the massive wooden table in the center of the room. Zaire was in Africa, all right. Until two years earlier, it had been the Democratic Republic of the Congo (DRC), and Lubumbashi had been Elizabethville. I knew both of those. My first introduction to the Congo had been when I was six years old and my father was stationed in Brussels, Belgium. At that time, the Congo was not a state but a Belgian colony, the Belgian Congo. My parents had a picture book of the Belgian Congo, and when I was eight or nine years old, I used to pore over it avidly.

The name had been changed by the country's president, Mobutu Sese Seko (formerly Joseph-Desiré Mobutu) as part of his nationalistic "authentication" campaign, called Zairianization. Lubumbashi looked like it was smack in the geographic center of the African continent. I thought this was simply too outrageous an opportunity to pass up, and I was very excited.

Not all of my colleagues shared my enthusiasm. Not too long after I received word that I had actually been assigned to Lubumbashi, I got a call from a friend who had recently been transferred from the Paris embassy to Washington. He was in the Office of Fuels and Energy in the State Department. The 1970s oil crisis was in full swing, and that office was the place to be for ambitious Foreign Service officers. He said they had been horrified to hear of my assignment and asked if I would like to return to work for them. He was confident they could get the assignment changed. I thanked him but said I was looking forward to the adventure.

***

Several months later, after home leave to visit my parents and a crash course in export promotion at the Department of Commerce, I arrived in Kinshasa. It was the middle of the night in September, and the temperature was sweltering. Someone from the embassy picked me up at the airport and dropped me off at the embassy guest house several blocks from the chancery. The ride in from the airport had not revealed very much, except that the roads were in bad condition. My greeter had offered to send a car to get me the next morning, but I said I would rather walk and would get directions from the manager in the morning. The air conditioner was on full blast in the room, which smelled like mold and air conditioner. I escaped onto the balcony and stood there in the dark looking out over the street. There were just a few dim lights and occasional people. "I made it! I'm actually in Africa!" I thought. "The Dark Continent, the Heart of Darkness!" This was "Reality!" This was "Experience!" It was a little like some of the places I had visited in Latin America—the humid heat, the contrasting sweet, smoky, and trashy smells.

It was also different—and the difference was in the people. I could tell that from what I had seen on the way in and from my limited vantage point on the balcony. The walk in to the embassy was interesting but not attractive. The people did not seem friendly. In Latin America, even when I was recognized as a *gringo*, I could feel a part of the society and the people. I could associate with them and imagine myself as one of them, leading their lives. I did not feel that way in Kinshasa that morning, and I never managed to feel that way during my tour in Africa, though I tried.

At the embassy, I checked in with personnel and called on the ambassador and the deputy chief of mission. The ambassador was Deane Hinton, already a legendary figure in the Foreign Service. He was brilliant, very tough—and gruff. He had a heart of gold, but that was not readily apparent to a newly arrived officer whose psycho-professional gyroscope was not yet fully functional. He scowled at me and snapped, "Your father was a pretty good Foreign Service officer. Are you as good as he?" I took a deep breath and replied simply, "I'm different." That seemed to be enough for him, and we had a good introductory visit until I moved on for more in-depth discussions with the economic section. There, I also asked permission to take the long way to Lubumbashi, the route that stopped in Kisangani (Stanleyville) and several other cities, rather than the direct flight to Lubumbashi. This was received with some amusement, and I was told that I had already taken long enough—it was time to get to work.

***

Shaba Province is in the southeastern corner of Zaire, and right in the middle of the African continent. Its name was Katanga before President Mobutu changed it to Shaba in 1972, and the name reverted back to Katanga when he fell from power in 1997. It is a high plateau, so the landscape, climate, and vegetation are completely different from most of the rest of the country. This is the region where the Zaire/Congo River begins, relatively narrow and fast moving, cutting through the plateau and down into the basin rain forests. To my eye, the people didn't look markedly different from those in the Kinshasa area, but they did speak a different language. The predominant language in the capital area is Lingala, a Bantu language that developed as a trading language in the Congo River basin before the Europeans arrived; it grew more prominent as the chosen language for the Congolese military officers before and after independence. In Shaba the people speak Kiswahili, the language in use by populations along the east coast of Africa when the Arabs arrived in that region in about AD 1000. It was brought to Katanga and the eastern Zaire region by Arab traders from Zanzibar. Kiswahili became a convenient common language for the many different ethnic groups that migrated to the region to work in the copper mines.

Perhaps the people in this region had been exposed to the outside world before those in the capital area. It seemed to me they had at least made cause with foreigners more than their brothers and sisters to the west. When the Belgians were pressured to give their colony back in 1959–1960, the European residents of Katanga objected. They were backed by big money. Katanga had vast mineral wealth and the mining company Union Minière du Haut Katanga (UMHK), owned by the Belgian holding company Société Générale de Belgique (SGB), had established and operated significant, state-of-the-art copper mines in Kolwezi and Likasi (formerly Jadotville). The owners of SGB, along with the European residents who had established farms and other supporting businesses for that core economy, believed they could defy the anticolonial trend. They and their African partners declared Katanga independent. It was an ambitious effort, supported by Belgian troops, though not formally by the Belgian government. Nevertheless, it failed in the face of world opposition—expressed through the United Nations and led by the United States.

The U.S. opposition had several reasons. First and foremost were political Cold War considerations. The United States wanted to deny the USSR any foothold in Africa and believed that it had to prevent the breakup of colonial entities as they became independent. It feared the proliferation of small states would be less viable and would increase opportunities for Soviet exploitation.

Second were economic drivers. The Congo is a region that is incredibly rich in strategic mineral resources: copper, cobalt, manganese, gold, diamonds, and uranium. American companies were actively seeking to expand their access and their presence in these areas, and they believed they were at a disadvantage in the former European colonies. Wittingly or unwittingly, the U.S. government was listening. A uranium mine in Katanga had actually supplied the high-grade uranium used by the Manhattan Project to make the first atomic bomb. All of this increased the strategic sensitivity of the province and probably increased U.S. reluctance to allow it to strike a path opposed to broader U.S. policies in the region.

Third, supporting and sometimes preceding these two reasons were popular ideological concepts of democracy and anticolonialism. Many, perhaps most, Americans believed that colonialism was oppressive and wrong. The end of World War II, the creation of the United Nations, the withdrawal of British colonial rule from the Indian subcontinent, and then the blossoming of the civil rights movement in the United States all enhanced the political energy of this belief and made it part of U.S. foreign policy.

I was familiar with most of this reasoning, having grown up with it and having studied it in school. At least part of my father's pride in American ideals and his skepticism of European culture and intentions had rubbed off on me. Sadly, these strategic, economic, and even humanitarian objectives gave insufficient consideration to the needs of the African populations. Independence was a noble goal, but these people and these societies were too unprepared, too vulnerable, and the natural and human forces arrayed against them were too vast. By the time I left Zaire in 1976, I had concluded that the people of Shaba would have been better off had the Katanga independence effort succeeded.

***

The town of Lubumbashi was deteriorating in 1974, but it was clear that it had once been an exceptionally attractive place. Because the altitude was more than three thousand feet, the climate was very comfortable in spite of being so close to the equator. The savanna air was dry, but there was sufficient water during the rainy season and in the rivers and streams to support agriculture and decorative vegetation. Bougainvillea thrived and covered many of the walls of residences and commercial establishments. Though many of the purple-flowering jacaranda trees that lined the streets had been cut down for firewood, those that remained gave the city an almost magical atmosphere.

The American Consulate in Lubumbashi had a prime location on one of those streets, right next to the provincial governor's offices. It was the largest of the three original consulates in Zaire. The other two were in Kisangani (formerly Stanleyville), halfway up the Congo River (and the destination of Joseph Conrad's protagonist in *Heart of Darkness*), and in Bukavu (formerly Costermansville) in eastern Zaire on Lake Kivu. The consulate in Kisangani had been closed before I arrived in Zaire. The consulate in Bukavu had been reduced to only one American Foreign Service officer and a few local staff. The consulate in Lubumbashi had been reduced in size but remained a priority because it was located in the nation's economic heartland. Virtually all of the wealth that sustained the government and the military, made Zaire a player in Africa, and attracted the interest of the world was located there in Shaba Province's portion of the copper belt that also runs through Zambia.

The consulate included four Foreign Service officers, a Foreign Service secretary and about twenty local African and European employees. My colleagues were very impressive people. The consul was an experienced and sophisticated diplomat who displayed both acumen for the local environment and compassion for the people. He was infinitely patient, had a wonderful sense of humor, and took great care of all his charges. The administrative officer was a smart, competent man who was also deeply interested in the African people with whom he worked and lived. The public affairs officer was an enthusiastic and energetic promoter of cultural ties. I was the economic-commercial officer, charged with analyzing the local economy, in the context of both larger U.S. strategic interests and more short-term business interests. The local employees, or Foreign Service Nationals (FSNs), were superb. They kept the mission going. They knew how to make things work, both within the consulate and with the government and society. This was particularly true of the senior African employee, whose contacts and management seemed to be able to overcome all obstacles.

                                    ***

The "national" economy of Zaire was supported almost exclusively by revenues from the copper industry in Shaba Province. The diamonds of the Kasai were lucrative but insufficient. The funding for the government in Kinshasa, the military, and most of the transportation and energy infrastructure was tied to copper. So the national copper company, Gécamines (successor to UMHK), was the first interest of the economic section in Lubumbashi. It was still functioning reasonably well, but international commodity prices were declining; and the company, like other sectors of the economy, was suffering from Zairian government efforts to replace European owners and managers with Zairians who had substantially less education and experience. I needed to learn how the company operated, how it was coping with the changes, and then try to extrapolate what this meant for Zaire's future. That meant traveling to the different sites and getting to know key European and Zairian figures in the company.

I quickly discovered that it was a lot more difficult to meet and talk frankly with company officials in Lubumbashi than it had been in Paris. The political atmosphere made it precarious for people to talk openly in general, and Gécamines was a national security concern for the government. The relationship between the government of Zaire and the United States was also rather tense, so even if the officials personally saw the United States favorably they had to be careful. Finally, the senior leadership of Gécamines consisted mostly of Europeans, and there was an element of at least perceived competition that made them more circumspect when meeting with us. It took almost two years for us to develop enough of a relationship to be trusted. Several months before I left, senior officials opened their books to me and confirmed many of the financial and managerial difficulties that we had been speculating about throughout my tour.

The rest of the business community was more relaxed with us. Those in the government-run transportation sector were perhaps under less scrutiny than those in the mining company. I spent a long time trying to understand how products were shipped in and out of Lubumbashi, which was about a thousand kilometers from the nearest port. The most direct railroad route, through Angola, had been shut down by the civil war there. The only national route, to Kinshasa and the port of Matadi, was riddled with corruption and theft. One businessman explained that to avoid theft they had containerized their imports and then welded shut the containers. The containers arrived safely, welded shut and weighing exactly what the bill of lading stated. However, when opened they were full of sand. There was a point on the route where the containers had to be off-loaded onto barges and moved upriver to the next railhead. The barges were fully equipped with sophisticated weighing and welding equipment, so . . . Most of Lubumbashi's imports and exports therefore went the long way, through South Africa.

Food in Lubumbashi and most of Shaba Province was very expensive, because it was mostly imported. The lack of food was not due to an inhospitable physical environment. When I was in Lubumbashi, there was a group of agricultural scientists working in Shaba from Centro Internacional de Mejoramiento de Maíz y Trigo (CIMMYT), the organization that had played a central role in Latin America's "green revolution." They told us that Shaba Province had the climate, soil, and water resources sufficient to feed all of Africa! Indeed, prior to independence the region had been agriculturally self-sufficient. The indigenous people produced their own food, and the mining towns were supplied by a network of farms run by Europeans that produced a wide variety of vegetables, grains, fruits, and meat. These had mostly disappeared by the early 1970s. A major factor in their disappearance, and in the decline of food production by the indigenous population, was the rapid deterioration of the provincial (and national) road system. Under the colonial administration each village had been required to maintain its section of road. The system of dirt roads was so good that one could drive from one end of the country to the other in an ordinary sedan. After independence, the road maintenance system was not enforced. The dirt roads quickly became problematic and often impassable even by four-wheel-drive vehicles. Even if villagers wanted to grow crops, they could not get them to market. Fourteen years after independence, basic foodstuffs were scarce and Shaba was importing not only meat but vegetables and flour from the internationally sanctioned Rhodesia.

When I arrived at the Lubumbashi airport in 1974, there was only one other large aircraft on the tarmac. It was a completely black DC-10 with no markings. My new boss explained that was the supply plane from Rhodesia. At the time, Rhodesia had incurred the righteous opprobrium of the international community with its "unilateral declaration of independence" from

Great Britain—essentially to retain unfettered white rule. I assumed that the criticism and anger directed at Rhodesia would be particularly strong from its black neighbors, but in Shaba Province the trade with Rhodesia was thriving. This was partly because the European expatriates had a good deal of sympathy for the Rhodesian political position. However, it was largely because Rhodesia was simply the best, most convenient, and least expensive source of a wide variety of food products. The market in Shaba Province was determined by need and money, not by race or political preference.

During the two years that I was there, our reporting chronicled a relentless decline in economic conditions, services, and virtually all aspects of functioning human society. The availability of food and other basic necessities, the condition of roads, the management of railroads, and even the management of the huge government-owned copper company were suffering. We did a report once on the state of Air Zaire, the government airlines, and called it "Fear of Flying" after Erica Jong's popular novel of the time. Air Zaire was going downhill in almost every way. Even maintenance was becoming problematic, in spite of the fact that it was contracted out to Pan American. The crew and most of the pilots were Zairian. They had been trained and were competent technical pilots—but their judgment was sometimes questionable. On one of my flights between Kinshasa and Lubumbashi, the passengers were disturbed by the presence of a large rat that was running up and down the aisle and meandering among the seats. I watched with some amusement, wondering how the crew would deal with the problem. They didn't. Instead, the pilot left his seat and proceeded to chase the rat around the plane with a hatchet for some twenty minutes. He got it, but . . .

***

The European expatriates were involved in all aspects of the economy, from the government-owned mining and transportation companies to the banks and small businesses. They had knowledge and relationships with those in power that we did not even dream about. Over time they shared with us their stories and their perspectives on the tremendous changes that part of the world, not just Lubumbashi, was going through. These included stories about the unsuccessful Katanga secession. I had an American perspective that had also been leavened by my year at the United Nations. I had read about UN Secretary General Dag Hammarskjöld's peace efforts and his death in a plane crash not far from Lubumbashi, and I had also met people at the UN who had been personally involved with that mission. The secessionists were "bad" people, but suddenly I was meeting them and spending time with them socially. They told stories about how during the day they would face off with the UN soldiers behind their respective fortifications shooting at each other from time to time—and then in the evenings they would all get together and drink and play cards. They spoke as if it had all been good fun.

They were good businessmen, knew their customers, and were very agile and flexible. They had found many ways to overcome the physical, cultural, and political obstacles to doing business in the middle of the African continent, and they had turned many of the political and economic developments of the first twelve years of independence to their advantage. They had developed elaborate ways of managing their financial affairs that enabled them to circumvent the currency restrictions and artificial foreign exchange rates imposed by the government. Some of these methods were of questionable legality; some of them were perfectly legal, just not very transparent. It was all quite an education for a young American who still believed assiduously in the moral imperative of the rule of law and the certainty that those who abused it would be caught.

I marveled at what I considered to be the sophistication and uniqueness of their methods, but some of them assured me that what they were doing was anything but unique. They described similar situations in Europe where special arrangements were made to avoid taxes, or bribes to officials were needed to facilitate ordinary transactions. Most of those I had missed—or chosen to ignore—during my two years in Paris. It couldn't be ignored in Zaire, where less and less worked according to laws and regulations.

Government services, including permits, licenses, telephone, electricity, water, fuel, customs, and so on often functioned only on the basis of individual entrepreneurship—or what we in the United States call "corruption." In Zaire, the payments were called *matabiche*. Official Americans were strictly prohibited from participating in this entrepreneurship—not by the host government, but by ours. However, just about everyone else had to. If they wanted to make a long-distance telephone call without interminable delays (days or weeks), they had to get to know someone in the telephone company. Then they would call their contact and arrange to pay for the service informally. If they knew the contact well, he or she would come to their house to collect. Sometimes similar arrangements were necessary to purchase airline tickets, and getting on an airplane was always a cliff-hanger, from check-in all the way to getting a seat and taking off. The personnel couldn't find one's reservations; they weren't sure the plane would arrive today or take off; the baggage looked too heavy; no, there was no one available with more information. If one wanted to be sure one would actually get a seat and that one's luggage would make it as well, one would go to the airport ready to "help out" whoever had not been included in the original payment. Establishing these connections and developing a proficiency at carrying it off was critical to success. If one was interested in people and alert to their sensibilities one could go far.

Expatriate society there was quite vibrant. The expatriates were mostly from Belgium and France, but there was also a significant Greek community as well as a Sephardic Jewish community that had originally arrived from Rhodes via East Africa in the early twentieth century. For the most part, they chose to be there. Many had been born in Katanga or elsewhere in the region. They lived a European life in an African setting that they had been able to control or at least orchestrate for more than half a century. Most worked closely with the Zairians. Many spoke Kiswahili and other local dialects, and they seemed to know their African colleagues and even their families well. However, they rarely socialized with the Zairians, often considering their race and cultural background to be a divide that could not be overcome. Among themselves, social life was very active. They were distressed by the changes that were taking place in Zaire, and most knew that their days in Africa were numbered. There were parties and dinners almost every night, and sometimes it seemed a little bit desperate. They were very generous in their welcome for newcomers from Europe or from America.

Life was pleasant, and it was also very expensive, particularly for the relatively junior American officials. The official rate for the local currency, the zaire, was $2 per zaire, while the real value was more like 20¢ per zaire. Official Americans were not allowed to change money at anything but the official rate, so for us local goods were five to ten times more expensive than for those operating in the real economy. Many of the expatriate businessmen had complex arrangements by which they made the transition between different currencies. Some of these involved their Zairian business partners, some did not. Some of the wealth they built up could not be transferred back to Europe—and that helped contribute to more conspicuous consumption of luxury goods. For those who would not or could not participate in this unofficial economy, "keeping up with the Joneses" was utterly out of the question.

This could make it difficult for official Americans to reciprocate the social generosity of either our expatriate or Zairian colleagues. Social occasions are the most effective place to make the contacts necessary to learn about and function effectively in a foreign environment. However, official representation budgets for the U.S. Foreign Service are generally very low, and priority goes to the senior person at post who has the heaviest responsibilities. In Zaire, the limited budgets were compounded by the exchange rate problem. On one occasion, a shipment of fresh crab arrived from Belgium. It sold out within hours of the plane's arrival, at a price of 250 zaires per kilo (about $225/pound). Needless to say, none of the official Americans purchased any, though some might have been invited to share it that evening.

We did have one somewhat unique tool that we used as much as possible. The Department of State sent commercial movies around to posts to use for recreation. In the mid-1970s there was no Internet, no DVDs, and not even any videotapes. These movies were 35mm movies on large reels, and each post had one or two projectors. When we received them we would invite as many of our local friends and colleagues as we could to our houses to watch them. They often were not very good films (probably the lowest priced the Department of State could find)—lots of violence, drugs, and sex—so they were not the most appropriate for official representation purposes, but most people didn't mind.

***

While life in Lubumbashi was interesting, it was not always relaxed. On one of my first trips away from Africa, a colleague in London aptly described it thus: "There is often a sense in Africa that life there is precarious." In Zaire that sense of precariousness was enhanced by an Alice-in-Wonderland sense of absurdity, which one seemed to encounter at every turn. Sometimes we were living on the edge of absurdity, and sometimes we would topple over the edge and flounder in it. Conversations with officials, soldiers, ticket sellers—almost anyone who held any kind of power—could appear quite nonsensical.

Sometimes they could not understand what we were saying. Sometimes they could understand what we were saying, but not what we wanted. Sometimes they chose not to understand, because they suspected it would be too much trouble to understand. Sometimes they knew perfectly well what we wanted but pretended not to as part of their bargaining strategy. Sometimes we didn't know what to ask for. Sometimes we couldn't understand the reply (perhaps for one of the above reasons). Sometimes we chose not to understand the reply or the request, because we didn't want to step into a negotiation. Whether the misunderstandings were real or intentional, it seemed generally that there was more misunderstanding than understanding.

That should not have been a surprise. This was a country, a people, and a culture in shock. The people were making a leap from a primitive social structure, a subsistence agricultural economy, and a nonparticipatory authoritarian political system to a complex, multicultural/international society, an appendage of an enormous global economy, and a political system that had many of the trappings of a pluralistic democracy. Most of the population was at the mercy of the more aggressive elements that understood and sought to control at least pieces of the social, economic, or political environment.

Everyone was struggling, including the political leadership. By 1965, when Mobutu seized power, the country was still owned and run by its citizens in name only. The real economic power was still in the hands of expatriates, and this meant that political power was heavily influenced and often controlled by them. President Mobutu tried to accelerate the transition process with political reforms that centralized his power and weakened the fledgling democratic institutions, and by stimulating nationalism. In the mid-1960s he changed the names of major cities. The capital Leopoldville, named after the former Belgian king, became Kinshasa (apparently named after a local village). Stanleyville became Kisangani (a Kiswahili word describing its location), and Elizabethville became Lubumbashi (probably after the local river).

In 1972 Mobutu stepped up his efforts with an African "authenticity" campaign. This was called *authenticité* in French, which ironically enough remained the national language and the language by which the *authenticité* campaign was promulgated. The government changed more names, starting with the name of the country and its features. The Democratic Republic of the Congo became the Republic of Zaire. This was supposed to be more authentic, more African. The name came from the Kikongo word *nzere* or *nzadi*, describing the Congo River and meaning "the river that swallows all rivers." But *zaire* was the Portuguese version of that word, so in reality the new name—for the nation and the river—was more mired in the colonial period than the original name. Katanga Province had taken its name from a nineteenth-century chief in the region, so it was already pretty authentic. However, its attempt at secession must have cancelled any claims to *authenticité* in the minds of Mobutu's officials, and it was renamed *Shaba*, a Swahili word for copper.

The president changed his own name, from Joseph-Desiré Mobutu to Mobutu Sese Seko Kuku Ngbendu wa Za Banga. Officially, this meant the "all-powerful warrior who goes from triumph to triumph." Unofficially, at least in Lubumbashi, it was popularly understood to mean "the cock that leaves no chicken untouched." Everyone else was ordered to follow suit—with the names, that is—and to adopt more "authentic" Zairian names. Most complied, but in the beginning at least there were reports of one rather significant holdout, namely the president's wife. Marie Antoinette Mobutu was a devout Catholic, had received her name at her christening, and was rumored to have refused to change her name or her children's names. She died of heart failure a few years later, and Mobutu's second wife was more "authentic."

UMHK had already become Gécamines (Société Générale des Carrières et des Mines) when it was nationalized in 1966, but in 1973 thousands more foreign-owned businesses were nationalized. Most expatriates who wished to continue operating in Zaire were required to take on a Zairian as an equal partner. Everyone did so, but the partners were rarely equal. They shared in the profits but rarely in the work. A façade was created to which everyone paid homage as real, and this just enhanced the absurdity of it all. George Orwell, in his novel *Animal Farm*, beautifully described the nonsense created by the combination of political ideology and political opportunism. Zaire was a real-life example. I used to recommend *Animal Farm*, along with Conrad's *Heart of Darkness* and Golding's *Lord of the Flies*, to visitors and Zaire watchers as the best descriptions of what was happening there. As time progressed, less and less was as it appeared to be. To some degree, this suited the purposes of both expatriates and Africans. Many expatriates did not want to give up their control, and many Africans preferred trappings to responsibilities. Things began to deteriorate. Inside the shell of appearance, the real economy rotted at an ever-increasing rate.

Life's precariousness was much more of a problem for the Zairians than for the expatriates. Things had been bad enough during colonial times. In those days, the local people—*les noirs*—were hardly even second-class citizens. They had virtually no say in their government, and for the most part they had access only to primary education and to manual labor jobs. They could work their way up to positions of some responsibility, but rarely to management, and never on a par with other races. Some labor was required, such as maintaining the local roads, and laws and rules were strictly enforced, including use of corporal punishment. However, during colonial times there had been order, very little crime, sufficient food for everyone, and jobs available for those interested in participating in the market economy. After independence all of that changed. Laws and procedures were arbitrarily enforced. The money economy declined steadily as businesses closed and jobs disappeared. Buildings, roads, and services deteriorated, and even food became scarce.

The declining economy not surprisingly undermined everyday security. While I was there, we were pretty safe. We all had night guards, but that was mostly to protect against theft rather than bodily harm, and the guards seemed to sleep more than we did. The police and military were unpredictable, and that could be rather unsettling. This seemed to correlate directly with the unpredictability of the paychecks they were supposed to receive. When things got particularly bad for them, the checkpoints around town would increase. Cars would be stopped—sometimes a reason given, sometimes not—and held until the occupants made an appropriate contribution to the well-being of those sworn to protect the nation's security. The soldiers in particular were not very well disciplined, and they were often drunk or otherwise inebriated. I was stopped once by a man who shoved his automatic weapon through the window into my face. He was so drugged and/or diseased that his eyes were yellow and vaguely inhuman, but when I told him (in retrospect rather stupidly) that the American Consulate did not allow us to pay *matabiche*, he simply shrugged and waved me on.

This precariousness could be official as well as personal. Once, the American defense attaché from the embassy flew the defense attaché's plane out to Lubumbashi from Kinshasa. He neglected to go through the established procedures for clearance. While he had called the appropriate office in Kinshasa for permission and had been told it was granted, he had no written proof of this. When he landed in Lubumbashi the plane was immediately impounded, and he and his crew were placed under house arrest. The consul and the rest of the consulate staff spent the next several days trying to secure their release. Everyone was on edge—which only added to the difficulty of resolving the problem.

***

Much of what I experienced professionally and socially in Zaire surprised me and altered the preconceptions of Africa I had brought with me. The one part that did not surprise me, but certainly lived up to the images I had from books and films, was the land. I was awestruck by it. It was huge and magnificently varied. My official travels took me from one end of Shaba to the other, and also down into Zambia. They gave me glimpses of the savanna and the forests, and of the human and animal inhabitants. I saw more, though, when I took time off from my official duties and got out into the countryside on my own or with others who knew it well.

I was fortunate to meet a few Europeans who had been born in the region and loved to get out into the bush to hunt and explore. We went out camping, hiking, hunting, and fishing. I am not much of a hunter, but I enjoyed going with them. One friend took me down with his family to a park on the southern shore of Lake Tanganyika just over the border from Shaba. We stayed in small cabins, where we were visited by a herd of elephants who seemed to come in just to scratch themselves on the cabin walls—which was a little like experiencing an earthquake when one was inside the cabin in question. We went spearfishing for tiger fish just off a small white beach about a half mile from the cabins. The technique was to swim out into about eight feet of water, submerge, and lie on the bottom as long as possible waiting for these very large fish to swim by. We didn't see any. However, after about an hour I thought I noticed a large, dark shape move slowly off to the side of us. My eyes are not very good without glasses, so I mentioned it to my friend, who just shrugged and said he thought it was time to leave anyway. The next morning when we returned by boat to resume our vigil, we found the entire beach covered with very large crocodiles—which ended my interest in spearfishing in Lake Tanganyika.

I got as far north as Goma in northeastern Zaire near the Rwandan border, and climbed the Nyiragongo volcano with a reluctant guide—reluctant possibly because he was carrying a gun that seemed to weigh more than he did. He said it was to protect me from elephants. It was a long hike to the edge of the crater and the view was magnificent, although there was no visible lava in the crater, just some steam or smoke. Several years later, in 1977, the volcano suddenly erupted and the lava flow killed thousands of people in the area.

My dream had been to get to the Rwenzori Mountains, also known as the Mountains of the Moon, which for centuries were considered to be the source of the Nile—and even rumored to have been the location of the Garden of Eden. The Mountains of the Moon turned out to be beyond my reach, but I was able to visit the gorillas in the forest west of Bukavu, and that turned out to be my most memorable African trip.

Before Diane Fossey publicized the lives and habits of the mountain gorillas in Rwanda, Adrien Deschryver, a Belgian resident of Bukavu on the shore of Lake Kivu, had done a great deal of work studying the lowland gorillas of that area and trying to protect them. Deschryver was the chief warden of Kahuzi-Biega Park, and he initiated tours for small groups of visitors into the forest to visit the gorillas. Midway through my tour in Lubumbashi I made a trip up to Bukavu, and the American consul there arranged for me to join one of those groups. Deschryver had gotten to know the gorillas well, in particular one old "silverback," the name given to mature males, whom he named Casimir. There were wonderful stories about Deschryver taking groups in to visit the gorillas, even share lunch with them. Unfortunately for me, Mr. Deschryver was away in Europe when I visited, and our group was led by one of his Zairian assistants. In addition, the old silverback Casimir had been deposed in the last year by a younger opponent who was less comfortable with human visitors.

A small group of us, both European and Zairian, left Bukavu in the early morning and drove out to the park. We were given a briefing on what to expect. They had a pretty good record of finding the gorilla family, but it was never a sure thing. They told us we were supposed to keep as quiet as possible in order not to alarm the gorillas, and if we did find them we were to be silent and stand very still. The guide explained that the silverback was likely to charge us to assert his dominance. This was an act, and we would be in no danger. However, under no circumstances were we to break and run, because that would put us in danger. Did we understand?—I guessed so.

In our case we had a relatively short walk of about an hour before we heard the first indications of their presence: rustling bushes and the sound of breaking branches or trees (some of which sounded pretty big). We walked for some time listening to that and wondering how close the gorillas actually were. Then, without warning an indescribable high-pitched scream exploded upon us, sounding like it came from right over my shoulder. The surprise knocked the breath out of me—but the person who was the most startled was our guide and leader, who jumped at least two feet straight up. That was less than reassuring, but after he collected himself we continued and eventually stopped at the edge of a very small clearing. After several minutes we began to notice movement in the bushes around the clearing. Some gorillas began to move into sight to get a view of us. The guide pointed to the side where we saw another shape almost twice the size of the others. "That's pretty big," I thought, and then it stood up. We had only been looking at his head. He seemed enormous, much bigger than anything I had seen in a zoo—and there were no bars between us. We all braced ourselves for a charge, but it never came. We stayed for about thirty minutes watching them minding their children and watching us, and then we headed back. On the way I began talking more with our guide and learned why he had been so nervous. On his last visit to see this particular gorilla, he had been charged—and had lost his nerve. He turned to run, and the silverback grabbed him by the leg, hurled him around, and bit his foot. He didn't know what to expect on this outing. I was rather glad that I had not learned that before we set out. I was also very impressed with our young guide's courage in returning to face his assailant. Perhaps we didn't get charged because the silverback recognized our guide and figured he had sufficiently made his point the last time.

***

The Zairians I met and got to know, from senior government officials to people who worked for me, were generally kind, polite, and friendly—in a distant, careful sort of way. Most of them were just trying to live their lives and survive. For some, survival meant getting enough food for themselves and their families. For some, it meant competing in the unpredictable—precarious—world of Zairian politics. For some, it meant getting and keeping a material lifestyle comparable to the Europeans. Most of them did not appear to think much beyond the box they were in. They either did not have, or were not willing to share with me, intellectual, cultural, or philosophical interests and aspirations beyond what was needed for survival at the time.

I was a little surprised that most of the Zairians in positions of power or influence with whom I talked had little appreciation for the natural beauty that surrounded them. Perhaps it was just too close to them. A Zairian friend who had attended college in California told me a story of a friend who visited him from Zaire and asked what there was to do in San Diego. When my friend mentioned the San Diego Zoo, his friend's comment was, "I grew up in a zoo. Why would I want to visit one here?" It was understandable but disappointing to me. I was trying to appreciate what they had. They were just trying to get away from it.

I'm sure that part of my perspective was the result of language constraints. I spoke French well enough, but I did not speak any of the African languages. Many of the ordinary people in Shaba Province spoke only a little French. Their language was Kiswahili or one of the local dialects. Even many of the more educated government officials had only limited French.

The European expatriates who spoke those African languages (usually Kiswahili) had much more substantial relationships with their Zairian counterparts than we did. This came with more than a little irony, since we arrived at least intending to live, interact, and work with the Africans as equals.

I had hoped to find a unique and rich culture in Africa, hidden from the world—or denied by it. I didn't find it, at least not where I was, and I hope that others have been more successful. Sometimes it seemed like the Congo Basin was a great hole in the world. Those born there had terrible difficulty getting out. Some tried to do it by climbing on the backs of their fellow countrymen, but that just bound them ever more tightly to it. Others, not born there, were sucked in, enticed with the possibilities of riches, adventure, or escape from different holes.

***

Those of us at the American Consulate in Lubumbashi did our job as best we could, representing our nation with its culture, aspirations, and ideals to as much of the local population as we could. We reported to the embassy in Kinshasa and to Washington what was happening in Shaba and what we thought that meant for our relations and our interests. Because that period was one of decline, much of our reporting was negative and cautionary. Because we were located in the heart of the country's economic engine, what we said was of some interest to our colleagues.

We assumed that it was of interest to the American business community as well, but after leaving Zaire my confidence in that contribution was shaken. I traveled to New York City with a group of State Department colleagues studying economics and met with the international department of a major American bank. During the discussion, they told us how enthusiastic they were about the prospects for working with lending to Zaire. When I expressed surprise and recounted some of what I had seen there, they seemed completely unaware of the problems and only marginally concerned.

I arrived in Zaire with my own set of preconceptions. I believed strongly that the Africans should be free and independent, and that they were capable of governing themselves if they were only allowed to do so. By the time I left, I recognized that that view was flawed. While it may be true that "all men are created equal," we are certainly not born into this world in equal circumstances. And while all men may be "endowed by their creator with certain inalienable rights," we are not all given the tools to realize those rights in the world of men.

I concluded that the people born into the Congo region of central Africa over the last two centuries were seriously deficient in their ability to pursue the rights we Americans believe they were endowed with. This was not only the result of exploitation by people from more powerful nations. They have been vulnerable to exploitation by outsiders not only because they have been less powerful, but because they have lacked the experience, support, wisdom, and discipline generated over time by more developed social and political cultures.

Efforts by outsiders to help these peoples will be short lived at best and very possibly counterproductive, until they can create or import sufficient depth and breadth of culture to provide a sustaining environment for themselves and future generations. The scope of the challenge is more than mind-boggling. France has been engaged in this process for more than a thousand years, and it has the further advantage of being an heir to Roman and Greek civilizations. China has been doing it for more than five thousand years. We in the United States, who say we want to help the underprivileged of the world, have only been building our own culture for several hundred years.

When I was in Lubumbashi most of us thought the situation was already very bad, and it was hard to imagine things getting worse. Sometimes we thought our reporting was somewhat iconoclastic. We did not realize that the unraveling had only just begun. Shortly after I left, the first invasion of Shaba Province took place by forces that included exiled soldiers from the former secessionist Katanga, and the precariousness that I had experienced turned to real violence and destruction. In subsequent years the economy and living conditions continued to decline almost unabated. When Mobutu, whom many considered to be the central problem, finally left the scene twenty-five years later, things got even worse, with the whole eastern part of the country exploding in a frenzy of violence and even talk of an "African World War."

American foreign policy often is neither as well informed nor as wise nor successful as most of us would like to believe. The United States helped prevent the breakup of the newly independent Democratic Republic of the Congo and stopped the growth of Soviet influence in the new country. In strategic geopolitical terms, that was seen as a success at the time. Would the secession of Katanga have made the region more vulnerable to Soviet influence? More importantly, might it have helped prevent the terrible violence that has infected the whole Great Lakes area of central Africa in recent decades?

Probably none of us are wise enough to prescribe a solution to the tragedy of this region. However, there is one relatively small change to our conduct of diplomacy in Africa and the world in general that would help to begin making a difference over time. That would be to expand our foreign language capability. Looking back at my time in Zaire, if I could do it over I would try to expand my contacts with Zairians in different walks of life to better understand their needs, their predicament, and their perspectives. I was charged with reporting on the economy that was important to the United States, and I went directly to the most important players. That was appropriate, but I missed many of the people behind them, who played some part in influencing them and wanted to and sometimes did replace them.

I don't think our diplomatic mission in Zaire really understood the depth of the challenges the country and its people were facing or what it would take for them to successfully meet those challenges (though I do believe that it was at least as well plugged in as the missions sent by other nations). Because most of us did not speak the indigenous languages or Kiswahili, we were not able to communicate with about 80 percent of the population except in the most rudimentary fashion. Communicating only with a country's elite is insufficient. The elite have their own unique perspective—and they may even be part of the problem. We need to be able to look beyond the major cities, below the surface and behind the face presented to outsiders.

It is difficult for most people to cope with and communicate with strangers, particularly if those people have relatively narrow education or experience, and if they see strangers only in extreme categories as enemies or saviors. The barriers created by looking different are formidable. If we talk differently as well, the barriers are likely to be insurmountable. Language creates a window through which we can exchange thoughts and perspectives. When the language we speak is comprehensible to others, they are more likely to welcome us into their communities and their homes. When their language is comprehensible to us, we are more likely to be comfortable in their environment and to see things and understand situations that otherwise we would not. Unfortunately, we did not then, and we do not now—with a few exceptions—train our diplomats in indigenous languages beyond official national languages. In many cases we do not even train our diplomats in the national languages of the countries to which they are sent. This is because the Department of State has insufficient resources to do so. Inadequate financial resources limit the number of teachers and classroom space. A shortage of Foreign Service positions makes it impossible to assign existing Foreign Service officers to more extensive language training.

Every study of how to improve American diplomacy that I have read recommends improving our language ability. Our diplomats, bureaucrats, politicians, and the general public all voice support for that finding. However, over the last five decades very little has been done to provide the resources and the structure for expanding our ability. We Americans take a minimalist approach to the study of foreign languages. It is given short shrift in our public school systems across the nation, and it is still terribly inadequate for public servants throughout the federal government. It is a deficiency within our own social and political culture that will cause us significant problems in the future.

Chapter Three

Introduction to China: Taipei (August 1980–July 1981)

In the late summer of 1980, I arrived at Chiang Kai-shek International Airport,[1] headed for the U.S. government's Chinese language school, newly located on Yangmingshan (陽明山 "Grass Mountain"), just north of Taipei (台北). For years, the school, which taught civilian U.S. government officials basic Chinese speaking and reading skills, had been located in the central Taiwan city of Taichung (Taizhong). In 1979, after the United States transferred its formal recognition of the government of China from the Republic of China (ROC) on Taiwan to the People's Republic of China (PRC), on the mainland, the U.S. government presence on Taiwan was consolidated. The embassy was shut down and replaced with the quasi-private American Institute on Taiwan (AIT), and the school was brought up closer to Taipei.

It was night and difficult to see very much as the car from AIT hurtled along the superhighway through the hills and along the river, but it looked crowded and busy. After twenty minutes, we left the highway and snaked up the mountain road to the little town of Shanzihou (山仔后 "Back of the Mountain") on Yangmingshan. On the way up, I remember seeing the gate lights of what looked like large houses, but little else. The driver dropped me off at a little row house that was to be my quarters, pointed out the general direction of the school for the next morning, and left me alone. I had finally arrived in the East.

It had been a long trip. I could have made a one-day hop west directly to Taiwan, but chose to go the long way. Going east through Europe, the Middle East, and India gave me the chance to see some old friends and made the transition more gradual. Looking back, it was probably a subconscious effort to say goodbye to my cultural and emotional ties with Europe, stopping in Stockholm, Paris, and Rome. I also wanted to go east through Istanbul and

43

see the Bosporus, which, in Western eyes at least, separates the European and Asian continents. While there a friend took me out to the southeastern corner of Turkey to climb the mountain Nemrut Daği and watch the sun rise silently over the desert from the tomb of Antiochus of Commagene, accompanied by enormous statues of Greek and Persian gods. That was a fitting way to take leave of the West. I then stopped for a week in India, where the colors, smells, crowds, and infinite confusion of past and present were quite overwhelming. Even though I had not yet seen much of my new home, I felt relieved that I had finally arrived in Chinese Asia.

The next morning I was up early, and I wandered in the direction that the driver had showed me. Eventually, I found a cluster of single-story, military-like buildings that were markedly different from the other buildings in the town, and I headed for the only door where there was a light and some movement. Inside, an attractive young woman was busy straightening up some books and papers. She was wearing slacks and a traditional Chinese blouse. I asked in my very elementary Chinese if this was the school, and she fixed on me a penetrating stare with piercing brown eyes that I remember thinking I could not see into. She answered yes and invited me to come in. She was called "Teacher Chen" (the Chinese, Chen Laoshi, sounds more distinguished), and she was more commonly known as "Little Chen." There were two teachers named Chen, so the older one was "Big Chen" (Da Chen) and the younger one was "Little Chen" (Xiao Chen).

All my life I have traveled. Being alone in a strange place is not new or troubling for me, since I have experienced it in Europe, Latin America, and Africa. However, Taiwan was different yet again. In almost every other place I had moved to, something specific assaulted my senses and emotions as soon as I arrived and influenced how I would continue to see my new environment. In France it was the smells of Paris. In Zaire, it was the oppressive and exciting damp darkness of the tropical night. In Argentina, it was the excruciating awareness that I was way south of the equator and on the edge of the fabled pampas. In Taiwan, however, I felt as though nothing seemed to stand out.

In fact, my formative introductory impression in China had happened. I just had not noticed it. It was my meeting with Xiao Chen—whom I married thirteen months later. I was too overwhelmed that morning, and I could only begin to piece it together as I became slowly accustomed to many other aspects of the environment. China, the Chinese language, and Asia were not things I could grasp quickly—either intellectually or emotionally. Thirty years later I'm still finding pieces to the puzzles. I began to realize then that I was skipping across the surface of something very deep, complex, and different.

***

Part of that initial impressionistic confusion upon arrival in Taiwan was simply inadequate preparation on my part. When I was sent to Taiwan for language training, my understanding was that it was considered to be a part of China but was different from the rest of China primarily for relatively recent political reasons. The island of Taiwan—also called Formosa, a Portuguese name from the sixteenth century—was where the government and army of Chiang Kai-shek took refuge after being defeated by the communists in China's long twentieth-century civil war. The government on Taiwan called itself the Republic of China and claimed to be the rightful government of all China. It had been supported in that claim by the United States from 1950 until 1979, less than a year before our group arrived in Yangmingshan to study Chinese. I was aware that a significant number of Chinese on Taiwan had only lived there since 1949. However, I was not aware of Taiwan's own complex history and social makeup.

Each of China's provinces has characteristics that endow it with unique identity. Taiwan's special characteristics include its demographics, being an island, coming relatively late to the "Middle Kingdom," spending fifty formative years as a Japanese colony, providing a seat for about thirty years for a pretender to the throne (supported during much of that time by the most powerful nation on the planet), and another thirty years as one of Asia's leading democratic and capitalistic societies.

There are actually three major demographic groups on Taiwan today. The newcomers are the Han Chinese who came to Taiwan between 1945 and 1950. They make up about 13 percent of the population, and from 1945 to the late 1980s held virtually all the political power. Those with the oldest claim to Taiwan are the aboriginal people. They are related to the Pacific Islanders, including the Hawaiians, and their ancestors have been on Taiwan for thousands of years. They make up only about 2 percent of the population. The largest demographic group is the Han Chinese whose ancestors arrived in the seventeenth and eighteenth centuries. They account for about 85 percent of the population, but they had little say in Taiwan's post–World War II government until the 1980s.

Taiwan was not dominated by Han Chinese until the mid-seventeenth century, and it did not formally become part of China until the end of that century. It had been pretty much the exclusive preserve of the aboriginal peoples until the early 1600s and was then dominated by the Dutch for forty years before one of the last holdouts of the fallen Ming Dynasty made it a base to continue his opposition to the Qing. The Qing Dynasty's interest in Taiwan seems to have been almost exclusively strategic defense—first against the Ming holdouts, then the British, the French, and lastly the Japanese. When China lost the First Sino-Japanese War in 1895, it formally ceded Taiwan to Japan.

The Japanese then ruled Taiwan as a colony for fifty years, intending to make it a stepping-stone for Japanese expansion to the south. While the first two decades of that rule were heavy-handed and sometimes violent, Japan eventually decided to prepare Taiwan to become an integral part of Japan. Most Taiwanese born before 1940 were educated in Japanese schools and spoke Japanese (many still do) as well as Hokkien. When I first met Xiao Chen's mother, she spoke Hokkien and Japanese but almost no Mandarin Chinese. Many Taiwanese served in the Japanese army and actually fought against China in World War II. Unlike most of their other Asian counterparts who experienced Japanese rule, many Taiwanese viewed Japanese rule positively and considered themselves Japanese subjects. During most of Japanese rule Taiwan was peaceful and prosperous. Most of Taiwan's original transportation and industrial infrastructure was created during that period, and the Taiwanese retained a great deal of responsibility for governing the island at all levels.

The early years of restored Chinese rule after World War II contrasted unfavorably. The Nationalist Chinese who arrived in 1945 were viewed as heavy-handed, poorly disciplined, and corrupt. Taiwanese industrial, commercial, and personal property was commandeered on a large scale by officials and on smaller scales by individual soldiers roaming the countryside. When the Taiwanese population revolted in 1947, the Kuomintang (KMT) military massacred tens of thousands of them in what is now known as the "228 Incident." In Chinese, foreigners are called *waiguo ren* (外国人 "outside country people"). In Taiwan, the mainlanders are referred to, not so affectionately, as *waisheng ren* (外省人 "outside province people"). For some Taiwanese, the *waisheng ren* are more "foreign" than the actual foreigners, and some older Taiwanese still view them as little better than thieves and ruffians.

For many years, the governments of the People's Republic of China and the Republic of China both claimed to be the legitimate government of all China, including Taiwan. Challenges to central government control of the vast Chinese empire are not new. They did not begin in the twentieth century but date back at least to the third century BC when the Han Chinese peoples were first unified by the Qin emperor. At one time or another, they seem to have come from virtually every part of China. While the challenge from the Republic of China on Taiwan now rings hollow, for a while during the Cold War when its claim was apparently backed by the United States, it had to be taken seriously. It certainly reminded the Chinese leadership in Beijing of the strategic importance of the island.

Today many Taiwanese espouse a different goal: independence. They have emotional, historical, and even some legal grounds for that quest, but it is unlikely to happen. It is hard to imagine any responsible leadership of China acquiescing to anything less than complete and irreversible inclusion of Taiwan in at least the broader strategic control of China's central government. Over time—perhaps a long time—most of those on Taiwan are likely to comply. The genuine grievances that the Taiwanese had against their invading cousins from the mainland in the 1940s and 1950s have been mitigated substantially by the democratization and economic progress that has taken place since 1990. Taiwanese have developed their own interests in greater China by investing heavily in mainland China in the same time period.

It is fascinating to speculate what Asia might have looked like today if Japan had been more patient and pragmatic about its twentieth-century expansion ambitions. Taiwan was securely in its control. Most of Oceania, excluding Australia and New Zealand, probably could have been overcome and secured with international acceptance, if Japan had left China and the United States alone. A pacific island empire might have changed both Asia and the Americas irrevocably.

***

After living and working on four different continents, I thought I was pretty cosmopolitan and experienced. I had adjusted to and come to enjoy many different kinds of sights, smells, and sounds. In France, I had been through the food, flower, and animal markets and come to appreciate the smelliest of cheeses. I had even gotten used to picking my way through gutters filled with cows' heads, when the animals were still being butchered at Les Halles in central Paris. In Panama, the mold and stale fish didn't bother me. Sleeping in a hammock for a month with the Indians on the San Blas Islands in the Caribbean and taking elaborate precautions with mosquito nets in Panama's Darien Jungle to keep out vampire bats were adventures, but I could take ownership of them. They were not foreign. Africa was definitely foreign but not surprising. China was both foreign and surprising.

Taiwan is a beautiful island. It is only the size of Belgium but has a huge variety of topography, from beaches to plains and rolling hills to mountains more than ten thousand feet high. Taipei in the north is about the same latitude as Miami. While it is noticeably colder than Miami, at least in winter, the southern part of the island is quite tropical. Most of the population lives in the lowlands, but excursions to the mountains are quite popular. I went out walking as much as I could in the Yangmingshan area, and the language school organized a three-day hike across the mountains in the middle of the island. The scenery is quite spectacular in places, even near the cities.

However, it was not quite what I expected. I had been heavily influenced by French culture, where appearance in some respects has been elevated to almost religious significance. I expected China, as a much older and more advanced civilization, to be similar. I expected it to be exotic and beautiful. While I knew that much of Chinese culture on the mainland had been destroyed by the violence of the twentieth century, I also understood that on Taiwan the Chinese had been able to preserve many cultural traditions and artifacts. However, when I arrived I did not see any public evidence of my concept of Chinese culture. Of course, all the signs were in Chinese, but most of the buildings in Taipei were either Western architecture or just boxes made from brick or concrete. Much of the "modern" city had been built by the Japanese in the first half of the twentieth century. A few newer government buildings and hotels had incorporated elements of older Chinese architecture or design, and the temples were traditionally Chinese. The urban areas were crowded and grimy, and the rural areas were littered. Even in the spectacular countryside, one would often come upon piles of trash or garbage. I did not yet understand that although the elite in China had refined just about every area of human endeavor to levels comparable to or beyond those of the West, aesthetics—at least at that time—were not a primary concern for most Chinese. The majority of the Chinese population was concerned first with survival, then family, then personal advancement, and only later aesthetics.

Temples were and are important centers of social, cultural, and commercial interaction. Buddhist temples are the most abundant and are often very crowded, particularly at the time of new and full moons. The big ones are resplendent with high curved roofs held up by massive pillars, often painted in bright colors and with deities of all sizes and aspects every way you turn. The visitors are pious and respectful, but not quiet. There is usually a constant hum of voices chattering or chanting mantras and sutras. There are gongs and drums and bells and firecrackers. Pervading everything is the smell of incense being burned as petitions to the deities, or paper money being burned for deceased ancestors (silver paper) or the gods (gold paper).

It is both spiritual and practical. People are coming not only to pay their respects but to ask for help. They are asking for good fortune, health, and protection for themselves and their families. They are also asking for information, using a system of divination that has been around for thousands of years. The petitioner first prays and makes offerings to the deities, then shakes a container of sticks until one falls out. Each of the sticks is engraved with a number that corresponds to a text, which must be interpreted in light of the question. Before seeking the interpretation the petitioner must throw another combination of blocks to confirm that is the right stick. The whole process can last a few minutes or many hours, depending on the petitioner's state of mind and the complexity of the question. Once we visited the Zhulin-

shan Guanyin Temple (竹林山觀音寺 "Bamboo Forest Temple to the Bodhisattva Guanyin") in Linkou, north of Taipei, with my sister who was there
from the United States. She had a question that she wanted to ask and went
through the process several times, but she kept getting stopped by the wrong
configuration of blocks in the confirmation stage. Finally she was told that
the "gods are laughing at you" and she needed to go back and clear her own
mind before asking again.

Other important centers of social and commercial interaction are the markets, particularly the night markets. In downtown Taipei, near the Longshan
Temple (龍山寺 "Dragon Mountain Temple"), there is a vast jumble of
single-story and occasionally two-story buildings. It is crisscrossed by alleyways, some fairly wide and some narrower than sidewalks. At night, people
come from all over the city and beyond to shop and to be entertained. They
are welcomed by a hoard of shop owners, vendors from the countryside,
performers, and purveyors of all kinds of services—sometimes licit, sometimes illicit, but almost always colorful.

These night markets can be found all over Asia. For many villages, towns,
and even cities they can be the social and business heart. The overhead is
very low. Anyone can come in to buy, and just about anyone can come there
to sell. Most of the goods are relatively cheap, but expensive antiques can be
found there as well. There is relatively little regulation, so it's a good place to
buy and sell counterfeit goods—obvious and not so obvious. When I first
arrived in Taiwan, about the only place in Asia where these markets could
not be found was in mainland China, because there still were almost no free
markets there. However, by the mid-1980s that too was changing.

The buildings are the same as in much of Taiwan—boxes made of brick
or cinderblocks that are wide open at one end with folding or sliding doors,
now more often roll-up garage doors. Storage is in the back. Sometimes
cooking takes place in the back, but often the cooking is right up front so you
can see what you are in for. Seating can be inside, but it often spills out onto
the sidewalk. Lighting is strictly fluorescent and mostly just bare bulbs.
There is very little attention given to aesthetics. This is partially just practical, as decorations cost money, but sometimes it almost seems intentional—
as if making it attractive would detract from the intrinsic value of the food or
whatever other product is being sold.

The smells are overwhelming. There is incense wafting from the temple
and from many shops. There is the cooking: pungent spices; hot cooking oil;
meat, fish, or poultry; charcoal smoke. There is the food that is stored to be
cooked. There are the live animals waiting to become food—and so on.

The crowds are heavy, but they are not rush-hour crowds. There is lively
bargaining and bickering. There may be some competition to get to the head
of the line, but there is little sense of a timetable. There is a carnival atmos-

phere, with endless variations of enticements to get the money from your pockets—and an occasional effort to take it out directly.

In this area there was one street (華西街 Huaxijie) devoted almost entirely to the purveyance of snakes. The stores or stalls were all open to the air and had tables and chairs either inside or on the street. Cages were piled in front of the stores, and they were full of snakes, mostly cobras. The snakes themselves would have been terrifying if they had not been so obviously terrified themselves. They were all waiting to become meals for passersby. The flesh was put in soups or other dishes. However, the most popular part of the snakes' anatomy was not the flesh but the gall bladder. We were told that it increased the sexual prowess of men. Indeed, "Snake Alley," as it was affectionately known to foreigners, was quite close to one of the city's red light—or in this case, green light—districts. The practice seemed rather cruel. The shopkeeper would open the top of one of the cages and hook out one of the deadly snakes using a short pole. She would slip a wire noose around the snake's head and hang it up on a clothesline. Then without any further ado, she would slit open the snake's throat, cut out the gall bladder and then drain the blood and the bile into separate glasses. These would then be served to the customer, who would usually down them quickly and leave. Often these shops had one or two mongooses in cages as well. While the snakes were terrified and just tried to get as far away from everything as they could, the mongooses were anything but terrified. The cages of deadly cobras were like honey pots to them. They would pace up and down, never taking their eyes off the snakes. They would stretch their forelegs through the bars of the cages trying desperately to reach the snakes. I have rather a horror of snakes, and the bizarre spectacle of the mongooses acting like they would like nothing more than to jump right into the middle of the snake cages heightened the exotic contrast of this market—and this culture—with everything else I had experienced.

***

Having arrived in Taiwan in August, I had my first major cultural experience at the celebration of Confucius's birthday on September 28. There is a *kongmiao* (孔廟 "Confucian temple") in downtown Taipei that was built in the 1930s on the site of an earlier temple torn down by the Japanese. It is an impressive structure of traditional Chinese architecture, similar to the Buddhist temples but with more subdued colors and a less chaotic atmosphere. Since September 28 is a national holiday in Taiwan, we were able to get away from our grueling class schedule to watch the ceremony. It was my first introduction to Chinese ceremonies, and in some ways my first introduction to Chinese cultural aesthetics. I didn't like it.

The temple and its environs were very crowded. Altars inside and outside the temple were heaped high with all kinds of offerings of fruit, vegetables, and meat, most of it displayed very formally. Some of the sacrificed animals didn't even seem real. Others seemed all too real, and I was glad that my two vegetarian sisters were not there to see it. My memory of the ceremony itself was that it was incomprehensible, interminably long, and boring.

If this was Confucius, I felt I could do without him, his thought, and his influence on Chinese history and society. Indeed, as the months progressed, I reacted quite negatively to what I perceived to be Confucius's influence on Chinese society. This included the deification of the national ruler, the inflation of government officials, the professed respect for rules of behavior, the slavish devotion to society, and even the pious respect for the elderly. It seemed to me they stifled freedom, independent thought, and creativity. While that may be true to some degree, I also came to realize that my "perceptions," in fact, were often as much the prejudices I had brought with me as they were observations of objective reality.

There was certainly respect for the president at the time. However, President Chiang Ching-kuo (蔣經國 Jiang Jingguo) was respected in large part because he was doing a pretty good job of leading Taiwan through a remarkable economic expansion and toward considerably more political freedom than his father Chiang Kai-shek had allowed. Also, while many of the Chinese who had followed Chiang Kai-shek to Taiwan from the mainland genuinely admired him, the former president's popularity and that of the Nationalist government was considerably less with the Taiwanese inhabitants of the island.

Respect for authority in general was also something of a paradox. While most people demonstrated respect for public officials and figures of authority—often with some obsequiousness—that respect did not seem to translate into any obvious social orderliness. Markets, traffic, and all kinds of other daily affairs seemed quite chaotic, sometimes every man and woman for themselves. There seemed to be a kind of centrifugal force at work constantly pulling people toward chaos, which was only kept in check by the central gravitational force of authority (in government, organizations, and families) advocated by Confucius and many other Chinese philosophers.

And yet, some of the chaos was not as chaotic as it appeared. If all the cars, trucks, buses, taxis, motorcycles, bicycles, and pedestrians were carefully following a set of prescribed rules, it was not obvious to any but the most sophisticated observer. Taipei traffic at that time was not like Rome traffic, which I found alternately exhilarating and terrifying. It was more baffling, with almost equal numbers of cars and motorbikes mixing together in some incomprehensible synchronicity. An American friend once commented that he loved driving in Taipei, because there was absolutely nothing he could not do, provided he did it slowly enough—and then to demonstrate, he proceeded to cut across six lanes of traffic (going both directions) without eliciting even one honk of protest.

Over the years I have come to see Confucius (孔夫子 Kong Fuzi) in a very different light. He was born in 551 BC during the latter years of China's Zhou Dynasty. During his life he compiled a body of thought, much of it records and commentaries on prior Chinese history, that has formed the organizational and behavioral principles that have dominated Chinese civilization for the last twenty-five hundred years. Occasional efforts like that of Mao Zedong's communist regime to stamp out Confucian influence have not succeeded. Much of what he taught concerns the political realm: relations between states and the organization of government and society. However, he also speaks profoundly to the spiritual cultivation of the individual, in the context of everyday life in society, and he is considered by many to have personally achieved a high degree of enlightenment. His own works are extensive, and commentaries on his work over the subsequent two millennia appear to be innumerable. Whether his ideas and pronouncements are his own or just compiled from others (he insisted it was the latter), he at least was responsible for making them convincing and accessible enough to provide the cultural glue for the world's oldest, and I believe most highly developed, living civilization.

***

In the 1970s the Foreign Service Institute's Chinese language school on Taiwan provided the second half of a two-year program in intensive Chinese language training for U.S. government employees assigned to work in Chinese-speaking places.[2] It had been there since 1955 and had trained most of the State Department's core of Chinese language speakers. In the late 1970s, as relations between the United States and the PRC began to pick up steam, the State Department began looking to expand its cadre of Chinese-speaking diplomats. I was lucky enough to be coming to the end of my four-year tour with the Bureau of Economic and Business Affairs at the time, and while looking around for another assignment, stumbled entirely by chance into the China field. I went to talk with another colleague in the Economic Bureau about taking his job, because he was leaving. When I heard he was heading for Beijing, I expressed fascination with the fact that he had previously studied Chinese, and he set me up for lunch with the deputy director of the Office of Chinese and Mongolian Affairs. That person, again by chance, had been the Chinese language officer assigned to the Paris Embassy for the U.S.-PRC contacts there seven years earlier, and we knew each other.

I had always wanted to go to Asia, and I was working at the United Nations in New York when "ping-pong diplomacy" broke upon the world.

My supervisor there was a very impressive Chinese-American woman who was absolutely thrilled with the implications of first contacts after more than twenty years of bilateral hostility. When I expressed an interest in studying Chinese, she looked at me with more than a little skepticism and told me I would have to make a commitment of five years for that study to be worthwhile. She had judged me correctly. I dropped the idea indefinitely.

The East Asian Bureau wanted me to start language training immediately. The Economic Bureau wanted to keep me a year longer. They split the difference by reducing the language training I would get in Washington to six months. This is a chronic problem at State. The department, its offices, and its people seem to be always scrambling to keep up. There is very little advance planning—but it is not exclusively the fault of the people at State. First, the department is *always* short of resources. It usually does not have the money to hire the people to do today's jobs, much less tomorrow's jobs, and certainly not for people to plan for tomorrow's jobs. This is largely because most members of Congress perceive little or no political benefit to directing tax dollars to the State Department that could otherwise go to roads, schools, or other contracts (e.g., defense contracts) in the districts that elect them. While most (not all) presidents eventually learn that the Department of State is critical to America's strategic interests, even many of them have not been willing to go to bat for the civilian foreign affairs budget. Over the years, good bureaucrats absorb this reality into their psyches and act accordingly. They stop planning and try to make do with less. So I went to Taiwan with only six months' preparation instead of a year. I didn't mind, since I got there earlier, and I still believed I could do it faster.

There were about thirty students at the school in Taiwan, most from State and other civilian agencies of the government. There were a few military personnel, but the military had its own schools and programs (all amply funded). The classes in Washington had been group classes, but in Taiwan they were all one-on-one tutorials. We had classes most of the day, and then usually had to study late at night to keep up. At the end of the year, I believe we all attained the three-point grade in both speaking and reading that was required for our next assignments. However, the pressure was tremendous, causing me to expand my Chinese vocabulary beyond political and economic subjects to medical ones, such as *wei kuiyang* (胃潰瘍 "stomach ulcer").

***

When I first joined the Foreign Service, during our orientation course we had a particularly outstanding presentation on the difficulties of cross-cultural communication. The lecturer, or more accurately the performer, was a man who walked into the room with a baseball bat on his shoulder and then proceeded to keep us in stitches for well over an hour on the ways we Americans misinterpret the rest of the world's peoples and misrepresent ourselves to them. We human beings often have great difficulty explaining ourselves to and understanding each other. Even those of us who grow up with the same language—and even the same family—sometimes find that language can become inexplicably opaque. How much more so when we have very different backgrounds and speak utterly different languages?

Chinese is a difficult language for westerners to learn. One of the most obvious reasons is the writing system. There is no alphabet that is used to construct words. Chinese characters are pictures that must be memorized. Our alphabet has twenty-six letters we need to memorize. The Chinese language has seventy thousand characters. You need to know at least five hundred to be able to read a newspaper (the easy articles), and at least four thousand to get through college.

The spoken language also has special difficulties. It is a tonal language. Not only does the articulation of the word convey meaning, but so does the tone. Mandarin Chinese (the "national" or "common" language) has four different tones—actually five, since some words have a neutral tone. The same word said with different tones can mean at least four different things. (Context also plays a role, but we won't even try to get into that here.) For example, the word *Ma*:

- Ma with tone (1), or high tone, means "mother"
- Ma with tone (2), or rising tone, means "numb"
- Ma with tone (3), or low tone, means "horse"
- Ma with tone (4), or falling tone, means "to scold"
- And Ma with no tone at the end of a sentence means the sentence is a question.

As difficult as it was for us students, Mandarin is relatively easy compared to some of the other Chinese languages. Hokkien, the southern Min language that is spoken on Taiwan and in Fujian Province, has six tones. Cantonese has eight. For someone who has grown up learning Chinese, this of course is very natural. For those who are introduced to Chinese at age thirty, it is anything but natural. Many of us westerners cannot even tell the difference between the tones, much less understand or apply them properly. This can be the source of much embarrassment, mirth, or other emotions—depending on where you happen to be standing.

After I had been in Taiwan for about three months, I rented a car and went on a short road trip with Xiao Chen. Before we set out, I noticed there was some rather noisy squeaking from under the hood, and so we drove into a local garage to ask a mechanic to check it. I assumed the problem was a loose fan belt. All the vocabulary I had learned was political and economic, not mechanical. Nowhere had I seen a word for "fan belt." I asked Xiao Chen, but she didn't know what a fan belt was. So I asked how to say "rubber band," figuring I would point to the fan belt as I said it and the mechanic would get the message. Armed with "rubber band," I bent with the mechanic under the hood and told him I thought there was something wrong with the fan belt. He turned his head slowly and looked at me with utterly uncomprehending eyes. I realized that I had gotten something wrong and walked back around to ask Xiao Chen what it was. She looked at me with a flat expression, said, "You just told him there is something wrong with your banana cookie," and then dissolved into giggles.

xiang (4) jiao (1) quan (1) rubber circle (band)
xiang (1) jiao (1) quan (1) banana circle (cookie)

The mechanic apparently saw little humor in it. He never changed his expression, told me there was nothing wrong with my banana cookie, and not to worry about it. He then closed the hood and went back inside. Much later we looked up "fan belt" in the dictionary: feng (1) shan (4) = fan; pi (2) dai (4) = leather belt. I guess it should have been obvious.

Many months later—when I thought my command of tones was better—we were visiting a rug factory. By this time, we were engaged. "Xiao" Chen actually had a name, Chen Chunzhi,[3] and we were shopping for a wedding present for ourselves. We had looked at all the different designs, and I was trying to describe to the salesman the combination that I preferred—and that I thought Chunzhi agreed with. I did fine with the center of the design and with the colors, but then lost it on the border. I explained that on the edge I wanted a "pearl border," which was a combination of circles and squares. I thought at that point the salesman would nod and politely say "Good choice," but instead all conversation stopped. He looked embarrassed, and I turned to Chunzhi to ask what I had done wrong this time. This time she didn't offer me any help, except to say pointedly that she didn't want any pig shit on *her* rug.

zhu (1) bian (1) pearl border
zhu (1) bian (4) pig shit

One of my fellow students had a much more embarrassing moment all by himself in a major department store. He wanted to buy a ballpoint pen, and he approached a counter where there seemed to be several on display. He smiled at the attractive salesgirl and asked in his best school-taught Chinese, "Please show me your pens." Much to his surprise, instead of responding graciously, as most salespeople there do, the salesgirl started scolding him loudly and vehemently. He could not understand what she was saying, but the shoppers around him obviously could, and he beat a hasty retreat—without purchasing his ballpoint pen. The next day, he explained to his teacher (Xiao Chen) what had happened and asked her what went wrong. Tones, of course:

bi (3) ball point pen
bi (1) vagina

***

Love is a very powerful thing. It can cross any boundaries—but crossing the boundaries does not eliminate them. When they are crossed, the environment and how it responds can be quite different from what we are accustomed to or what we are anticipating. We might see the boundary and leap boldly (or recklessly) across. We might not see it at all and stumble unknowingly into a quite different rabbit hole. Sometimes it is a blinding revelation—an *aha!* or *oh no!* Sometimes the recognition comes only months or years later.

After less than three months in Taiwan, I had decided that I wanted to marry Xiao Chen. I was pretty sure the feeling was reciprocated, and we had talked around the subject for some time. I have always been a sort of romantic person, and I looked for a setting to make a formal proposal that would be memorable. I succeeded, but not entirely in the way I intended.

We would often meet in downtown Taipei after school, wander around the shops, and spend time in a little coffee shop talking and sometimes studying. There was a park there that had lovely trees, walkways, ponds, and traditional Chinese bridges and pagodas. We would sometimes walk there in the afternoon. I picked an evening when it was still warm, and there was a full moon. After we finished dinner and were getting ready to head back to our respective homes, I suggested we walk through the park. She said no, that was too much trouble; let's just head for the bus station. However, I insisted, and she reluctantly gave in.

About halfway through the park I suggested we sit down on a bench that had a nice view of the water and the moon. Again, she said no, let's keep moving. Again, I insisted, and she accommodated me. So we sat down, and I gave my little speech and asked her to marry me. She was not the least emotional and replied that would be fine with her—but she thought that I needed to think about it some more—and now could we please move on to the bus station? It was not quite the momentous romantic moment that I had anticipated, but the deed was done.

Sometime later when we looked back on that evening, she finally explained to me how different the experience was for her.

- First of all, she said the park was not considered a safe place. She had never told me this before, and it seemed perfectly safe to me. There were even plenty of people strolling around. However, she had been distinctly uncomfortable, had not wanted to go in, and had been very anxious to get out as quickly as possible.

- Second, the full moon was anything but romantic for her. The full moon is considered to have a destabilizing effect on people and often to bring out their worst qualities—enhancing in her mind the likelihood that the park was dangerous.
- Third, I had picked the absolute worst month of the year for our visit. This was the month when in traditional Chinese cosmology, the gates of Hell are opened, and the disturbed spirits are free to roam the earth and take revenge on the living. (Actually, there she was mistaken. The ghost month usually occurs around August.)

In sum, I first put her in an absolutely terrifying situation and then asked her to leave her family and everything familiar to her—and spend the rest of her life with me, a man whose judgment was appearing increasingly questionable.

***

I come from a large extended family. My mother's family of Marshalls, Porters, and Lees is Southern, from North Carolina, Virginia, and Missouri. Their history in America stretches back to the 1600s. My father's ancestors were Scots-Irish, who arrived two hundred years later and settled in Pennsylvania and Ohio. The families fought on different sides of the Civil War. Both families have retained an extensive sense of history and family, and reunions of each usually include sixty to a hundred people from all over the United States and beyond. There are almost always at least four generations present physically, and five or six present in spirit. This is relatively unusual in the United States, where the concept of family is usually limited to two or three generations. Nevertheless, the size of my family and the extent of our traditions are insignificant in comparison to the importance of family in China.

Family is a central concept and dynamic in virtually every area of Chinese culture: philosophy, education, economics, politics, and even security. China's most famous philosopher and teacher, Confucius, described the family as the basic building block of society and politics, detailing the obligations between husband and wife, parents and children, and so on. He detailed a hierarchical structure that led all the way up to the emperor. If families were well managed and cultivated, he taught, the social and political health of the nation would be assured—if they were not, then the reverse would be true.

Family members depend on each other and are responsible for each other. In particular, children must respect and obey their parents, and they must care for them in their old age—as their parents cared for them. The oldest son bears the heaviest responsibility, while daughters owe their allegiance to the families into which they marry. Every individual is responsible to someone else: children to parents, wife to husband, husband to ruler. No one is independent—no one is ever completely "free" in the sense that many Americans value so highly. Traditionally, family members are even held to account for each other by the political and legal systems. If an adult individual commits a crime, his family's reputation will certainly suffer, and the family can be held legally responsible as well. If the crime is political the repercussions are even greater. It was not unknown for an emperor to execute several generations of a family for the crime of a single individual.

Mao Zedong tried to destroy the traditional Chinese family, reasoning that it interfered with loyalty to the state and obstructed progress toward a new China. During the Cultural Revolution, he set husbands against wives and children against their parents—but in the end the family survived. Today, in both mainland China and in Taiwan the economic, political, and social lives of members of a family are inextricably bound together. The traditions that do this are extensive, elaborate, and sometimes enormously complicated. For an outsider it is sometimes opaque and always confusing.

***

Chunzhi grew up in a very large family, even by my standards. Her grandmother had thirteen children (that lived), of which Chunzhi's father was the oldest. Chunzhi in turn was the oldest grandchild, and for several reasons she was sent to grow up with her grandparents at the family home. She was almost as old as some of her aunts and uncles, so she straddled the generations. She watched at close quarters all the joys and problems a large family produces. In the process, she became very sensitive to personal relations within the family and to how to manage issues to prevent them from developing into significant problems.

Marrying an American was one of those issues that needed to be managed. The family was not entirely unfamiliar with Americans. There was an American base nearby on part of the family property. One of Chunzhi's uncles, who was himself in the military, had struck up a friendship with an American officer who visited often enough to make a lasting impression on a very young girl. They called him "Tang Shushu," which to the kids meant "Uncle Soup," but was probably a homonym for "Tom." He drove a bright red Jeep and wore big black boots—both very unusual and exotic. Notwithstanding that friendship, when one of Chunzhi's younger sisters later married an American military officer there was considerable family disapproval, which had not entirely dissipated by the time I arrived. Chunzhi was determined to avoid a similar situation.

I was introduced gradually, first visiting with a group of her students from the language school. We were treated as honored foreign guests. Several of the uncles joined us and were extremely gracious, even though most of us had very rudimentary Chinese. Some of the family, like Chunzhi's mother and grandmother, actually spoke primarily Taiwanese. It certainly helped that we were Chunzhi's students. Being a teacher is a much honored profession in China, and they were rightfully proud of her. It also helped that we were government officials. Traditionally, a government posting (civilian, not military) is the highest of all professions in China, and Chunzhi's great-grandfather had been an official in the imperial bureaucracy of the Qing Dynasty. Among government posts, diplomats are well regarded as well.

I visited several other times after that—low-key visits, no pressure, and no fanfare. I never really understood what was going on. It all seemed perfectly natural to me, and by the end of a year they were all familiar with who I was. At some point during the summer Chunzhi's grandfather asked her, "Well, are you going to marry a foreigner?"—and with that the principle was approved. I, however, still needed to be approved. That required two tracks, male and female.

The female side was predictable for me, since I was familiar with the importance accorded to astrology. Chunzhi's mother and grandmother took my statistics to an astrologer and came back with a positive answer. Among other things, I was born in the year of the rat and Chunzhi was born in the year of the dragon—considered an excellent match.

The male side was more of a surprise. Chunzhi's grandfather, A-Gong, was a very distinguished man. He was a landowner, with beautiful bucolic property in the hills near the CCK International Airport. His profession was Chinese medicine, carrying on a family tradition that was more than a hundred years old, and he maintained a clinic in a nearby town for many years. His seven sons had been carefully educated and directed to professions that would benefit and support the family. The oldest, Chunzhi's father, had been a businessman until his untimely death in an accident when she was only ten years old. Second Uncle was a politician and local government official, Third Uncle was a teacher and school principal, Fourth Uncle was a businessman, Fifth Uncle had gone into the Navy, Sixth Uncle was a Chinese doctor, and Seventh Uncle was a biochemist.

A-Gong was also blind, an affliction that had come upon him gradually as a result of migraines that neither Chinese nor Western medicine had been able to control. When I met him, he was already ninety years old. He could still walk around with help from his wife or sons, but most of the time he would sit at a small table similar to ones Chinese doctors use for consultations, just inside a door that led out to the home's large central courtyard.

Many family members and many friends would enter and leave by this door rather than the larger, more formal entrance in the center of the courtyard that led to the altar to the ancestors, and during large family dinners this was the room where most of the younger children would congregate to eat and to play. Also adjoining this room was the bedroom that he shared with Chunzhi's grandmother (A-Ma). In this central location A-Gong would listen to—and keep track of—the people coming and going and respond to questions, often with a big smile that would crinkle the corners of his eyes, and light up his face as if he could see again.

One day, Chunzhi brought me into his room and announced my presence. He said something to her, and she led me over to him, directing me to give him my hand. He took it and carefully felt my hand and fingers. His own hands were strong, but very soft and warm. Then he gave my hand back and said something else to Chunzhi. "He approves," she said—and it was done.

I wondered what esoteric science, what discipline developed over thousands of years of Chinese civilization, had given him the ability to make this kind of assessment—and also what he had learned about me that allowed him to make such a quick and categorical decision. After we left, I expressed my wonder and admiration to Chunzhi and asked for more explanation. Her answer was short and simple, "No calluses. You are an intellectual, not a worker."[4]

***

That approval meant the three generations of women returned again to the astrologer to pore over our collective statistics and pick the most appropriate, auspicious day—which turned out to be October 24.

We decided that I would pick up Chunzhi at the family home early that morning, where we would go through the ritual of her saying goodbye to her family. Then we would drive downtown to the Taipei City Hall where we would be officially married in the company of our immediate families and friends—including a venerable eighty-six-year-old American woman who was a friend of one of my uncles. Traditionally, wedding ceremonies took place in the groom's family home, but I had no family home in Taiwan. Also, we needed the official government documents to present later to U.S. authorities when we applied for Chunzhi's U.S. citizenship. After our ceremony, we would go and get pictures taken, and then that evening we would hold a reception for her extended family and our colleagues at the school.

I had read one account of a Chinese tradition that required the groom to have a mock battle with the bride's brother, in which the groom had to assert and prove himself. Chunzhi had a brother and also many male cousins, and I was not sure exactly what to expect. Chunzhi was not much help. When I asked she would reply that she did not know because she had never done this before, or simply tell me not to worry about it. The latter was right, but I didn't or couldn't do it.

I arrived at her home early that morning, driving a small Fiat sports car lent to me by a fellow student, who was my best man. The sun was up and burning off the mist that still hung in places along the valley road that snaked through the hills. Everything was fresh and beautiful, and just a little chilly.

The family greeted me pleasantly. There was no gang of youths blocking my entry. They ushered me into the central room of the house where there was an altar to Guanyin and photographs of the ancestors. Chunzhi and I stood before the altar with her mother, held burning incense sticks, and bowed three times. Third Uncle was officiating and telling us what to do. He spoke in Taiwanese, and Chunzhi relayed the instructions to me in a mixture of Mandarin and English (leaving a good margin for misunderstanding). Then Chunzhi and I faced her mother. Third Uncle was saying something very official, and we bowed three times to each other. Her mother started crying and Chunzhi started crying. We were then led out of that room and into the courtyard.

When we got to the door, Chunzhi looked down at the threshold, and said in English, "Jump over." Traditional Chinese houses have a threshold that is about twelve inches high. You can't just walk through but have to step over it. I thought the idea of the two of us jumping over this threshold was rather striking—me in my formal pin-striped suit and Chunzhi in her long, skin-tight white Chinese *chi-pao* with the skirt slit up the side. I looked quizzically at her, but I was prepared to do what I was told. Then, she stepped demurely over the threshold. I hesitated for an instant and decided it was better to do too little than too much and also stepped over. Everything proceeded normally, and I breathed a big sigh of relief. Apparently "jump" was just the first verb that came to mind. Later, I thought with horror what would have happened if I had actually jumped. Would everyone have been mortified? Would A-Gong have had second thoughts about his positive pronouncement?

As we crossed the courtyard, escorted by Second Aunt, who held an umbrella over our heads even though it was sunny and cool, firecrackers started exploding all around us like artillery fire. Once in the car, with gunpowder smoke filling the air, I turned to Chunzhi and asked, "What was that all about?" She smiled gently and replied, "We just got married."[5]

***

I suppose many people don't understand everything that is said during their wedding ceremony. However, most at least understand the general drift. I had not had a clue. I didn't object, and I felt more like I had been given an

extra gift, but it still took a while for me to understand the enormous significance of the moment for Chunzhi.

When we burned incense and bowed before the family altar, for me it was
a gesture of respect. For her it was of a very different magnitude. This was
the altar to the spirits of her ancestors who looked after and protected the
family. She had bowed respectfully before it countless times before, with her
grandmother, her parents, and many relatives. This time, however, she was
not just greeting the ancestors respectfully and asking for their blessing on
our marriage. She was saying *goodbye* to them and walking out from under
the umbrella of protection they had provided for her whole life. Similarly,
when we bowed to her mother, we were not just thanking her for giving birth
to Chunzhi and raising her. She was *leaving* the family.

Traditionally, in China—as in much of the West—when a woman marries
she leaves her family and becomes a member of her husband's family. In
modern times this has changed a great deal in both China and the West. It is
often more symbolic than real, and many women even retain their original
name. In traditional China, however, it could be a true separation. Many
brides rarely saw their parents again after they married. Some would only go
back on the second day of the Chinese New Year (which is reserved for that
occasion), and then only with permission from their husbands. Chunzhi's
family experience had been much more traditional than modern, and her
perspective was more traditional. It was intensified by the knowledge that
within two days she would not only leave her family but would physically
leave behind her country and everything that she had known up until then.

***

We drove into Taipei to City Hall, where we were to go through another
ceremony. My family and our friends were already there, and we dove into
the bureaucratic part of it. There were rooms full of tables full of officials.
We had to sign and seal our documents. For the latter we had each had
personal seals made—and we used them to stamp what seemed like an endless series of documents (none of which I could read, of course, because my
newspaper reading instruction had not covered that kind of language). The
rooms where all of this activity was taking place were absolutely jammed
with people. Eighteen other couples were getting married that morning, and
all of them had family with them as well. It was utterly chaotic, and the
others didn't seem to understand it any better than I. Nevertheless, we all
managed to get to where we were going, and faster than I anticipated.

When the paper signing was complete, we were lined up in the main hall.
We first faced the officials and bowed to them as they made more pronouncements I could not understand. Then we bowed to each other. Then we

all turned and bowed to our families. Suddenly, it was done. More pronouncements were made, and everyone was clapping and mingling, and our families and friends were all around us. We gradually squeezed out into the alleyway, headed for the cars, and someone asked about the rings. There had been no provision in the ceremony for exchanging rings, and I had forgotten all about it. So, Chunzhi and I stopped right there in the alley. I pulled out the box with the rings in it, and we put them on each other's fingers. I can still see Chunzhi there with her immaculate white *chi-pao* and her hair pulled back, standing in high heels on bumpy cobblestones, in a dingy alley with my mother, her mother and sister, and eighty-six-year-old Mary Horsley, all beaming. It seemed a perfect mix of order and chaos, anonymous crowds and close family—very Chinese?

That night for the wedding dinner we rented the banquet hall at the Grand Hotel, a huge bright red hotel that had been built by Madame Chiang Kai-shek in traditional Chinese style on the northern edge of Taipei. The banquet hall was an enormous room supported by massive red pillars much like some of the temples. We needed a large room because with all of Chunzhi's family—who came in from the countryside in chartered buses—and our fellow students, teachers, and friends, we had well over a hundred people. It all went without a hitch, except for when one of Chunzhi's uncles discovered that I was drinking tea for the traditional toasts instead of rice wine (to protect my stomach) and expressed his strong disapproval. That, too, seemed an appropriate continuation of my education.

***

In Taiwan I got my first exposure to the world's oldest and most extensive living culture. It was not at all what I expected, at least not at first. I was still influenced by my experience—or my interpretation of experience—with French culture. I put a high premium on the obvious, physical manifestations of culture like architecture, art, order, physical appearance, food, and so on. In Taiwan I did not immediately find what I was looking for.

Outward appearances in my new environment were heavily influenced by the level of economic prosperity at the time, and by the years of turmoil and change that Chinese on both sides of the Taiwan Strait had experienced for at least the last century. It took me longer than I expected to adjust to a cultural environment that was more profoundly different than I expected. The social order was incomprehensible to me. It seemed more chaos than order, and it took me years to begin to see the predictability of some of that chaos—or to begin to appreciate the disorder. I was not culturally ready to appreciate the garish local temples. I did not have a sufficient level of artistic awareness to appreciate the wealth of creativity in the painting and calligraphy available all around me. Food was another huge adjustment. Intellectually, I could appreciate how much refinement went into the preparation, presentation, and complementarities of the cuisine, but it took much longer for my senses to accept and enjoy the assault of all those new smells and tastes.

This society also seemed to accept more obviously, and at face value, the social mores, values, and disciplines handed down by its culture than do we—and even more than did the French. Whereas French youth excelled in overt revolutionary challenges, Chinese youth seemed far more circumspect.[6] Respect for parents, older people in general, and authority were a given. In many circumstances—in a home, in a government office, in a school—behavior was programmed to be overtly respectful. On the other hand, overtly respectful behavior did not always carry over to the rest of one's daily activities. There was also a contrasting element of first demonstrating one's show of respect and then going ahead and doing whatever one could get away with.

The strongest cultural imperative that I saw was the family. Perhaps this was because I was given glimpses of it through my encounters with Chunzhi's immediate and extended family. There is tremendous loyalty to family. You support it, and it supports you. The immediate family is most obviously important, but extended family relationships and influence are pervasive. Parents have an obligation to nourish and train their children. When one is young, one is obliged to obey one's parents. The obligation to obey becomes at some point in adulthood an obligation to support and care for one's parents until—and even beyond—their death. Notions of freedom and self-expression are distinctly secondary to these familial and social obligations.

In Chinese culture the natural bonds of family have been strengthened and extended to an extraordinary degree. Twenty-five hundred years ago one man in central China, Confucius, articulated a set of mutual family and social obligations that found extraordinary resonance within his culture. Several hundred years later, the Han Dynasty emperor Han Wudi (漢武帝), who had already experienced major success militarily in solidifying the security and political unity of the Chinese peoples, decided to use Confucius's teachings as the framework for the political structure of his dynasty. Over the ensuing two thousand years, those teachings have been refined and imprinted on the Chinese individual and collective psyche to a degree that seems unmatched anywhere else in the world.

The weight and discipline of that culture was playing an important role in Taiwan's economy at that time. My first assignments in France and Zaire had strengthened my impression that some depth of culture is essential to social stability. However, I still believed that too much cultural tradition tended to restrict economic development, because it inhibited the ability of individuals and society to adjust to changing circumstances. In Taiwan I began to revise that belief.

When I went to study Chinese in Yangmingshan in 1980, Taiwan was a "developing" country. Its industrial and technological capacity was still in the early stages of growth, though it was already known as one of the "Four Tigers"[7] of Asia's economic miracle, under way since 1960. Taiwan's economic growth seemed really to take off when it emerged from under the umbrella of U.S. government development assistance in 1965. It accelerated even more after the United States switched its formal recognition from the ROC to the PRC as the government of all China. To some this seemed counterintuitive. Why would the lack of foreign assistance and political support actually stimulate growth?

Part of the reason was cultural. Through most of the last two thousand years of Chinese history, government has been authoritarian and directive rather than democratic and responsive. The government of the Republic of China took a leading role in Taiwan's development by managing the financial system and credit and by undertaking major infrastructure development projects (some using U.S. assistance) within the context of a broad economic plan. The latter began to come online in the 1970s. The government had established a platform that made a national economic takeoff possible. This was supported by the extraordinary importance that Chinese culture places on education. Local schools and universities expanded prodigiously. Existing and prospective government officials were sent to the best universities in the United States and Europe to study science and engineering, and that education was applied to the management of this development process. Taiwan's entire population was growing in size, in education, and in a mindset that was beginning to envisage the potential ahead for individual and communal growth.

Probably more important, the Chinese people on Taiwan—and on the mainland—were finally beginning to emerge, as a people and as a culture, from the chaos and destruction of the twentieth century. On the mainland, that culture had been burned to the ground by the fires of Mao's revolution, but its roots were amazingly still alive. On Taiwan, much of traditional Chinese culture had been preserved, surviving hundreds of years of imperial Chinese neglect, close to a century of Japanese rule, and the bitter clash of compatriots when Nationalist forces fled to the island in the late 1940s and imposed themselves on the local people. On Taiwan, Chinese culture finally began its successful emergence onto the modern world stage.

China's cultural heritage would provide the identity and the social cohesion necessary not only to cope with the late twentieth century's accelerated pace of change but also to successfully ride and direct it into the twenty-first century. These people were not disoriented, intimidated, and compromised by the advent of a new world. They were not just seeking personal survival or gratification in the short term, like many of their African counterparts. They were beginning to take charge of it, on a scale that most of us could not anticipate.

***

My experience in Taiwan was very different from that in my previous two overseas posts. I was studying, not working. I was watching and trying to absorb and understand my new environment, but I was not trying actually to sync what I was seeing with interests or perceived interests in Washington. I was not in operational mode.

That doesn't mean it was easy. Struggling to learn the language was exhausting. In some respects it was like becoming a child all over again, where one knows nothing, can't make oneself understood, and must take what the teachers/adults say without question. That was mitigated somewhat by the pronounced respect we were given by the teachers—partly because we were foreign officials, and partly because they were just extraordinarily polite.

This was my second experience of formal training within the Foreign Service (not counting our introductory training as junior officers). The first had been several years earlier when I took an economics course given by the Foreign Service Institute (FSI) that crammed a full undergraduate economics major into six months. I had been impressed, because we were kept under such pressure during that time that it was impossible to get bored even with the "dismal science." Eighteen months of Chinese language was a different kind of pressure. There was no question of boredom, but anxiety was an entirely different matter. One begins to question whether one's brain is actually working!

In both instances, FSI and the Department of State did a very impressive job. I was not as competent a student as some of my colleagues. I learned enough to communicate on a daily basis, and to communicate formally with government officials. Some of my colleagues have become true scholars of the language and culture. Even those performances, though, fall short of what we need to do. The Department of State teaches Mandarin Chinese to most Foreign Service officers assigned to China. Mandarin Chinese is the official language—both on Taiwan and on the mainland. It is taught officially in all schools; all officials speak it, and most Chinese in the significant population centers have at least some knowledge of it. However, on Taiwan the mother tongue of most of the population is Hokkien. If one does not speak Hokkien, as much as half of the population and political activity is not directly accessible. On the mainland, it is far more complex. In terms of languages, China is more like Europe than America. Hokkien is spoken in Fujian Province; Cantonese is spoken in Guangdong Province; Shanghainese is spoken in Shanghai; and Hakka is spoken by the Hakka peoples spread throughout China. These are different languages—as different as French and Spanish. There are also hundreds of dialects that, even though they may not qualify as different languages, are for all intents and purposes mutually incomprehensible.

Over the ten years that I worked in the area, the American officials in China seemed to be at least as well prepared linguistically to live and work in China as other foreign diplomats there. On the other hand, the Chinese officials did a substantially better job with their English than we did with our Chinese. They begin their study far earlier than do we. In Taiwan, English language instruction is available in some kindergartens and in many elementary schools. On the mainland, foreign language training also begins in elementary school. Chinese on both sides of the Taiwan Strait are learning to speak our language, which gives them extensive access to our culture and society. In order to deal with China and the Chinese as equals in the future, we are going to need to be able to speak their languages. The U.S. government will need to train more diplomats in Mandarin and other major Chinese languages. Our national education system, public and private, will need to train lots more Americans—officials, businesspeople, academics, and so on—in all of the major Chinese language groups. This is not just a challenge for the Department of State, or even the federal government—it is a challenge for our nation and our culture.

NOTES

1. The name was changed in 2006 to Taiwan Taoyuan International Airport.
2. It is now provided at multiple locations on the mainland.
3. In Chinese, the family name comes first, followed by the given names. Most people have two given names, which are meant to be significant in several ways. In this case *Chunzhi* means "pure weave." The first given word, "pure," was also given to all of her sisters and identified them as being in that particular generation of that particular family. This is sometimes called a "generation name" and traditionally was set by an ancestor or an official who composed a poem or song with characters that he (usually a male) considered significant in some way for his family's future. The characters were assigned to the generations one by one (though male and female members often have different generational names). When the poem was finished it could be started again or a new one created. On occasion, an emperor honored a family by creating a general poem for them himself. This tradition may be weakening. In the case of Chunzhi's family, the poem was written by an ancestor several generations back. It may have ended with her generation, because not all branches of the next generation have been given generational names.
4. Much later, Chunzhi told me that he had also commented, "At least he is not a *waisheng ren*"—a mainlander.
5. The protective umbrella was to ensure that our marriage endured through rain or shine.
6. At this time, I was only dimly aware of the important role that Chinese youth have played throughout Chinese history in protesting government policies, participating in and even leading rebellions and successful overthrows of established government authority.
7. Hong Kong, Singapore, South Korea, and Taiwan.

Chapter Four

The Last International City: Hong Kong (August 1981–June 1984)

My first Chinese assignment was to a British colony. In the fall of 1981, the largest U.S. diplomatic mission in a Chinese language area was the consulate general in Hong Kong (香港). Before heading off in 1980 to Chinese language training in Taiwan, I had been offered a choice of two post-language-training assignments: Hong Kong or Taipei. The Taipei position was more senior, because it was the head of the entire economic section. Taiwan had made impressive economic strides, and I also assumed there was a greater repository of knowledge about Chinese history and culture there than on the mainland after the ravages of the Cultural Revolution.

However, the Hong Kong consulate general was working not only with Hong Kong itself but also on issues relating to mainland China. I thought that, with the recent reestablishment of diplomatic relations between the United States and the People's Republic of China, the Hong Kong experience would probably be more valuable. I also wanted to see Hong Kong up close. For some time, I had had the idea that there were really only two cities on the planet that were more international than national: Beirut and Hong Kong— places where interests, preferences, faiths, talents, experiences, and energies from different places and cultures all around the world mixed together in one place, creating something new and different. I had missed my chance to see Beirut back in the early 1970s, and by 1980 the international city of Beirut seemed lost. I wanted to get to know Hong Kong before it changed too.

In Hong Kong, working with some of the U.S. government's most knowledgeable and competent China analysts (both American and Chinese), I was given a wide range of foreign policy exposure. We watched China from just outside its borders. At that time Hong Kong offered more accessible opportunities for an American official to understand what was going on in China than did being in the Beijing embassy or the consulates, where contacts were extremely restricted. I got an introduction not only to the enormous changes that were developing in the PRC but also to how the Chinese watched and interpreted each other's statements and activities.

***

Hong Kong sits astride one of the best natural harbors in the world. The setting is spectacularly beautiful, and the city's location has made it and many of its inhabitants spectacularly rich. In Chinese terms, this metropolis is relatively young, having existed less than two hundred years. Before the mid-nineteenth century there was little Chinese or Western interest in the island that is now Hong Kong or the adjacent mainland region. The political, economic, and demographic center of southern China was in Guangzhou, located on the Pearl River about two hundred kilometers to the northwest. Ships from Arabia and Europe had brought trade to China for more than a thousand years, but the volume of the trade was limited, and Guangzhou's port at the head of the Pearl River Delta had been sufficient to handle it. China itself had only once built up an extensive fleet, and after a brief experiment the emperor at the time put an end to it. [1] Without a sizable navy, the Chinese empire had no need for a deepwater harbor, and most in Beijing probably were not even aware that they had such a resource.

Hong Kong, or *Xianggang* (香港 "Fragrant Harbor"), was discovered and developed by another empire whose interests, unlike those of China, were inextricably bound to the sea. Great Britain saw the harbor's strategic potential, carved the territory out of China, and established a colonial administration that presided over the extraordinarily rapid growth of an enclave combining some of the most dynamic elements of Western and Eastern civilizations in cooperation, competition, and contradiction. Many westerners have looked to Hong Kong as a jewel of order, dynamic productivity, and even civilization perched on the edge of a continent mired in poverty, corruption, and decaying cultural arrogance for the last several hundred years. On the other hand, there are Chinese who see it as the product of more than a century of deceit and violent abuse by a barbarian empire—the world's first global drug cartel—that deliberately corrupted and poisoned the Chinese population.

Hong Kong is all of those things. While it has served the interests of both Western and Chinese governments (and peoples) over the last century and a half, the circumstances of its birth were less than glorious. British merchants trading with China in the early seventeenth century had to pay for unique Chinese products like tea and silk with silver, because there was little Chinese interest in Western products. That created the first severe trade imbalance between China and the West, putting strains on both the merchants and the British treasury. Then the British discovered that there was a product the Chinese wanted and didn't have—opium. For more than a hundred years the opium trade grew steadily, managed by the British East India Company under a monopoly sanctioned by the British crown. Three successive emperors banned opium and the opium trade, but the Western traders, which by the early nineteenth century included Americans, were undeterred. By 1838 they were selling fourteen hundred tons of opium annually to Chinese consumers. When the Chinese government finally tried to crack down, executing Chinese merchants, blockading British merchants, and seizing and destroying their opium stocks, the British Empire responded by declaring war. British forces quickly overwhelmed the defenses of the Qing Dynasty and obtained a treaty[2] that legalized the opium trade, vastly expanded British trading rights in China, and ceded the island of Hong Kong to Britain in perpetuity—forever.

***

I was not disappointed in my search for an international city. In 1981 Hong Kong most certainly was a mixture of influences visually—a bustling city, simultaneously gleaming and dirty, sprawled around the harbor, edging up the mountainsides on Hong Kong Island and pushing back across the flatter peninsula of Kowloon from the docks. Most of the buildings were nondescript twentieth-century functional office and apartment buildings. Some skyscrapers were rising above them; British colonial buildings still stood out in the central part of the city, and occasionally there were Chinese temples or ordinary buildings that had been given Chinese architectural façades. In the commercial areas of the city, neon signs in both Chinese and English were everywhere. The major streets were choked with traffic, mostly Japanese Toyotas but with plenty of British Rolls-Royces and German Mercedes, all of which negotiated their way around British-manufactured double-decker buses and trams. The alleyways were jammed with stalls selling anything from clothing to antiques, and perpetually filled with clouds of steam from Chinese fast food. The people were all colors and sizes, dressed in Chinese, European, Indian, and a multitude of other fashions. The harbor itself was a constant movement of ocean liners from Europe and Scandinavia, container ships from all over, ferries from Britain, Chinese sailing and motorized junks, and of course pleasure boats from tiny sailboats to opulent yachts.

The population was predominantly Chinese, from many different parts of China. Most were southerners (Cantonese, Chaozhou, and Hakka). There was also strong representation from Shanghai and somewhat less from the more northern regions of China. There were many British: officials who dominated the government; military, who still had a prominent position; and businesspeople throughout the commercial, financial, and transportation structure. There were plenty of Americans: businesspeople, tourists, and consulate officials, and also some military since Hong Kong was an important port of call. There was a large Indian community that had played an important role in Hong Kong's business development, and there were plenty of others from other European and Asian nations.

The economy was international. There were huge British, Japanese, and Hong Kong Chinese department stores, and more newly established ones from the People's Republic—experimental expanded versions of the "Friendship Stores" that the communist government managed for foreigners resident in cities like Beijing, Shanghai, and Guangzhou. The smaller stores were a mixture of local Chinese, British, and some Japanese, though the Chinese stores vastly outnumbered the others. British, American, and Hong Kong Chinese banks were prominent. The British banks built the first real skyscrapers—Charter Bank and the Hong Kong and Shanghai Banking Corporation built side by side. The Bank of China, which was originally in a centrally located, colonial-style building when we arrived in 1981, hired I. M. Pei to design what would become Hong Kong's tallest building and the signature piece of its rapidly changing skyline.

The art world was well represented. There were performances by visiting European symphonies and ballet and opera companies, public libraries stocked with both English and Chinese language books and magazines, and endless antique stores filled with mostly Chinese and some European artifacts. There were galleries and stores filled with recent and ancient Chinese painting and calligraphy. Our Chinese language teacher at the consulate was well-known for his beautiful paintings and distinctive calligraphy. There was a booming Hong Kong Chinese film industry led by the Shaw Brothers Studio, which among other things gave Jackie Chan some of his earliest roles.

Food was international. There were high-end European restaurants in the major hotels, some of which would have compared favorably with those in France and Italy. There were even more exalted Chinese restaurants that produced banquets modeled on fare served to past emperors—very expensive fare. There were more ordinary French, Italian, German, and Greek restaurants; traditional Chinese restaurants from most of the different regions of China; and huge dim sum restaurants that were virtually impossible to get into on weekends. There were also some older teahouses that sold traditional Chinese food served with a wide selection of Chinese teas. One small teahouse, not far from the consulate, mimicked the dark wood décor of its ancestors and had menus exclusively in Chinese. Even if you could read the Chinese characters (which were not the standard political and economic vocabulary we studied), the names of the dishes rarely gave us westerners any clue as to what the dish actually was. Then there were the massive, multistory floating restaurants in the harbor on the southern side of the island. They were accessible by water taxi and were factories devoted to feeding masses of tourists and local residents—and to mahjong. The food was good, and the noise—from human revelry and clashing mahjong tiles—was simply unbelievable. Quieter and more exclusive repasts could be had—for members and guests—at the social clubs. There were ethnic clubs like the Shanghai Club; professional clubs like the Foreign Correspondents' Club; and sports clubs for tennis, golf, and yachting. There was also, of course, the Hong Kong Jockey Club, founded in 1884 to promote horse racing and endowed a century later with the monopoly on legal gambling in Hong Kong. Sadly, none of them were affordable for a mid-level Foreign Service officer.

Since Hong Kong was a British colony, the Church of England was prominent. The Anglican Cathedral was right in Central, just above the Hilton Hotel, and just below the American Consulate. It was a beautiful, traditionally styled building with arched ceilings, stained-glass windows and regimental coats of arms in the woodwork. Somewhat less traditionally, it also had ceiling fans and windows that opened onto tropical gardens. I was raised in the American Episcopal Church, and attended Anglican churches when my father was posted to Europe and Latin America. I was very familiar with it and was therefore surprised to see that the new dean of the Church of England's cathedral was an American—and not just an American but a former Baptist missionary! Paul Clasper had served for many years as a missionary in Burma and then began writing and teaching comparative religion, with a strong emphasis on Eastern religions. He had been teaching at the Chinese University of Hong Kong when he was invited to take up the post of dean at St. John's Cathedral. My wife and I became close friends with him and his wife, Janet. He baptized Chunzhi after we moved to Beijing, and later baptized our son, Charles, when our paths crossed again in Virginia where he was teaching at the Episcopal seminary in Alexandria.

Hong Kong also hosted a retreat center that drew from several centuries of interaction between Christian missionaries and Chinese traditions. The Tao Fong Shan (道風山 *Dao Feng Shan*: Tao Wind Mountain) Christian Centre was established in 1930 by a Norwegian missionary. It adopted as its symbol a cross (Christian) rising out of a lotus (Buddhist) that had been first conceived by Nestorian Christians in the sixth or seventh century. Persian missionaries reaching Changan (now Xian), the capital of the Tang Dynasty, in AD 635 had been welcomed by the Tang emperor. They crafted their message about the teachings of Jesus of Nazareth in Chinese language and symbols, meshing it with the Taoist, Confucian, and Buddhist traditions that were already well established. They were perhaps the first to build a serious connection between these different religious traditions. They were also perhaps the most successful Christians in China, as their work carried through both the Tang and the Yuan dynasties. The later Ming and Qing dynasties were less welcoming and more restrictive. While most of the Christians in the seventh through the twentieth century were primarily interested in promoting their religion *over* the others, people like Paul Clasper saw the existence of Tao Fong Shan as a statement of dialogue and mutual growth.

In Hong Kong the different peoples cooperated and competed. The mixing of different cultures created harmonies and disharmonies. We Americans were part of both. Being a port with a water-oriented economy, Hong Kong enthusiastically celebrated the traditional Chinese holiday Duanwu Jie (端午節), better known internationally as the Dragon Boat Festival. Today the custom has spread around the world, and there are even Dragon Boat races on the Potomac River in Washington, DC, but in the early 1980s it was new to most of us at the consulate. The major Dragon Boat races took place in the harbor near Kowloon, and the participants were almost all Chinese, though some of the boats were sponsored by multinational corporations. There were smaller competitions as well. One of them was organized off the south side of Hong Kong Island rather than in the main harbor, and it included foreigners. The American Consulate General fielded a team, which I joined for each of the three years that we were there. We made a point of recruiting the consulate's Marine guards, since they were in far better shape than the rest of us and the paddling was strenuous. On one occasion we managed to fill half the boat with our military colleagues, which gave us tremendous power. There was only one problem: the dragon boats had been made for small, wiry Chinese men, not for bulked-up Marines. Additionally, the bay was less protected than Kowloon harbor, or the rivers where many Dragon Boat races take place. There was some surf—and waves. With our sizable Marine contingent, our boat was very low in the water, and our enthusiastic start pushed us under rather than through the waves. But the camaraderie was great, between as well as within the teams. Setting aside almost drowning, it was a lively and harmonious mix of cultures.

Somewhat less of a mix was the "Hash House Harrier" runs. The Hash House Harriers were originally started in pre–World War II Malaysia by a group of British military and foreign businessmen for the dual purpose of getting exercise and socializing. They got together for runs along courses set by "hares" through any kind of environment, ending with beer drinking and socializing. The custom has since spread around the world. In Hong Kong, our chapter was organized by some British military and Hong Kong government officials. We would meet once or twice a week at a designated location and run through every conceivable Hong Kong setting: through the countryside and rural villages on the islands, New Territories, and Macao; through the city streets, alleyways, and markets; and even through department stores and other establishments with the runners merrily yelling "On! On!" and blowing their bugles. While fun, this was distinctly foreign—at least the chapter that I was in—and while individual runners were usually polite, the mob was not always respectful of the environments through which it surged—more an example of disharmony.

***

The U.S. Consulate General in Hong Kong was larger than most American embassies. There were about a hundred American employees from many different U.S. government agencies, managed by the State Department but including the Immigration and Naturalization Service, the Department of Commerce, the Department of Defense, the Drug Enforcement Agency, and so on. There were also about two hundred Foreign Service nationals. The consulate's size was justified by the fact that it supported not only U.S. interests in things Chinese, but also other posts in the Pacific and Southeast Asia.

Hong Kong was a transportation and communications hub for the whole region. Most commercial airline routes in Asia and the Pacific led to Hong Kong. It was the largest port and shipping center in Asia, and it was the second largest financial center, after Tokyo. The British colonial government had successfully kept the territory's borders open—for people, goods, and finance. The political structure, while fundamentally colonial and authoritarian, was relatively transparent and provided considerable opportunity for participation by Hong Kong residents. The media, both English and Chinese language, was dynamic, inquisitive, and relatively free from censorship or recrimination. It was an open and free-flowing environment in which people and organizations with a multitude of different backgrounds could pursue their interests and feel free to share their knowledge. In Hong Kong, we had access to both Chinese and foreign businesspeople who traveled in and out of China on a regular basis and had commercial and personal ties with individuals in key positions around China that we officials could not get close to.

***

Shortly after I arrived in Hong Kong, I was asked to make a trip up to Shanghai to visit the consulate there and get my first introduction to mainland China. Before going up I spent a few weeks calling on local businesspeople who did business with Shanghai to get a little better understanding of the environment there.

On one of my calls, when I explained what my plans were, my host said, "Well, you must visit my parents while you are there." I was very touched but said I did not want to do anything that would get someone into trouble. He assured me there would be no trouble and said, "They will invite you to their house for dinner and you should accept, because they have a very good cook." I thought one of us had misunderstood. I was traveling to Shanghai, in Communist China, which had just emerged from the Cultural Revolution a few years earlier. People didn't live in their own houses (I had read *Dr. Zhivago*)! And how could they possibly have their own cooks? He smiled, gave me their telephone number (they had their own telephone too?), and said he would contact them to let them know that I was coming.

When I got to Shanghai, the consulate had made a reservation for me at the Jin Jiang Hotel, an old hotel from the 1930s. It was (and is still) located on the edge of the old French District, and it is very elegant though at the time a little threadbare. The lightbulbs—the few that were on—were a very low wattage so it was a little somber. In fact, the whole city was somber and quite dark at night. Near the hotel there were only a few streetlights. It was quiet and peaceful. People strolled on the sidewalks and bicycles passed by on the street, but there were almost no cars. It was a little like being on a country road, but with lots more people. The French District was quite love- ly. The buildings were mostly European, and the streets were lined with trees, often London plane trees (like sycamores), with light-colored bark and branches that arched over the streets and sidewalks and leaves that let the sunlight play patterns on the pavement. It was like Paris—obviously.

The evening that I arrived, I made my call to my new friend's parents, assuming that they would be busy and would politely beg off. To my sur- prise, they said they were expecting my call, and if it was all right with me they would call on me at the hotel. They arrived a little later—one of the most elegant couples I had ever met: gray haired, well dressed, very polite and considerate, and very well educated. We had a pleasant visit. They asked me what my plans were and gave me some suggestions of places to see. Then, as predicted, they invited me to their home for dinner. So, the next day after I had finished my meetings, I set out to look for their home. The hotel called a taxi for me, and I gave the driver the address. He didn't recognize it, but I had been instructed to tell him it was just off of a nearby boulevard. As he was driving slowly down the boulevard trying to read the cross-street signs, a man came out of an alley on the right and signaled us to pull in. We followed him in, and he stopped at a door in a high wall, at which point the driver exclaimed, "Oh, it's them!" I stepped through the door into a well- manicured garden surrounding a very nice Tudor-style house.

Nothing that I had read or been told had prepared me for this. I was entering the home of one of Shanghai's most prominent prerevolution capi- talist families. After the revolution, they had sent their children out of the country, but they had stayed. They suffered considerably during the Cultural Revolution, but amazingly they had been allowed to remain in their own house—and now they were both playing an increasingly important role in China's economic and political life. They did have an excellent cook and we had a very enjoyable dinner, during which they told me stories of some of their experiences during the Cultural Revolution. Their life during that time had been precarious. They were "reeducated" and visited periodically by officials or groups of Red Guards who would question them, threaten them, and take things from the house. They pointed to a small painting on the wall and explained that it was a very old and very valuable piece of art. On one occasion when the Red Guards entered and began taking or destroying some of their things, the husband had stood watching, with his back covering the painting. During the several hours the Guards were there he didn't move, hoping they would not notice the painting. They didn't. When they left he took it down and hid it in the basement, bringing it out again only after that period had passed.

On that trip, I had a number of meetings with officials and made a visit out to Wuxi on Lake Tai and the Grand Canal. However, nothing made as deep an impression on me as the dinner that I had with that most impressive couple. It was one of many reminders that China was not and would not be what I expected. These were people who had participated in the twentieth-century westernization of China, contributing to and profiting from the economic growth that took place particularly in Shanghai. They were "western-ized" by their associations and their education—he was educated at MIT. But they had both also received a classical Chinese education and were very much Chinese. That included a love for and a commitment to their country and their culture. They did not believe in communism, but they chose to remain in China after the revolution and to contribute to their country in whatever way they could. They suffered, accepted their suffering, and when things finally began to turn around they were there to support and encourage changes that would benefit China—a China beyond the definitions of twenti-eth-century political thinking.

***

Some of the businesspeople in Hong Kong with ties to and expertise about the mainland were actually American. The American business community in Hong Kong was quite large. The finance, transportation, chemical, and petro-leum sectors were particularly prominent. Some had their Asian headquarters located there. In the early 1980s they were all watching developments on the mainland and wondering if change was really coming that would offer them opportunities to tap the world's largest potential market. Some of the American companies were represented by individuals with strong Chinese language skills and considerable knowledge about China. Some of the American journalists were accomplished Chinese linguists and very active in their pursuit of stories and a better understanding of what was taking place in

China. There were also a few American lawyers who were China experts and were anticipating an eventual sea change in the rule of law on the mainland.

The rest of the American businesspeople, however, knew relatively little about either the culture of China or the potential business opportunities that it offered them, in spite of their proximity to it. Most of the American companies were concentrating on Hong Kong and other parts of Asia, not China. The American Chamber of Commerce in Hong Kong was very active; it had a committee focused on China that held regular meetings and engaged in broad-ranging discussions on developments there. However, the Americans were distinctly risk-averse compared to their Hong Kong Chinese counterparts, the Japanese, and other Asians. With the exception of a few large corporations that retained China experts on their staff over the years, the time horizon of the American companies was just too short even to get to know the Chinese environment, much less to develop the opportunities that it hid.

***

While the United States government does a little better than the American business community in this category, it too has a notoriously short attention span in foreign affairs. Both the Department of State and the CIA managed to sustain a working level of Chinese expertise through the three-decade period when there were no diplomatic relations between the United States and the People's Republic of China—but only barely.

The Department of State's capability was severely damaged by domestic political witch hunts in the 1950s. Some China Hands were treated to our own democratic brand of persecution. Others were sent off to jobs that had nothing to do with China, at least partially to protect them from persecution. I met one, Philip Sprouse, when I was six years old in Brussels. I only learned many years later that he was an exiled "China Hand," but I remembered him because he was the friendliest and most elegant man I'd met—and because he gave me a tip for taking his coat at one of the endless receptions my parents hosted there.

The CIA was less of a target, and during the Cold War built up the U.S. government's most extensive group of China analysts. It had the resources and the mission to allocate more attention to long-term analysis, and by the 1970s the CIA certainly had the strongest ability to analyze the Chinese economy. However, in the 1980s the agency appears to have made a conscious decision to shorten its focus—again to be more responsive to more short-term political interests in Washington. Its budget benefited, but in my view the quality of its analysis declined.

In those decades following the communist takeover of China, when active U.S.–Chinese relations were confined largely to the relationship with the

Chinese on Taiwan, many of the U.S. government's "China Hands" became primarily "China Watchers." When the United States reestablished ties with the mainland, first with the Liaison Office in 1972 and then with formal recognition of the PRC government in 1979, there were even a few "China Hands" still left who had been born and raised in China.

My colleagues in the Foreign Service who had chosen the China field over the previous twenty years were for the most part an extraordinarily intelligent group of people. I found some of them to be quite awesome. They were perhaps a little more intellectually inclined than their Foreign Service peers. This was partially because so much study was required to master the language, and partially because there were limited opportunities to actually practice diplomacy. The China Hands' activities tended to be more cerebral. They had to be less ambitious. Before the PRC embarked on Deng Xiaoping's reforms in 1979, a diplomatic career in the China field was almost by definition more intellectual than operational, more passive than active. There were limited positions for Chinese language officers, and they were almost entirely in Taipei and Hong Kong.

The China Watchers were, of course, well informed and personally very interested in Chinese politics, life, and culture. Some were able to get below the surface and develop a true understanding of it. Only a few really got beyond the curtain that separates the Chinese from foreigners.

***

One of the most important analytical assets the consulate general had was its Chinese Foreign Service Nationals (FSNs). Most were born and raised in Hong Kong, but some were Chinese who had left China back in 1949, alone or with their families, and sought refuge in British-governed Hong Kong. Some had traveled directly to Hong Kong, and some had gone first to Taiwan. When I was sent to Hong Kong those individuals were the core of the consulate's analytical ability. They could pick up on seemingly obscure statements or events and then extrapolate what was behind them and what that presaged for the future, and they were teaching a younger generation of employees who had never known life on the mainland. These were impressive people. My senior economic Foreign Service national was probably the most knowledgeable person about the Chinese economy (and all its political aspects) working for or associated with the entire U.S. government at the time. Washington-based analysts and American academics who had spent a lifetime working on China would seek him out during their visits to Hong Kong. (They also sought him out because he knew all the best restaurants.) He watched the historical personalities and the up-and-coming ones. He analyzed their speeches and publications, as well as when and where they appeared—or did not appear—in public. Unlike his counterparts in the political section, he also watched the numbers (industrial and agricultural production, trade flows, budget allocations, etc.) and how the government played with them. Few Americans had the language ability of these employees, and none had their personal experience. I did not encounter any Americans who had achieved a similar level of intuitive ability.

It was these consulate analysts who were the first in the U.S. government to pick up on the fact that the Chinese leadership was going to give ordinary people in China the opportunity to engage in private commercial activities. This was several years before other observers outside China—or even inside China—accepted that possibility. The Hong Kong Consulate—and most other China watchers—spent an inordinate amount of time analyzing leadership struggles inside China. This was justified because, for as long as anyone could remember, those struggles (and relationships) were what Chinese politics and society were all about. The watchers at the Hong Kong Consulate, however, were among the first to assert that the constant political maneuvering had taken a secondary place to Deng Xiaoping's preeminence and the implementation of his post-Mao economic policies.

For the Chinese communists, these policies were revolutionary—or more accurately, counterrevolutionary. They opened the door to free-market economic forces and ended the communist stranglehold on individual initiative and material gain. What fewer observers recognized was that Deng was overturning not only thirty years of Chinese communist policy, but several thousand years of imperial Chinese foreign policy.

Deng committed China to integration with the international community. For the last several thousand years, China had been the largest, most advanced, and most powerful entity on the Asian mainland. It was invaded at various times by non-Han peoples and was conquered two or three times, depending on how one counts them. However, it always eventually succeeded in repelling or absorbing those invasions. China was in many ways a world unto itself. It set the rules. Other nations were expected, usually with good reason, to pay tribute to China and to obey whatever rules applied to them. With a few exceptions, China was far more interested in its own internal affairs than in what was happening beyond its borders. China did not participate actively in the world beyond its borders, and foreigners were a curiosity or a nuisance. China's rulers during the late Qing, China's last imperial dynasty (1644–1912), were arrogantly dismissive of non-Chinese cultures and capabilities, and eventually paid a severe price for that arrogance at the hands of equally arrogant but more powerful Japanese, British, and other Europeans (including Americans). Mao Zedong's People's Republic chose a foreign ideology (Marxism) and dabbled with the export of Marxist revolution, but to most practical purposes it was isolationist. Deng's contribution was different. Not only did he open the door for individual, nonstate entities to pursue commercial activity, but he also declared that China would learn from the rest of the world and adopt what it had to offer. He not only opened the door for non-Chinese influence to enter China, but he opened the door for China to influence the world. China would not just passively accept foreign influence but would become integrally involved globally—for the first time in its history.

***

In the best of Chinese traditions, there was plenty of bickering between different China Watchers in the consulate, particularly between the political and economic sections. In fact, there was quite a rivalry between the two sections, and I admit to being drawn into it. Some other sections thought it was amusing or silly, but to some degree the competition was useful. It stimulated everyone to make an extra effort, and the different perspectives and opinions kept us on our toes.

We would regularly take our contrasting viewpoints up through the consulate hierarchy to the consul general or to his deputy for arbitration. This was usually an instructive experience that would correct our intellectual trajectory and/or broaden our perspective. On one occasion, we were surprised by a new deputy, who himself had many years of China experience. After listening to our respective arguments, which were particularly heated that day, he made his decision. I can't remember who won, but then he told us, "Look, China is an extraordinarily large, old, and complex culture. It would probably be possible for you to say virtually anything about China and be right to some degree. So don't get too carried away." My first reaction was to think that was an extraordinary cop-out. Many years later, however, the truth of that statement stands out far more than our respective arguments, which have long since faded into obscurity.

In those years, the consulate in Hong Kong provided more numerous and more accurate assessments of developments in China than did the posts actually in the PRC—because it had better opportunities to do so. Our colleagues in Beijing and the consulates in Shanghai, Shenyang, and Guangzhou had to establish an American presence there. They had to live in the local hotels, under constant surveillance, adjust to a limited (by American standards) diet, and work in very restricted circumstances. They were "on the ground." They could see, hear, smell, and feel the environment. They could read the local papers and guess at what they meant. They could call on some local officials and get direct statements from them—but those statements were rarely revealing. They had difficulty developing contacts and producing reports that added significant insight to developments there. On the whole, I found the reporting from those posts to be solid but not very interesting. There was one exception. The consulate general in Guangzhou at one point sent in a report that analyzed recent leadership travels, and extrapolated from that analysis some significant predictions—both political and economic. I thought it was a brilliant report. It was fascinating to read, exciting to think about the implications, and generally inspiring. Unfortunately, it turned out to be completely wrong, which was a good lesson that the "interesting" is sometimes more seductive than real.

In Hong Kong we did have the opportunity to make contacts. Sometimes we could even make contacts directly with officials traveling from China. While there was some competition between Hong Kong and the posts in China, I think it was outweighed by mutual respect for the jobs each was doing with the material and the challenges it was handed.

***

We also, of course, worked with the Hong Kong government, which was British. Our relationship was very close, on all levels. We had close personal relationships, and a large measure of trust and understanding. It was still a relationship between governments, however. The U.S. and UK governments had similar interests in the region—but not exactly the same interests. We had our disagreements, and each had confidences that it did not share.

The early 1980s was a critical time for Hong Kong. The PRC and the UK maneuvered, considered, negotiated, and finally agreed to end the UK sovereignty over the region that had existed unchallenged since the middle of the nineteenth century. It was a time of turmoil and doubt for the non-Chinese communities, organizations, businesses, and individuals who lived and operated in and around Hong Kong. It was a time of personal crisis for many Chinese residents, particularly those who had taken refuge in Hong Kong after the communist takeover of the mainland in the late 1940s.

The prospect of an end to British rule seemed to many foreigners, myself included, a prescription for disaster. Hong Kong was a Chinese place that for two hundred years had been administered by non-Chinese. This combination of Chinese population and energy with non-Chinese government had seemed to work well in different places around the world. In Asia, Chinese populations in other nations like Thailand, Indonesia, Vietnam, and even Burma were the driving economic force in their respective countries. As long as those incredibly effective investors and merchants were not in the government (with all its responsibilities and temptations), all of their energies went into economic productivity. However, it seemed that when government was thrown into the mix, the equation changed and things began to go wrong.

Early and mid-twentieth century mainland China, with its extraordinary imbalances of wealth and formidable corruption, was one example. In the late 1970s and early 1980s, Taiwan seemed to be working its way out of that mold, but it had not yet achieved the dynamism of Hong Kong. The Hong Kong economy was as capitalistic as any economy on the planet. A visiting American banker once commented to me that Hong Kong was his dream city—because one could work twenty-four hours a day, seven days a week there, totally connected with the rest of the world! One could eat or be entertained twenty-four hours a day, though sometimes at one's own peril. A Western friend of mine visiting from the mainland embarked by himself one evening on some social spelunking, and he woke up the next morning $3,000 poorer and with no memory of the previous night. He hoped he had had a good time, but he didn't feel like it. I had to go down into Kowloon and rescue him.

Many thought that without the British overlay, the Chinese would not be able to preserve the freedoms that had allowed Hong Kong to prosper for so long. These freedoms included not just the freedom to make commercial decisions, but also things like freedom of speech and movement, which were critical to foreign investment and participation.

Many believed that the—until then—ideologically dogmatic and totalitarian government of the People's Republic of China would find those freedoms anathema. Even if the leadership were able to accept the ideological implications of such freedoms, we thought they would be subjected to irresistible pressures from their own domestic politics. We also thought those officials, most of whom had only had experience with a command economy, would be unable to resist the temptation either to interfere in the economic process, or to soak the territory for immediate gains (for country or for self). If that assessment were correct, a turnover to the PRC would augur a precipitous decline in economic health, commercial activity, and social and political stability.

The senior British leadership did not think so. Most of the American government was ambivalent, but leaning strongly to the pessimistic view. The new American consul general in Hong Kong, however, was not ambivalent. His performance was my first real view, after ten years in the diplomatic service, of how one person's leadership could make a significant difference in American policy and in historical events.

***

Burton Levin arrived in Hong Kong in 1982. He was one of the U.S. government's most senior experts in Chinese affairs. He had previously served in Taiwan, Indonesia, and Thailand. His Chinese language was excellent, and he had a deep and abiding interest in things Chinese. After arriving in Hong Kong, he started taking regular language lessons with the consulate's language instructor. Many of us were studying Chinese with this man. The difference was that Levin's course material was the Chinese political classic *Romance of the Three Kingdoms*—a quantum leap beyond what any of the rest of us were studying.

Shortly after arriving, the new consul general called all of the American employees to a meeting to introduce himself and give initial guidance on his priorities. This meeting, however, was different from anything I had previously experienced. He was gracious and pleasant, but he read us the riot act. He declared that the standards of the consulate's work had declined, and he expected everyone to work their tails off to turn that around. From now on, we would have to meet *his* standards. He also declared he would personally review every report that went out. I thought his presentation was rather arrogant and that there was little chance he would live up to it. I moaned in horror at the last statement, as the clearance process was already tortuous, and I thought this would make it impossible. I was wrong on both counts. He managed everything, and the quality of work at the consulate really did pick up.

He immediately and forcefully made clear the U.S. position concerning the UK–PRC talks, first to the consulate staff and then to the public. It was simple: the United States had full confidence that the UK and PRC governments would resolve the future of Hong Kong in a way that would ensure the stability of Hong Kong and the region, and protect both the freedoms and the prosperity of the people living there. To everyone, he made clear his firm belief that the Chinese government had the understanding and the discipline necessary to carry this out over time. His position was not just for show. He convincingly articulated the historical, political, economic, and psychological reasons for this belief. Within the consulate, he informed us, we were free—and encouraged—to challenge this position. Outside the consulate, however, there was not to be a whisper to the contrary.

His conviction and his persistence were catching. He had a decisive impact on Washington and a strong supportive impact on public opinion in Hong Kong. Even in the worst time, when public confidence and the Hong Kong dollar were plunging, he was a calm center of stability. Both the press and the business community were accustomed to diplomatic prevarication. They were surprised by his confidence and the thoroughness of his defense. The business community wanted to hear it. The press, I think, was a little disappointed because it gave them less to speculate with. Without that kind of support from the consul general, however, the task of the Hong Kong and PRC governments would have been considerably more difficult. It is even possible that the outcome would have been less propitious. As things have turned out, he was right. Today, almost thirty years later, Hong Kong is as prosperous as it ever was, and it has retained almost all of its freedoms. It is having to adjust to an influx of new millionaires and new workers from the mainland, and the character of the newer authoritarian Chinese rulers is somewhat different than that of the previous authoritarian British rulers. Perhaps, however, the major negative from Hong Kong's perspective is that it is no longer the most exciting economic environment in Asia. That place is being snatched by Shanghai, something most in Hong Kong back in the early 1980s would have found very improbable.

***

Hong Kong was my first Chinese assignment, not including language training. It was my first assignment on the Asian mainland. Even more important, it was my first Foreign Service assignment as a married person. Getting married, of course, is a huge milestone for most of us who go that way. We have chosen to share our lives, to give up the freedom to make decisions by ourselves and for ourselves, and we have taken on responsibility for each other's well-being. In the Foreign Service the impact is magnified for all concerned. For Chunzhi it was even more momentous. Everything was foreign to her. Hong Kong was British. The Chinese people there spoke primarily Cantonese, not Mandarin or Hokkien. The principal Chinese influence and focus was mainland China, which during most of her life had been portrayed as a threat. And on top of everything else, her new husband was American. She took on an official English name, Ginger, and six months after our marriage we made a trip to Hawaii where she was naturalized as an American citizen.[3] That is a lot of changes to get used to in a very short period of time.

When I started Chinese language training the teachers at the Foreign Service Institute gave each of the students Chinese names. These were chosen first to be close in sound to our English names. However, during much of the twentieth century foreigners associating with Chinese were often given Chinese names that only mimicked the sound of the English. They were immediately identifiable as foreign, whether read or spoken, sometimes seemed quite strange in Chinese terms, and occasionally were intentionally insulting. The teachers at FSI tried to ensure that the names they chose were both Chinese and complimentary. My assigned name was 艾德, pronounced "aye de." 艾 was an established family name, and 德 meant "virtue." We chose "Ginger" for Chunzhi because it sounded close to her Chinese name. I thought it fit her too, because ginger is both a spicy and a healing plant. My father was particularly fond of ginger from his years in India, and I thought that was appropriate too.

It can be difficult enough for one person to adjust to a foreign environment. I found it even more challenging to do so as two. I had spent my life adjusting to new places, people, and cultures. To a certain degree, I would do so by just letting go of what I had before and immersing myself—by going with the flow without necessarily knowing where the flow was headed. It was easier for me to do that by myself than to reassure and help Ginger do it.

The Foreign Service can be very demanding time-wise—and not always in a predictable way. A difficult report or a local crisis can keep one in the office far past the 5 p.m. or 6 p.m. closing time. In Washington or in Paris I had sometimes worked until 9 or 10 p.m. When single that just meant a lack of sleep, but when married that can be very unsettling for the other person. Most of the time I could explain to Ginger what I was doing and why it was necessary to stay late, but often it was my choice to do so—and that meant a more difficult choice or explanation for why I had chosen the office demands over her. Much of Foreign Service work is done outside the office and outside normal working hours. That means directing personal time that would otherwise be spent relaxing together to getting to know other people—sometimes people neither of you find interesting or even palatable. This can be difficult for any person married to a Foreign Service officer, even more so if one is newly married and newly separated from almost all familiar supports. It had happened to my mother when at age twenty-one, married only one year to a man fourteen years her senior, and with a newly born infant, she moved to Rio de Janeiro and took on a role that had her out of the house for social obligations almost every evening, often in the middle of the day, and mostly in a language she had never spoken before. She at least had the advantage of being married to someone from her own culture who had the same basic understanding of their respective marital roles.

When we arrived in Hong Kong, it didn't even occur to me that Ginger might be uncomfortable. I assumed that she would be able to adjust more easily than I to all aspects of Hong Kong's Chinese environment, and I was so impressed with her in general that I thought she could handle just about anything. Then, the first thing I did was to make her adjustment more difficult with my selection of living quarters. I had been given a choice between an apartment with a spectacular view or one more convenient to the city. I chose the former and thought that Ginger would see it my way. Our apartment certainly met my needs for the spectacular. It was halfway up the mountain and had a literally unbelievable view of Hong Kong, the harbor, and Kowloon. I was in heaven. It was halfway up the mountain but not a long drive from downtown. Unfortunately, Ginger didn't drive. She had never had the need to drive, so initially she was isolated up there on the mountain.

She soon discovered, however, that there was a minibus that she could flag down in front of our building that would take her right to the Star Ferry pier at the harbor downtown. This had the additional benefit of delivering her right to the doorstep of Hong Kong's main public library. She began checking out a wide variety of books in Chinese and English. She also discovered the Hong Kong Chinese language magazines, which provided extensive insights into not only Hong Kong issues and society, but the mainland as well.

Ginger spent the first year of our tour in Hong Kong doing everything she could to be a good wife. Before we met she had already established her independence, first in business and then as a teacher. However, all of her family and cultural education had placed a clear priority on her first responsibility as a wife. That role just was not quite so clear being married to a foreigner in Hong Kong as it might have been being married to a Taiwanese in Taiwan. In traditional Taiwanese society the husband is responsible for supporting the family and for all matters outside the household. The husband is the head of the household, but the wife is responsible for all matters inside the house. Traditionally the wife has limited dealing with affairs outside the home. In the United States—in current times at least—there is much more emphasis placed on equality and shared responsibilities both outside and inside the house, and even a certain aversion to assigning specific roles and responsibilities. The result may be more opportunity but also less clarity and more stress. During that first year, Ginger worked on establishing her traditional Taiwanese role within the home, but she also stepped outside that traditional role to participate in every possible social function related to my work: lunches, dinners, receptions, events with other diplomatic spouses, and so on. She enrolled in the British Council to study English and in the Alliance Française to study French.

By the end of that first year, she began to shift her focus, attending less of the diplomatic functions and expanding her own circle of contacts. The people that we naturally chose to associate with were different. While this was sometimes a minor source of difficulty, it was mostly a plus both personally and professionally. In Paris and in Lubumbashi, I had intentionally sought out people who were not directly associated with my work, in an effort to get to know those places better and to expand my own horizons. In Hong Kong my professional challenge was considerably more difficult, and almost without noticing it I began to seek out people personally and socially who could directly impact my work: officials, businesspeople, journalists, and so on. I was becoming compromised in a way that I had aggressively criticized my father for when he was in the profession. Intentionally or unintentionally, Ginger didn't let me get away with it. She met people I would not have connected with at all: Chinese professionals who had escaped China after the Cultural Revolution, Chinese spouses of American and European businessmen who were not oriented to the American Consulate, and artists and musicians. At one point she was invited to a charity benefit for a well-known Chinese feng shui[4] (風水) master, Lin Yun, who was visiting Hong Kong from Berkeley, California. She took some of his courses and then began avidly studying on her own.

Our preferred activities were different. I chose the secluded walking trails on the mountains. She chose to explore all of the crowded alleys downtown. I thought the beaches and the old colonial Repulse Bay Hotel on the other side of the island were exotic and romantic. She preferred the antique stores and the night markets. I wanted to try the fancy Western and Chinese restaurants. She was happier with street food and coffee shops. I wanted to explore the farthest reaches of the islands scattered around Hong Kong. She was perfectly content to explore the depth of the city. I was looking at the hills. She was looking at the signs. I was trying to understand Hong Kong in relationship to China and the rest of the world. She was trying to understand what made Hong Kong tick. In the end we saw twice as much.

Among other things, Ginger also gave me my first real introduction to the power and sophistication of Chinese medicine. Several months into our tour, I came down with a kidney stone and was placed in a local hospital. At that time, Western medicine offered very little except strong painkillers to help the agonizing journey of a kidney stone down the urethra. After five or six hours of watching me suffer in the intervals when the painkillers wore off, Ginger decided a different approach was necessary. Having grown up watching her grandfather treat patients with Chinese medicine, she knew there were alternatives. So she called a taxi and asked the driver to take her to the best Chinese doctor in the city. She explained to the doctor what the problem was, and he asked one question, "Has there been an X-ray, and how big is the stone?" She gave him that information, which confirmed for him that it was physically possible for the stone to pass through. He then gave her a prescription and sent her to a medicine store nearby. They gave her an assortment of ingredients and instructed her to boil them together down from six bowls to one. She went home, followed their instructions, and then came back and presented me with a large bowl of thick brown goop and told me to drink it. I thought that anything would be better than what I had been going through so far, so with some difficulty I drank it. Precisely thirty minutes later my right side began to contract gently, exactly where the pain and the spasms had been for the last several hours. I was impressed that a doctor who had not even seen me could target the correct side. The contractions lasted thirty minutes. As they progressed I became enormously thirsty and began drinking prodigious quantities of water. Shortly after the contractions stopped on the right side, they resumed on the other side, for another thirty minutes. When that was finished I was pretty tired, but they immediately began again; and this continued for another two hours, each time getting stronger. I was not in pain, but it became progressively harder to catch my breath. When after about two and a half hours the contractions showed no sign of letting up— actually quite the contrary—I decided we should confess to my doctor what we had done. He was Chinese, with Western medical training, and he was amused rather than annoyed when we recounted our story. Then he looked at the ingredients, whistled, said "That is pretty strong stuff," and gave me a muscle relaxant. Twenty minutes later I passed a very nasty-looking stone— but with no pain. I do not know how long it would have taken to pass that stone without the Chinese medicine, but I still believe that I would have been in that hospital for considerably longer and would have suffered more. Clearly the Chinese doctor knew what he was doing, and I was most grateful.

***

Hong Kong was a transportation hub for most of Asia, and it was easy to explore from there. We took advantage of that to visit two places that rated high on the exotic scale: Bali and Nepal.

Our trip to Bali in particular highlighted more of the differences in perspective that Ginger and I were learning to share. I made the arrangements and after interviewing a number of friends (westerners) who had been there, reserved a small cottage right on the beach. Ginger was skeptical. Why would we want to stay right on the beach next to the water? Was it safe? Wouldn't the dampness be unhealthy? We arrived on a Friday night. It was gorgeous, with warm weather, a gentle breeze, and a full moon. The full moon should have been my first warning, but my romantic proposal of marriage was already two years behind me. The cottage was charming, made of bamboo with the bedroom opening onto a veranda no more than fifty feet from the water. I couldn't imagine a more perfect setting. Ginger was not so sure. It was out on the beach, away from the hotel. What if someone tried to break in? What if the waves got bigger and reached the cottage? I slept well that evening. She had nightmares. In particular, a bizarre mask kept appearing in front of her face.

The next day I wanted to rent a motorcycle since I had read that was the best way to get around. Ginger didn't think that was a good idea. Luckily, I failed my motorcycle test, and we looked around for another means of transportation. We met a young Chinese-Indonesian who spoke Mandarin Chinese; he offered to drive us around and show us the island. Everything changed then, and we began to see Bali quite differently. Ginger asked him about her dream, and he was not surprised at all. The face she had seen was familiar to him. He explained that black magic is deeply ingrained in Balinese society, and the most intense rituals are conducted at the edge of the sea—on Friday night.

As he drove us around showing us both current and historical sites, he recounted many stories of how people try to use black magic to improve their own lives and to hurt those with whom they compete—that was the reason behind the very high rate of traffic injuries. The beautiful, calm, and polite surface that we and other tourists saw in Bali masked something quite different in the lives of its inhabitants. He also gave us some insights into life in Bali as a Chinese. We knew that the Chinese community had suffered under both the Sukarno and Suharto regimes and had been terrorized in the 1960s. Our guide was too young to have personally experienced that, though he confirmed that there was still discrimination and underlying hostility. He made it clear that Bali was not an idyllic melting pot, and that there were more than enough interethnic tensions to keep everyone on their toes. If I had gone to Bali on my own, my experience would most certainly have been very different. I doubt that I would have gotten very far past the surface presented to a white westerner, though I might have gotten a better tan.

Nepal was a different kind of challenge. I had long wanted to go trekking in the Himalayas, and Ginger had done a good deal of hiking in Taiwan so she was up for it. From Hong Kong it was a doable trip. We flew via Bangkok to Katmandu with a colleague from the consulate and friends from Shanghai, an American couple with two children aged eleven and nine. Hal, from the consulate, had been to Nepal before and had some contacts in the Tibetan community in Katmandu who helped us find a Sherpa. After meeting Mingmar and collecting our gear, we flew to Pokhara, spent the night, and hit the trail the next day. It was very civilized, almost luxurious. Mingmar hired porters to carry our gear, and all we needed to carry was our day packs. The porters would precede us (moving much more quickly in spite of their relatively heavy loads) and at the end of the day would be waiting at our designated stopping point with the tents already pitched. We trekked for a week, spending a glorious Christmas Day in the Annapurna Sanctuary graced with a foot of snow that had fallen the night before. The views in the Himalayas were in fact more spectacular than Hong Kong harbor. On our first night we sat around a campfire and gazed at a mountain that looked remarkably like the Matterhorn, but almost twice as high. The trails were well worn and easy to follow, and we encountered almost no difficulties—except one of our own making.

On our second day we stopped for lunch at a small restaurant idyllically situated by a rushing mountain stream, just where the trail curved and began the ascent into the sanctuary. We saw many small teahouses along the trail where they sold "milk tea" and lentil soup to trekkers. Usually they were just shacks, but this one looked like a small Swiss chalet and even had a deck beside the stream and a menu in English. It included lentil soup, bread, and— "hash pancakes." We looked at each other and commented that must be corned beef hash, right? Then, out of curiosity, we ordered some. It was not corned beef. I ate a quarter of one and decided to stop, but Don ate two whole pancakes. As we headed out it became clear to me that a quarter of a pancake was more than enough, and my four-hour hike up the next several thousand feet was a rather spectacular experience. A short way out, though, Mingmar explained to us that we should go on ahead until we caught up to the porters, but he needed to stay close to Don. We arrived without incident. Mingmar and Don arrived several hours later. Don would never have made it without Mingmar, who had to prevent him repeatedly from straying off the path, which followed a cliff. Don was seriously out of commission for the next two days. At the time I thought it was amusing, until he explained to me that it had in fact been quite terrifying. We all made it back alive, though our plane back to Katmandu was canceled and we had to charter a bus—a very old and bumpy bus—to get us back in time to catch our flight back to Hong Kong. Overall it was a wonderful trip, though by the time we got back to Katmandu everyone in our group had to battle some form of intestinal or flu-like illness—everyone except Ginger. While the rest of us were scrambling up side peaks, pushing ourselves to see that extra temple, or avidly trying a new exotic dish, Ginger kept her enthusiasm in check. She was more careful about what she ate, didn't push herself beyond her limits, and resisted the temptation to take off her jacket in the high-altitude sun. She stuck closer to the "middle way," and her reward was nursing the rest of us back to health.

***

The "international" city that I was looking for when I chose between the jobs in Hong Kong and Taipei was not entirely what I expected. It was certainly international in that people and cultures from all over the world mixed there. However, the government was decidedly British, and the population, while Western-oriented for many commercial and some social reasons, was decidedly Chinese. I also came to realize that my concept of "international" was limited by my experience, which was centered almost exclusively in European culture. While the European character of Hong Kong was prominent, it was more like a point of rock being submerged in a steadily rising Chinese sea.

One of the most striking elements of this Chinese sea was the elite population of business tycoons who had risen to commercial prominence in Hong Kong and the world. These were, and are, some of the most industrious, innovative, and successful businesspeople on earth. Their activities stretch across the whole gamut of economic activity: trade, investment, banking, manufacturing, and so on. Some are very cosmopolitan and Western-oriented, with Western educations and lifestyles. Some, while their businesses are global, remain very Chinese by education and preference. Some made their fortunes in Hong Kong and the West, keeping their distance from the communist mainland. Others nurtured relationships with the mainland throughout the worst times of the Great Leap Forward and the Cultural Revolution. Some profited directly from the decades of animosity between China and the West by maintaining licit or illicit channels of communication and commerce for governments and other actors. I was fascinated by the stories of some of these individuals. One or two of them seemed to be almost real-life manifestations of Joseph Heller's Milo Minderbinder in *Catch-22*.

As I grew more familiar with China and things Chinese over the next decade, I began to discover that what I was admiring was in fact a very small piece of a larger reality. I met a fair number of Chinese businesspeople while in Hong Kong, but when I moved on to the mainland and then elsewhere in Southeast Asia I saw more and more of their vast reach and influence. The Chinese communities throughout Southeast Asia are easily the most dynamic economic forces in the region. They influence the economies of their respective countries directly, and the political and social structures sometimes directly, and always indirectly. They dominate trade, finance, and investment. They are equally proficient in both formal and informal economies. Where the banking systems are limited by a lack of development or an excess of political control, the Chinese communities run informal financial networks. These networks can handle both small and multimillion-dollar transactions— in any currencies. The Hong Kong Chinese businesspeople have their own lines into most of these communities.

The opportunities seemed limitless at the time, but there are also downsides to all of this opportunity and wealth. Chinese culture, like many older traditional cultures, relies heavily on informal systems of personal and family relationships, called *guanxi* (關係) in Mandarin Chinese. Chinese culture is older than just about any other living culture today, and so that system is perhaps more complex and pervasive than in other cultures. A very wise and well-informed Chinese scholar told me once that no Chinese businessperson can be successful beyond a certain level in Hong Kong (or any other Chinese environment) without using and participating in this network of relationships. As they do so, they incur personal debts. The more successful they are, the more debts they incur. These personal debts can be very open-ended. They might be collected in money, introductions, or other favors—and more often than not, with no questions asked. If a colleague, friend, or benefactor asks for a million dollars for three months—and you can afford it—you give it. Your money or the doors you open could be used for just about anything— good or bad. In this way, he explained, almost no senior Hong Kong businessperson is free of association with illicit activity, be it narcotics trade, war financing, the exploitation of other human beings, and so on. They may not have explicit knowledge of how they have assisted, but they have assisted, and therefore they bear personal responsibility. In many societies, wealth is seen as both a blessing and a curse. It is possible that in Chinese culture, with its extraordinary interconnectedness, the downside of wealth becomes more serious.

***

The U.S. Consulate General in Hong Kong did a good job during the early 1980s when the territory and its people were embarking on that momentous and unexpected journey to return to the "motherland." It did more than simply watch and report on issues of interest to the U.S. government. It made a real contribution to the stability of the region. I don't think that contribution would have been as substantial had the consul general been a different person. Burt Levin's language ability, his extensive knowledge of and appreciation for Chinese culture and history, and, finally, his personal confidence and extroverted personality made him uniquely qualified for that role. In my experience, it is relatively rare for American diplomats (perhaps for diplomats of any country) to play prominent, wise, and effective roles at the same time. Diplomacy by its nature is more safely applied quietly and out of the limelight. Diplomats have to be careful with anything that they do or promote, because the impact and fallout from actions in the international arena can be so far-reaching. Career diplomats also tend to be careful in defense of their own careers. In this case an individual with very solid qualifications took the initiative to forcefully implement something he believed in, and it worked.

The consulate general also did a pretty good job of analyzing and reporting on the rapidly evolving economy of the PRC. This was due in very large degree to the extraordinary Chinese employees rather than to the Americans, no matter how educated we may have been. I personally relied very heavily on my Chinese colleagues. My own contribution to the reports that really mattered consisted of interrogating my staff relentlessly about their assessments or speculations, and then editing the reports to make them more understandable and relevant to Washington interests. Neither my Chinese nor my knowledge and understanding of China were sufficient to produce insights of my own that could compare with what they did. Formal academic education didn't necessarily help.

On one occasion we made a trip to the first of China's new "special economic zones" immediately to the north of Hong Kong's New Territories. These SEZs were meant to be discrete areas where China could experiment with market economic forces in a controlled way, limiting their impact on the communist economic and political system at least for a while. Elements that worked—and were judged not to be a threat—then might be applied to the broader Chinese economy. Shenzhen was a significant experiment. It was a fishing village in the late 1970s, and it was transformed in a very short period into an urban area with roads, high-rise buildings, and modern communications. When we visited, the roads had just been built, and there were only a few buildings that were inhabitable. However, people were already flocking to the new area to try their luck. We spent a day exploring the nascent city and talking with officials and some of the new arrivals, and then we returned to Hong Kong to report our observations. One of my colleagues, a PhD economist, confidently declared that the area as then conceived would be a failure, and that the Chinese instead should concentrate on very simple labor-intensive areas in which they had a "comparative advantage." That was wrong. Today, Shenzhen is a city of fourteen million people, with per capita income over $13,000; the second-busiest port in China; and one of the fastest-growing cities in the world. Of course, we didn't need PhDs to be wrong. Most of us, including our Chinese colleagues, believed that, in spite of the impressive effort that Deng Xiaoping was making to reorient the Chinese economy, his stated objective of quadrupling China's gross national product by the year 2000 was highly unlikely. That happened also to be the conventional wisdom of most American observers. In the early 1980s, I can recall only one American official who not only believed it was possible for China to achieve that goal, but was confident that it would do so. That was Chas Freeman, who had been the director for Chinese affairs at the Department of State when diplomatic relations were reestablished, and who in the early 1980s was the deputy chief of mission in Beijing. He was right, and all the rest of us were wrong.

Hong Kong is an interesting example of the old adage that there is a good and a bad side to everything. The British colony was created because of and by the largest narcotics operation the world has ever seen. It is hard to imagine a more serious crime than a century of promoting drug addiction in a foreign land. However, Hong Kong then grew beyond that. It became a place where economic forces from around the world coalesced to generate a productive dynamo for the entire Asia-Pacific region. It became a place of refuge and hope for those fleeing a period of frightful physical, psychological, and cultural violence on the mainland. Many of those seeking refuge in Hong Kong have since returned to China to help rebuild it and set it successfully on its new path. All of these things would seem to be good. We do not yet know to what degree forces of greed, selfishness, and cultural disrespect are also carried with this dynamo and what damage they may do at some point in the future.

NOTES

1. In the fifteenth century, the Ming Dynasty built an enormous oceangoing fleet of more than two thousand vessels, led by a eunuch admiral named Zheng He. After almost thirty years of exploration that reached at least as far as Africa, and possibly even into the Atlantic, two successive Ming emperors, Hongxi and Xuande, decided for a variety of reasons to stop the expeditions and dismantle the fleet. Efforts during the late nineteenth century under the Qing Dynasty to build a modern fleet were not successful.

2. The Treaty of Nanjing, 1842.

3. Generally, one can be naturalized as a U.S. citizen only after five years of residency in the United States. However, there is a provision in the law that allows this requirement to be waived in the case of persons serving the U.S. government overseas, once all of the necessary health and security investigations have been completed.

4. Feng shui is the ancient Chinese science of placement (buildings, furniture, works of art, etc.) to bring optimum positive energy to bear.

Chapter Five

The Middle Kingdom: Beijing (August 1984–June 1986)

When I was first assigned to Hong Kong, I did not intend to spend more than three years in China, at least not all at once. I reasoned that three years dealing with one subject in one part of the world would be enough, and I should move on. However, after those three years in Hong Kong it was clear to me that I was not even scratching the surface, and when I was offered a job in the economic section in Beijing (北京), Ginger and I both thought that staying in China was the right thing to do.

We also thought that it would be exciting to actually experience Beijing, in spite of whatever hardships the limited living conditions there might have to offer. Beijing means "Northern Capital" in Chinese. It has been the official capital of China off and on for more than seven hundred years, including during four imperial dynasties and the current People's Republic. It has existed as a city for more than three thousand years, has been inhabited by Homo sapiens for twenty-seven thousand years, and was the home of Peking Man more than two hundred thousand years ago. That combination pretty much put it beyond anything any continent other than Asia had to offer. In addition, the scale of its dominion—in terms of geography, population, and culture—dwarfed anything else on the planet. Beijing was and is completely unique, and we thought we had better seize the opportunity that was being offered to us.

***

When we moved to Beijing in 1984, the city—and the country—was just beginning to wake up from a nightmare that had lasted thirty years. The establishment of the communist People's Republic of China in 1949 was one in a series of efforts by the Chinese to stem the decay and disorder that had begun in the nineteenth century as the Qing Dynasty began to decline. By the early twentieth century, reformist intellectuals like Sun Yat-sen had concluded that the only solution was to dismantle the imperial Chinese governmental system and establish a republic that would incorporate Western democratic ideals and mechanisms. Given that the Chinese imperial system of government and political philosophy had been responsible for maintaining order in the largest, richest, and most developed human community on the planet for more than two thousand years, Sun's conclusions were at that time very radical. They were also insufficient to prevent China's plunge into catastrophic violence—first with postdynastic warlordism, then the Japanese invasion, and, finally, the civil war between Chiang Kai-shek's nationalists and Mao Zedong's communists.

When Mao took over in 1949, he started China on a path of change, destruction, and trauma that went way beyond Sun's radicalism. Sun Yat-sen's model for government was a democratic republic rooted in the eighteenth-century thought of the French philosopher Rousseau. That model had manifested successfully in the United States and some of the European republics. Mao's model for government was a communist state, rooted in the thought of the nineteenth-century philosopher Karl Marx. The only functioning example was the Soviet Union, which by the end of World War II had been successful in political and military terms, but far less so economically. Mao preached that both Sun's republic and Stalin's Soviet Union had not gone far enough. To successfully address China's troubles, dismantling the political system would not be enough. Mao believed that even the nature of man had to be changed, for which it was necessary to dismantle the very foundations of Chinese culture. That included the philosophic and religious underpinnings of Chinese thought, the semisacred family structures, and even the language.

Mao was an incredibly talented and inspirational leader—which, as the twentieth century demonstrated in numerous examples, is not always a good thing. Hundreds of millions of Chinese enthusiastically followed Mao like lemmings into disastrous endeavors like the Great Leap Forward and the Cultural Revolution. It is estimated that between thirty and seventy million people died from persecution, widespread violence, or famine between his accession to power in 1949 and his death in 1975. Before it was over, the Chinese landscape had been vastly altered. Culturally, countless historical sites, palaces, temples, and even whole cities had been destroyed. Libraries, museums, books, documents, and artwork were eradicated. Artists, musicians, scholars, landowners, and countless others were persecuted, terrorized, or executed.

After Mao's death in 1975, Deng Xiaoping rose to power. Deng was a founder of the Chinese Communist Party and a longtime associate of Mao during the party's twentieth-century struggles. However, in the 1950s and 1960s, he also became identified with more moderate elements of the Communist Party, and as a result he was punished and humiliated during the Cultural Revolution. After his reemergence, Deng softened and even reversed some of Mao's internal policies. He set aside many elements of communist doctrine and radically altered China's economic policies, promoting market forces and setting China on a road that would make it a global economic power before the century ended.

***

When Ginger and I arrived in Beijing, five years after the initiation of Deng's new policies, many people were still wondering how these policies would manifest themselves, whether they would work, and whether they constituted a long-term trajectory or just another short-lived experiment.

While many changes were taking place, that which remained unchanged was greater than what was changing—to the uninitiated eye, at least. One thing that seemed unchanged was the omnipresent state security apparatus, which we had heard about for some time. During our time in Beijing, we were acutely aware that "Big Brother" was watching us. After all, we arrived in 1984, and George Orwell's novel of that name had imagined a world in which the government watched and controlled virtually every aspect of every individual's life.

For several years leading up to 1984 it was fashionable to speculate on just how accurate Orwell's futuristic portrayal was. The United States seemed to have avoided Big Brother, the novel's omnipresent government authority. Nazi Germany and the Soviet Union were another story, but China may have come closest to the total control that Orwell envisaged. There was very little privacy in China. Everyone was watched. Conformity of expression was essential, and conformity of thought was advisable. The most extreme manifestation was during the Cultural Revolution, when the slightest deviation from behavioral norms could result in persecution or death.

As foreigners in 1984, we were not expected to conform to Chinese behavioral norms. In fact, much of the population seemed to believe, in a charming sort of way, that it was simply impossible for foreigners to do so. For many, we were bizarre creatures to be tolerated or marveled at. We were a nuisance, or an entertainment, or both. For the security apparatus, foreigners were a potential danger, and foreign diplomats were a particular concern. As representatives of foreign governments we might present a greater threat. As official guests we also had to be protected from all harm. We were therefore carefully watched and restricted in where we could go, what we could do, and who we could see.

In the years immediately following the establishment of relations and the opening of the embassy and consulates, most official Americans lived in a few select hotels. In Beijing, everyone lived in the Beijing Hotel. The rooms, of course, were all bugged. The lack of privacy added to the personal stress of living and working there, though there was some humor as well. When lightbulbs burned out in the room, diplomats found that if they complained distinctly about it within the room, it was not long before a group of work-men showed up to replace the bulb (and possibly replace the bug). The offices were bugged, and we assumed that most public places like hotel dining rooms, bars, restaurants, and so on were as well.

While the electronic surveillance was pervasive, the most effective form of surveillance was by the people themselves. That included those who worked for us at the embassy, and those who worked in the hotels. It also included virtually everyone else in the society who came into contact with us. Since we did not blend in very well at that time, it was pretty easy for people to pick up on us, watch us, and then report what they saw or heard. For many of us this felt quite oppressive, and it tended to color how we saw and interacted with all of our hosts.

After about a year, Ginger and I flew to Hong Kong for a few days. As we exited the airport after passing through immigration and customs and started looking for a taxi, we both commented that something was different, and it was not the weather, the crowds, or the scenery. In spite of the noise and the traffic and the pollution, we felt more relaxed and at ease. Then we realized that neither of us felt like we were being watched or had to be careful about what we said and where we said it. We had only carried that burden for a year—imagine the impact on people of a lifetime of such circumspection!

It also tended to obscure the fact that there was another element of this that was less ominous. That was the desire to be helpful. For me it was, and still is, difficult to determine where the line is between personal choice and social obligation. Perhaps it is rarely a clear line. Chinese custom, like that of many traditional societies, includes a strong obligation for the host to protect and care for guests. In 1984 that custom still existed, and perhaps was being resurrected after the excesses of the Cultural Revolution. The government told virtually all members of society that they had an obligation to play a combined role of helping, protecting, and reporting on visitors. That was very specific for those working at the embassies and consulates, and for those working at the hotels where we lived. It became more generalized as it filtered out into society. It also became more complicated, since ordinary people were expected to help without being too friendly. Since for most people it was unclear how this was supposed to work, many people just tried to avoid contact with foreigners in those years.

All of the embassy's Chinese employees were actually employed by a Chinese government agency, the Foreign Affairs Services Office, and then contracted to the embassy. When we arrived in 1984, the economic section had two Chinese employees assigned to us. They were very nice, competent people, who worked very hard to help us do our job. Their most important contribution was helping us find and connect with a wide variety of government agencies working on issues of interest to us. Communicating with these different agencies was difficult for them sometimes as well. They had to convince their counterparts that dealing with us was first, allowed, and second, worth their while. It took me about a year to realize just how hard their job was. When I first arrived, I resented having to depend on them and often thought they themselves were the obstacles. Perhaps on occasion they were, but I grew to realize that they had a much greater professional interest in making the U.S.-China relationship work than in obstructing it.

When I arrived at the embassy, I was also told by some that there was one particular Chinese employee (in another section) to whom all the others reported—the chief spy, if you will. Most people recommended I avoid him as much as possible, and I was inclined to do so. Ginger's approach was just the opposite. She showed him extra attention and respect, and recommended I do the same. He turned out to be extremely helpful and very competent at working through obstacles that would stump others. It was certainly a two-edged sword, but without Ginger's encouragement, I would only have seen the negative edge.

***

In fact, Ginger's approach to many of our challenges was different, more effective—and more fun—than that of many official Americans. She had certain advantages, having been born a Han Chinese and being a native speaker. Actually, Mandarin Chinese was not her first language, because growing up in Taiwan her mother tongue was Hokkien. However, when she did learn Mandarin, she learned it without the pronounced accent of many of her Taiwanese compatriots. In the early 1980s in Beijing, coming from Taiwan also had its advantages, as the mainland Chinese were being officially encouraged to welcome their brethren from Taiwan. Being a native Taiwanese was an additional point of interest, since they were less associated with the ruling Goumindang (Kuomintang) Party on Taiwan and might have more potential to be wooed. Visiting Taiwanese were given a special compatriot status that allowed them to pay lower prices for a variety of services like transportation and entertainment than did most other "foreigners."

Nevertheless, being both from Taiwan and married to an official American was also problematic. Before moving to Beijing, we had heard many stories from other Taiwanese and Asian spouses of American diplomats that they encountered some hostility from the local population and constant harassment from the security forces. In particular, they often had difficulty gaining access to the embassy buildings, the diplomatic residential compounds, and even the major hotels. This was partly because the Chinese security forces guarding the diplomatic establishments—and some of the hotels—had instructions to carefully screen any Chinese seeking to enter to make sure they were not threats (to the diplomats or to the Chinese government). However, many suspected that there was also some resentment of "overseas" Chinese who had achieved a more privileged status.

Knowing that this would be a challenge, Ginger confronted it directly. A few days after our arrival—when I was at the office—she made the rounds of all the guards posted at all of the embassy buildings and the diplomatic compound. She dressed simply (though at that time any Western clothing stood out), except for one thing. She wore a hat. It was not a remarkable hat, but it was cute and had a little picture of a duck on it. She stopped at each post, introduced herself to the guards, showed her ID, explained who she was, and told them that she would be visiting all of those places periodically. She said she was introducing herself to them to avoid any confusion and to avoid causing them any inconvenience. If they were willing, she engaged them in conversation. All of them were surprised, some were amused, and some were completely flummoxed. But it worked. For the next two years, Ginger was not stopped once at any of those checkpoints, while many of her colleagues continued to have trouble. I noticed on more than one occasion that when she showed up the guards would smile broadly—when for most of us they were professionally stone-faced.

***

Living in Beijing in the mid-1980s was a special experience. Accommodations were limited. The government was working hard to expand the limited housing compounds for the diplomatic community, but still had a ways to go. There were only a few hotels at that time that were considered suitable for foreigners. When the U.S. Liaison Office became the U.S. Embassy in 1979 and began expanding rapidly, most of the U.S. staff was housed in rooms at the Beijing Hotel, a Soviet-era construction with spacious rooms and basic service. By the time we arrived in 1984, many U.S. employees were put up at the newer Jianguo Hotel, a prefab construction on the order of a nice American motel, with suites and pleasant Western restaurants as well as a fancy Chinese restaurant.

Ginger and I were fortunate. We were only in the hotel for a month, and our suite was very pleasant. Then we moved into a nice one-bedroom apartment in the diplomatic compound. It was substantially smaller than our Hong Kong apartment had been, and the view did not compare—parking lots versus the international harbor—but it was fine for the two of us.

On our first visit to Beijing in early 1982, there had been no Western restaurants, and Chinese restaurants that would serve westerners outside the hotels were a rarity. Those that did had to keep separate sections reserved for the non-Chinese. Was it to prevent us from fraternizing with the Chinese customers, or to make it easier to listen to our conversations, or to make it more comfortable for us? I don't know, but it was probably a combination of the three.

In 1984, the separate sections rule was still applied, but the number and variety of restaurants were growing. There were Western restaurants in all the new hotels and in several of the older ones. While we were there, Maxim's of Paris even opened a restaurant—with Parisian prices. There were several Japanese restaurants as well, and the quality of the Chinese restaurants was improving. Ginger and I would seek out the Western restaurants on the weekends as escapism. But the blossoming Chinese restaurants were really the most interesting.

Three of them stood out in particular. The first was a vegetarian restaurant called Gong De Lin (功德林). It applied a centuries-old art of simulating meat dishes from strictly vegetarian products. Sometimes it was quite convincing. Many kinds of meat can be mimicked using bean curd, and the sauces can come very close to the originals. The most impressive, however, was a whole steamed "fish" that when cut open revealed an entire skeleton—carved from potatoes. The second was a restaurant, which I believe was associated with the ancient pharmaceutical company Tong Ren Tang, that applied Chinese medicinal herbs to elaborate dishes—actually designed to address specific illnesses or physical deficiencies. These were dishes that used to be prepared for the emperors and other senior officials. The last was the Quan Ju De (全聚德), which was an enormous restaurant that specialized in Peking Duck, where the duck is carefully roasted and elaborately carved at the table, producing a variety of dishes using every conceivable part of the duck. This restaurant is very well known to foreigners—and probably came closest to shortening my career and life as any experience in China. In 1984, an American mountaineering group, led by Lou Whittaker from Seattle, came through Beijing on their way to attempt a climb of Mount Everest from the Tibet side. They were hosted in Beijing and at the Peking Duck Restaurant by the Chinese Mountaineering Association and Wang Fuzhou, one of the three mountaineers who made the first Chinese ascent of Mount Everest in 1960. For some reason, the senior leadership of the embassy was unable to attend, and I was asked to represent them. I sat next to Wang Fuzhou, who was a fun, charming man who loved to tell stories—and loved to drink. They served the Chinese white liquor, or baijiu (白酒), which is essentially straight grain alcohol, served in little shot glasses. Each course, each new friend, each story, each whatever was an occasion for a toast proclaimed with a hearty *Ganbei* ("Drain the glass"). Wang Fuzhou was very accomplished at this sport. I was not, but I was (stupidly) very determined to keep up with him. After nineteen glasses I was both proud and surprised that I could actually stand up and walk away from the table unassisted. I also proudly (and stupidly) boasted to Ginger of my accomplishment when I returned. She was distinctly unimpressed. When I reached our room and became violently ill, I understood why. I had managed to stay on my feet long enough to get back to the hotel, but it took me three days before I could stand upright again. Ginger forgave me, sort of, but my liver has neither forgiven nor forgotten.

The early 1980s were like very early spring for Beijing's market economy, which had been utterly forbidden before 1979. The mountains of cabbage on the sidewalks, where in 1980 and 1981 farmers had deposited the sole crop in amounts too great for the government distribution system to handle, were gone. Some varieties of vegetables were beginning to manifest themselves in street markets or small private or semiprivate stores in nooks and crannies along side streets. They were few and far between, but it seemed that each time we went for a walk, a new store would appear—or an old one would expand. While the Western restaurants in the hotels still imported much of their food, local farmers were quick to cater to their needs, and huge makeshift greenhouses began to sprout along the roads outside the city. Just as someone from Florida visiting Vermont in early spring might be unimpressed with the first signs of warmth and life returning, we coming recently from Hong Kong to Beijing were initially not as perceptive as we should have been. However, as we became more acclimatized, we began to appreciate the extraordinary changes that were taking place.

The opening of the antique markets had preceded our arrival, and we were told by many that we had actually missed the chance to purchase really valuable things at bargain prices. I had very little understanding of antiques and art, and virtually no experience in that market. Ginger understood it much better—all aspects of it—but she was more interested in learning cultural phenomena than in acquiring more possessions, so we mostly just admired what we saw.

For me the most fascinating of all the markets that were appearing were the bird and fish markets at the north of the city. There were actually less new than the others, because in many ways they were less commercial and had existed for some years as places for people—mostly men—to share their hobbies with each other. I had seen bird markets before—but never anything quite like the goldfish market. First, I had never imagined that there were so many varieties of goldfish. I particularly liked the ones with multiple fins and bubbles around the eyes. More importantly, I had never seen fish so domesticated. These fish were truly pets, elaborately trained, and even content to be picked up and fondled, hanging over their masters' hands like contented cats. The time and attention that went into the care and appreciation of these air and water dwellers must have been simply extraordinary.

***

Though Ginger was head and shoulders above me in her understanding of Chinese culture and history, neither of us had the education to fully appreciate and take advantage of where we were. We dabbled. We visited the Forbidden City, the Lama Temple, the Altar of the Sun, and other obvious points of historical interest. Mostly we walked, wandering through old commercial and residential areas of the city and the parks. Armed with a copy of *In Search of Old Peking*, published in 1935, we searched, sometimes successfully, for old monuments and buildings. Unfortunately, Beijing as a historical city seemed significant almost as much for what was no longer there as for what remained.

The foreword to *In Search of Old Peking* decries "the indifference of the Chinese themselves, more especially of their authorities, toward the historical monuments in which Peking is so rich," noting that "the loss by vandalism and utter neglect has been proceeding at such a rate that, on repeated occasions buildings and historical monuments have actually disappeared while the authors were still writing about them." But the destruction that the authors decried was nothing compared to what took place thirty years later under the rule of Chairman Mao. While *In Search of Old Peking* bemoaned the loss of individual buildings, Mao led a destruction that made the ancient city almost unrecognizable.

In Beijing the regime tore down almost the entire wall encircling the ancient Chinese and Tartar cities.[1] The wall surrounding the Chinese city had been thirty feet tall and twenty-five feet wide at the base. That surrounding the Tartar City had been forty feet high and sixty-two feet wide at the base. The top had been over thirty feet wide, sufficient to drive two chariots abreast. They must have been magnificent. By the early 1980s almost the only evidence of their previous existence was a few gates left standing by themselves. However, much still survived those cultural pogroms. The Forbidden City—seat of hundreds of years of imperial rule—was still standing, and available to the public. The Ming Tombs, located not far outside Beijing, were overgrown and in some disrepair, but had not suffered significant damage during the Cultural Revolution.

One of my favorite sites was the Yong He Gong (Palace of Concord and Harmony), also known as the Lama Temple. It was special, not just for its architecture and its Tibetan art, but because it was a functioning religious establishment right in the center of Beijing—and a Tibetan religious establishment at that. Originally, it had been a palace inhabited by the fourth son of Emperor Kangxi in the early Qing Dynasty. After Prince Yinzhen succeeded his father, becoming the Emperor Yongzheng, part and eventually the entire palace was dedicated to the Tibetan Buddhist religion. The Yong He Gong and the three emperors most closely associated with it (Kangxi, Yongzheng, and Qianlong) played a significant role in Chinese-Tibetan relations, and their contributions are particularly relevant to the international controversy surrounding that relationship today—as is discussed further in the section on Tibet in chapter 7.

***

I had been interested in Tibet and Tibetan Buddhism for many years, though still knew relatively little about it. Ginger knew much more about Buddhism in general, both from experience and from studying it academically. While we were in Beijing she found several opportunities to pursue her Buddhist studies. Some of them were at the Yong He Gong.

Early in our stay, Ginger was invited by a friend to attend a public blessing by a senior lama at the Yong He Gong. Since 1979, the Chinese government had declared that people were free to practice religion as long as their practice did not cross the line into political activity. Proselytizing was often considered to be political, while individual devotion was not. On this occasion, the lama who was visiting from Tibet was available in the courtyard of the Yong He Gong to those who wished to enter and receive a blessing from him. Quite a lot of people showed up on this occasion, and Ginger waited about forty-five minutes in line before she got to the lama. His blessing for most of the people in line was short and perfunctory, and most of the time his eyes remained closed. However, when Ginger reached him he stopped, opened his eyes, and examined her quietly for a while before giving his blessing and presenting her with a Buddhist baptismal name.

During that time she also met several other monks whom she was able to visit periodically in their temples to talk and study with. This was made possible by the president of the Buddhist Association of China. I called on him to discuss an upcoming trip to Tibet, and Ginger accompanied me to the meeting. When he found out that she was interested in Buddhism, he arranged meetings for her with prominent monks. One of them had himself recently translated a Tibetan language sutra into Chinese. Another had only one arm—just like the second Zen patriarch, Huike (慧可)—and he helped her significantly with her study and practice.

***

When we were in Beijing we did not take many long trips around China. My job kept me pretty much tied to Beijing, but we did take one trip to Tibet. Travel by foreigners in China was sensitive in those early days, and travel in Tibet was perhaps the most sensitive of all. However, it was open, and many were doing their best to make it work.

We needed to get permission from the government to travel there, and we needed to get plane reservations. The Chinese staff at the embassy helped obtain the tickets for the first leg of the journey, but the Ministry of Foreign Affairs had assured us that since Lhasa was now an "open city" no permit was needed. We had to pass through Chengdu, the capital of Sichuan Province, and the city from which most foreigners enter Tibet. Road travel from Qinghai Province and Yunnan Province was theoretically possible, but we had neither the time to travel those longer routes nor the time to obtain the permission, which we assumed would be very difficult.

We flew to Chengdu, only to be told there that of course we needed a permit, and there was nothing anyone could do, not China International Travel Service, the hotel, the Public Security Bureau, or the Foreign Affairs Office, each of which we dutifully visited. We had to call back to the embassy. In the end it was our Chinese staff there that prevailed, calling first the Ministry of Foreign Affairs and then the Chengdu Foreign Affairs Office. We soon received word from the Foreign Affairs Office that we could go directly to the airlines to buy the tickets, which we then did without mishap.

At the Jin Jiang Hotel that evening, which I think was the only hotel in Chengdu open to westerners, we met an American woman traveling alone who asked if we would like to share a taxi to the airport the next day. Together we made our way to the airport, boarded an old Boeing 707, and flew to Lhasa. Our arrival was spectacular. It was brilliantly clear and sunny, and the air was delicious. There just was not enough oxygen in it, which I discovered when I tried to sprint to the only outhouse before the only bus of the day left the airport. I had learned two years earlier on that trek into the Annapurna Sanctuary in Nepal that altitude was difficult for me. That was fourteen thousand feet. Lhasa was only twelve thousand feet, but I was going to stay in Tibet for a week, whereas I had stayed in the sanctuary for only half a day.

When we arrived in Lhasa and claimed our luggage, we had to register with China Travel Service where we intended to stay. A modern Chinese hotel had just been built, and the officials recommended we stay there. However, we had heard of a Tibetan place called the Snowland Hotel, and the Tibetan man taking the registration was noticeably pleased when we voiced that preference. Ginger made friends with him rather quickly when she showed him a picture of the Dalai Lama, and he arranged a taxi to take the three of us on to the Snowland. It was the right choice: three stories high, built around a courtyard, and painted in bright, happy colors—a stunning change from the rest of China, where most buildings were a grimy gray color. The social environment was rather different too. When we entered the courtyard there was a raucous water fight going on between some of the young western men and the young Tibetan women staff. It encompassed all three stories, with much screaming, peals of laughter, and streams of water arching from the balconies and sparkling in the sun against the dark blue sky. Everyone was drenched, the men in their T-shirts and jeans and the women in their multicolored Tibetan dress, and it seemed that as much of it was from tears of laughter as from the buckets of water. Ginger and I had seen nothing like this in China—nothing anything like it.

I have two other memories of the Snowland Hotel that I will never forget. One was being wakened each morning by the bold singsong voice of a woman selling fresh yogurt in the courtyard. She brought it in buckets and sold it in big bowlfuls. I was full of admiration for the aesthetics, although I have always been a little ambivalent about unsweetened yogurt. The other was suffering through a nightmarish sleepless night with an altitude-induced headache that would not respond to anything I tried, including one of Ginger's migraine pills. Luckily, the next day I was scheduled to call on the director of tourism for Tibet, and he took me to his organization's doctor. She had a polite but no-nonsense manner that reminded me of a nurse at an English boarding school. She told me reassuringly it was nothing serious— my heart was just not working properly(!)—and she gave me a plastic baggie filled with rough brown pills. Either the tough love or the pills worked like magic and returned me almost to normal.

On our first evening in Lhasa we wandered the main street looking for a place to eat. We stopped at a small local place with tables on a front veranda. The menu was in Tibetan and the owner spoke no Chinese or English, so we experimented with sign language. There was a sheep grazing in the dusty front yard, and we pointed to it. The owner smiled, nodded vigorously, and headed back to the kitchen. Then, while we were complimenting ourselves on our newfound communication skills, someone else came out, grabbed the sheep, and dragged it around to the back of the house. Our self-satisfaction changed to consternation, but we had no idea how to communicate a change in our order. About an hour later we were served a tasty dish of very tough mutton, and we spent the rest of the evening saying prayers for the soul of the sheep that we assumed had been dispatched for us.

In Lhasa, we visited the Potala Palace and the Jokhang Temple. We were accompanied by official guides who were both sent to help us and to watch us. At the Potala, Ginger had won the confidence of the senior lama, praying at each of the shrines, and giving the lama a picture of herself with the Dalai Lama. He was inviting us to take pictures everywhere without paying, and our guide objected. She also told us that foreigners were not permitted to give away pictures of the Dalai Lama. If we wanted to make a gift, she said, it had to be to the Travel Service, and they would pass them on. Impolitely, we called her bluff, and with a group of younger monks watching eagerly we handed the guide several pictures and asked her to pass them on. She couldn't do it. In retrospect it was probably quite unfair of us to put her on the spot like that. As we walked on, with our guide caught up in explaining the policy to the head lama, I watched as Ginger quietly followed with her hands behind her holding the pictures. The young monks came up one by one, each taking a picture and bowing deeply to her departing back.

On that visit we also traveled to Zedang in southeastern Tibet, the only area outside of Lhasa open to us at the time. Zedang is supposed to be one of the earliest settled areas of Tibet and has some of its oldest temples and monasteries. Many of these were severely damaged during the Cultural Revolution, and some were completely destroyed. We were accompanied on our trip by two guides from the China Travel Service, one a young Chinese man who was originally from Sichuan, and the other a young man from Lhasa who was half Tibetan and half Chinese. They got along well together, but a little less well with the third guide who was added to our retinue by the Travel Service in Zedang.

In the Yarlung Valley there is a fortress-like temple called Yangmulak-hang, built high on a promontory that juts out into the valley. Everything is spectacular: the valley, the mountains, and the temple. Yangmulakhang was once the residence of Tibet's most famous king, Songtsen Gampo, and his wife Wencheng, a Tang Dynasty Chinese princess who is credited with taking Buddhism to Tibet in the seventh century—and who is believed to have become one of Tibet's premier deities, the White Tara Bodhisattva. Yangmu-lakhang was later dedicated as a temple, and it survived the devastation of the Cultural Revolution relatively unscathed. It was not very big and was in some disrepair when we visited, but functioning. We had to climb a ladder to get to the main floor where there was a statue of the Buddha. In front of it there was a large flat rock lit by sunlight streaming in through an opening high above. Ginger said there was a tremendous amount of energy focused there, and it reminded her of some descriptions of the Egyptian pyramids. We were the only visitors. There were three monks who were chanting in a room on the second floor. They ignored me but stopped and smiled when Ginger came in and talked with them. As we were leaving they gave us some *tsampa*, ground barley mixed with Tibetan butter and formed into small cones.

The monks also gave Ginger a yellow *hada*. The *hada* is a thin silk scarf that is given as a greeting and a blessing in Tibetan culture. There are similar traditions among some African and Native American peoples. There is a story that the tradition was brought back to Tibet by a lama who visited the

Mongolian court of Kublai Khan, the first emperor of the Yuan Dynasty. Our guides told us that the yellow *hada* given to Ginger was quite unusual. Most *hadas* in Tibet are white, and our guides thought the yellow ones were reserved for high officials.

In fact, in spite of the daily frustration of dealing with official bureaucracy, we had to admit that we were treated a little like royalty during our visit, by both Chinese and Tibetans. They took care of us when we were sick, and they did everything they could to take us where we wanted to go within the parameters of what was permitted and possible. When we crossed the Tsangpo River on the way to Samye Monastery, our guides negotiated the Tibetan fee instead of the tourist fee. At the end of our stay, when we finally arrived at the airport and discovered we were booked on a nonexistent return flight, our guides and the Lhasa Foreign Affairs Office mounted an assault on the airline office. The Foreign Affairs official went through the front door, while our guides worked the "back door" with a friend of theirs. We got the last two first-class tickets out, and there were many less fortunate than us. It is possible that having two official Americans in Tibet was just too much of a headache for everyone at that time, and they were willing to move heaven and earth to get us out—but there was a great deal of personal kindness there as well.

***

Right near the Yong He Gong in Beijing was a less touristy but even more interesting entity, the headquarters of the China Academy of Traditional Chinese Medicine. Located in an old building across the street from the wall of the Forbidden City, its job was to preserve, coordinate, and regulate the practice of medicine according to knowledge and principles developed over five thousand years of Chinese history.

Ginger had made friends with a woman who was the only female student of one of the most senior and well known of the Academy's doctors, a man known as Xia Lao. Her friend urged her to visit Dr. Xia to see if he could help her with the migraine headaches from which she had suffered since she was child. Xia Lao—Lao means "old" and is a title of respect for respected elders—was in his late eighties and had a very severe demeanor. He used acupuncture to treat Ginger for her headaches and to treat me for kidney stones. The results of those treatments were limited, because neither of us could go the course. I dropped out during the first treatment. I have always had a phobia of needles, and in this case it required lying on my stomach while he put needles in the back of my knee. This was the first time I had experienced acupuncture, and my phobia combined with the sensitivity of the knee and being placed in a helpless position was just too much for me.

Afterward, Ginger told me that he in fact had only used one needle and had moved it from place to place without even taking it out. I did not believe that at the time, and I still am skeptical—but now after more than thirty years of association with things Chinese I am prepared to accept the possibility of almost anything. Ginger's headaches became worse after the initial treatment, and she too decided to drop it for the time being.

Then something else happened that sent her back to Xia Lao for help and guidance. She became pregnant. We were both very pleased, and we initially consulted with the embassy doctor and with doctors at the Beijing Capital Hospital and the Chinese-Japanese hospital. We were comfortable with the doctors there, and the Chinese gynecologist at the Japanese hospital was particularly supportive. However, we encountered the limits of our more "advanced" Western medicine when a sonogram after several months indicated a condition of placenta previa. This is a condition where the placenta is located in the lower part of the womb covering the cervix, rather than on the side of the womb. It can cause bleeding, and serious complications for the mother and fetus at birth. In Western medicine there is no way to correct this. Bed rest for the mother is prescribed, and the doctors essentially hope that the condition will correct itself—which most apparently do over time. If they do not, the doctors often resort to a cesarean section, sometimes before term.

Ginger's friend suggested we go back and consult with Xia Lao, and we did. He said the condition was easily corrected and not to worry. He then taught Ginger how to use moxibustion. Moxibustion is a procedure in which a small amount of a certain type of herb, in this case Chinese mugwort (ai cao艾草), is placed on a particular acupuncture point and gently burned using an incense stick. The smoke is drawn into the acupuncture point and helps correct the body's energy circulation, removing whatever blockage is causing the problem. The acupuncture point in this case was on her big toe, and Ginger did it religiously once a day at a strictly appointed time for two weeks. At the end of that time she went back to the Capital Hospital for another sonogram. The fetus had turned around and was completely normal. The doctors at the hospital were quite surprised.

Xia Lao was an extraordinary man who had been classically educated. The traditional Chinese educational system required that capable students become proficient in a wide range of subjects. They studied the three major schools of philosophical thought: Confucian, Taoist, and Buddhist. They studied mathematics, science, arts, and music. They also studied and practiced meditation and various forms of martial arts. Xia Lao was in his eighties and had clearly benefited from that education before Mao's regime tried to dismantle it.

He became a kind of father figure to Ginger, giving her a range of counseling and advice on medical, Buddhist, and classical studies. He had told us, before the sonograms showed it, that the child would be a boy. We had already decided that if it was a boy we would name him after my father. My father had named me for my mother's father, because there were no male children in her family to carry on the name, and we thought we should make that up to him. However, we had not decided on a Chinese name, and Ginger invited Xia Lao to give him one. He thought about it for a few days and then gave him the name Li Yu (立宇)—which as close as I can translate it means "to establish a great space." Xia Lao had assured Ginger that she could give birth in Beijing and he would take care of her. However, she decided that Charles should be born in the United States. This was not for medical reasons, but so that Charles, as the child of a mixed marriage, would have no doubts about where his home was—and also so that he could be elected president. Ginger returned to my parents' home in Stuart, Florida, where I joined her just two weeks before Charles was born. Remarkably, in Charles's birth picture, taken minutes after he was born, he has the face of an old man that looks stunningly like Xia Lao. Unfortunately, when we communicated this information back to China, we learned that Xia Lao had died.

***

When I was invited to go to the Beijing embassy, there were two positions available in the economic section. One was responsible for studying and analyzing China's economic development, essentially what I had been doing in Hong Kong. The other dealt with bilateral U.S.-China economic relations. I was offered my choice, and I chose the latter. I had spent the previous three years analyzing the PRC economy. I did not think I could do as good a job at it in Beijing as I had in Hong Kong, because of the limitations on contacts and the lack of help from our Chinese economists, and I wanted something more action oriented.

Between 1972 and 1984 direct trade between the United States and China had grown from zero to over $6 billion a year. During most of the 1970s the United States had enjoyed a trade surplus, primarily due to substantial agricultural exports to the People's Republic. However, by 1984 the U.S. account had slipped decidedly into the red—a deficit of almost $400 million. It has remained in the red ever since (in 2005 China's trade surplus with the United States was over $200 billion).

That the United States would have a trade deficit with China early in its economic relationship was not surprising. While the United States had capital equipment and technology to offer the newly developing nation, it faced formidable competition from the Europeans and, most importantly, from Japan. Japan was closer to China, and the languages were more compatible. More importantly, Japanese corporations were willing to make long-term commitments to the China market, and they were willing to take risks. Japanese businessmen seemed more willing to take on the personal hardships of working in that alien culture—alien as much because of its thirty-year communist history as because of any cultural differences. American businesspeople thought they might have an advantage due to the terrible legacy of Japan's invasion of China in the 1940s. They probably did, but they did not successfully take advantage of it.

While the trade deficit was not surprising, it was already becoming controversial. The embassy's commercial section was trying to help interested American companies make contacts and find niches. The economic section was concerned with the structure and rules of the growing relationship. There was much concern in the United States that China would do what Japan had so successfully done: develop its export economy to take advantage of the West's relatively open markets, while restricting the accessibility of its domestic market to Western products.

One way of discouraging that approach was to encourage China to begin playing by existing international trade rules as early as possible. Many in the U.S. government believed that China should be encouraged to apply for membership in the General Agreement on Tariffs and Trade (GATT) as soon as possible—and that the GATT should do everything possible to welcome China into the fold. The embassy's economic section worked hard to encourage the Chinese government agencies to choose this path. Some Chinese officials readily agreed that this was the way to go. Others were more skeptical. There were clearly some advantages to holding out as long as possible, particularly if China was not facing too many barriers to its exports at the time. One of those advantages was avoiding confrontation with the multitude of local interests and the enormous communist bureaucracy that spanned the entire country. The GATT would require the imposition of standard regulations, not only on the customs processes at the borders but also on government support and regulation of economic activity. In a centrally planned system like China's, the entire economy was government regulated and supported. It would be years before China's economic activity—and political perceptions of it—would develop to the point where conformity to "non-Chinese" rules and standards would be politically acceptable or practically possible. As it turned out, China did not officially join the GATT's successor organization, the World Trade Organization (WTO), until 1999. In the mid-1980s our work was confined to many conversations with foreign trade officials and government think tanks.

Many of our discussions about the balance of trade unfortunately were futile wheel-spinning exercises, because U.S. statistics were substantially different from Chinese statistics. In the early years, when U.S. statistics showed a U.S. trade deficit, Chinese statistics showed the opposite. It proved quite difficult to examine this objectively. A major part of the discrepancy, however, seemed to be how each country treated the trade that passed through Hong Kong. The U.S. statistics treated trade that originated in China and simply transited Hong Kong as imports from China, not from Hong Kong. Chinese statistics treated those shipments as exports to Hong Kong, not to the United States. American officials, including myself, saw this as Chinese manipulation of the statistics. To some degree that was probably true, but we also tended to see Chinese entities as being part of a cohesive whole, while in fact many of them were more independent—either intentionally or de facto. The statistical discrepancy still exists more than twenty years later. U.S. statistics show the U.S. trade deficit in 2005 was $202 billion, while the Chinese statistics show (only) $114 billion.

On a more immediately practical note, we did have one agreement that was intensely active: the U.S.-China Bilateral Textile Agreement. In the early years of U.S.-China trade the most rapidly growing Chinese export was textiles. The United States has long protected its domestic textile industry by imposing an intricate and extensive system of quotas on many textile products. This system is mandated by Congress, and the quotas are set for individual countries through bilateral negotiations. As early as 1984, China was already chafing at these restrictions and aggressively seeking to expand access for its exports. While the negotiations themselves were conducted by delegations coming from Washington, led by the Office of the United States Trade Representative, the embassy's economic section did much of the preparatory work, and always participated as a member of the delegation. The importance of the exports to China meant that the officials with responsibility for the bilateral agreement were far more accessible to American officials than were most other officials of the Chinese government. In this regard, we in the economic section had more dynamic and personally rewarding interaction with our counterparts than did many other sections of the embassy.

This was somewhat less true for civil aviation, where the challenge was dynamic, but the personal and bureaucratic interaction was very frustrating. American airline companies were very interested in expanding their access to China. To land in Beijing or Shanghai, the only two airports open to U.S. airlines at that time, they needed landing rights accorded under a bilateral civil aviation agreement which had been first signed in 1981.

These landing rights were basically done on a reciprocal basis. Since China at the time had only one international carrier, operated by the Civil Aviation Administration of China (CAAC), it initially tried to restrict landing rights to one U.S. airline, which was Pan American. That was unacceptable to the United States, which did not have a single national airline and needed to provide equal opportunities for all American airlines. Just before I arrived in Beijing, China had agreed to add Northwest Airlines. However, the permit that China gave to Northwest was only valid for six months. Northwest had to resubmit its application every six months, and the CAAC would wait until the last minute to renew the permit, putting Northwest in a very risky position in terms of accepting reservations from passengers. That meant that every six months Northwest had to mount a campaign, which included regular—and sometimes frantic—appeals to the embassy for help. At these times the economic section would work overtime, calling on the aviation authorities and appealing to the Ministry of Foreign Affairs and other senior government officials to help prevent a break in service. The rest of the time we would demarche the government on a regular basis asking that Northwest be given a longer permit—and that other U.S. airlines also be given the chance to fly.

Dealing with this agency was extremely frustrating. It was difficult to get appointments, and when we did the meetings tended to be debates rather than an effort to find common ground. The situation was admittedly difficult for the Chinese. Chinese airspace was controlled by the military, with limited routes provided for civilian purposes. The opposite is the case in the United States, where most airspace is managed by civilian agencies. Allowing foreign carriers to fly in to China was probably very traumatic for Chinese military and civilian security officials, as well as challenging for the nascent civil aviation bureaucracy. But there was also an element of providing an unfair competitive advantage to the single Chinese airline. Our job was to try to keep the playing field level.

This was my first real experience with the use of "reciprocity" as negotiating leverage. It was not easy. The United States has a multitude of complex and competing domestic interests that make it difficult to establish a clear negotiating position and to enforce an effective trade-off of bilateral interests. Our competing private companies could put a variety of pressure on the U.S. government that might weaken our own negotiating position. While in the beginning China wanted to restrict its entry points to Beijing and Shanghai, the U.S. government faced pressure from both airline companies and different cities to provide access to more U.S. cities than just New York and Los Angeles. There were of course competing interests within China, but they were less transparent to us than ours were to them.

Senior U.S. officials responsible for U.S.-China relations were very reluctant to use the reciprocity tool. Actually, most American diplomats tend to be reluctant to use punitive measures in the exercise of diplomacy. I can still remember clearly one meeting with our ambassador to China, Art Hummel. It was a particularly frustrating time in our bilateral aviation relations, and I raised the possibility of restricting some of the Chinese airlines' operations in the United States to correspond to difficulties our airlines were having in China. He firmly rejected the idea, saying, "I am not going to be talked into more 'China bashing.'" At the time, I thought that was just wimpy diplomacy, where we were avoiding anything that would cause our Chinese colleagues to be annoyed with us. However, as I thought more about it, I realized there was good cause for being careful.

First of all, the concern that such action would cause a costly reaction had some justification. This was an early phase of our developing relationship with China, and there were many elements in the Chinese bureaucracy or the political power structure that were at best ambivalent about the more positive track our relations were on. The authoritarian nature of China's government also meant that it was able to take action in a wide variety of ways to make things more difficult not only for U.S. officials and U.S. policy, but also for American businesses trying to establish their own relationships.

The second reason was perhaps even more important. It lay on our side, and it was the concern that caused Ambassador Hummel to use the term "China bashing." There were (and still are) many forces in the United States who were ideologically opposed to improved relations with the PRC. There were also many forces that feared a growing Chinese economy—some for geopolitical reasons, and even more for protectionist economic reasons. The U.S. democracy is not an efficient, rational system that carefully considers the nation's strategic interests and adjusts policy and actions to address those interests. It was built to limit the concentration of power in government, and to protect and respond to local interests. Protectionist interests are strong, and when specific policies are put in place to satisfy those interests, they can be very difficult to dislodge. We have very little flexibility in the exercise of such policies as incentives or disincentives to influence other nations. We therefore have a very limited arsenal of tools to deal effectively with nations that can exercise significant centralized authority, like Japan and China.

In the 1980s the major economic challenge was coming from Japan. At the time, we knew that China with its vast territory, population, and resources could theoretically dwarf the challenge presented by Japan. However, we also believed that China's size, complexity, and socialist experimentation would hold it back significantly. That was logical and clever—and so far is proving to be wrong.

***

Unless something completely unforeseen happens, like either the United States or the PRC suddenly disappearing from the planet, the U.S.-PRC relationship will be the most important and influential relationship between nations in the twenty-first century—whether it is good or bad. I was not present "at the creation." The current relationship was conceived in the late 1960s and born in the late 1970s. The period when Ginger and I were in Beijing was more akin to the formative period of infancy. This infant was not neglected. Both sides gave it a high priority, and both assigned competent envoys to guide and nurture the relationship. Both sides were able to control the forces that wished the infant ill. I think the United States did the right thing in the early years—reaching out, committing energy to the relationship, and expanding training for Chinese language officers. We also chose some outstanding people with extensive knowledge about China to lead the effort, like Ambassadors Arthur Hummel and Stapleton Roy, and Deputy Chief of Mission Chas Freeman.

Looking back over the last twenty years, I think we have been less successful in keeping China where it should be in our strategic perspective. In the simplest part of that equation, our cadre of Chinese language officers with experience in China is still too small. More importantly, if we are to deal successfully with China—either as a friend or a foe—we will need to address some fundamental weaknesses in our national education and in our economy, which supports everything that we are and do.

The American public is woefully unfamiliar with the reality of China. Our national education system will need to prepare our population to be able to interact successfully with China, because the government's involvement isn't enough. Even if our politicians are willing to provide the Departments of State and Defense with sufficient funds to train sufficient future diplomats and military personnel in Chinese language, that is too late a point at which to start. Our schools need to offer, or even better, mandate Chinese language to students at an early age—like elementary school. The Chinese language is just too different and too difficult for all but the most highly gifted to learn as adults. We also need to teach the intellectual, social, and moral traditions that have molded our future neighbor and might provide useful lessons for our own society. These foundations are needed by government officials who deal directly with the Chinese, by businesspeople who sell to and buy from them, by academics who study them, by scientists who need to learn from them, and by politicians who will make the laws and appropriate the resources that we need to work with them.

We also need to take a giant step beyond the constant political mantra of "growing" the economy and give more consideration to guiding and maturing our economy. Our economic system needs guidance in preparing for challenges beyond the horizon that our stock exchanges and marketing gurus can't see because they are afflicted with a kind of selfish myopia imposed by increasingly short-term demands of our peculiarly American kind of capitalism. That does not mean that we need a command economy. After working for the government for thirty-five years, I am well aware of its limitations. Bureaucracy does not produce efficiency; politics only occasionally produces fairness and almost never wisdom. However, government needs to manage a healthy regulatory system to protect individuals and the nation from excesses in the profit-driven private sector. It needs to anticipate future strategic needs and to provide incentives for the private sector to direct its energies to addressing these needs.

We need some protection from erosion in our industrial base resulting from private sector unwillingness to allocate resources to staying ahead of the curve rather than just soaking the present for profit (witness the American automobile industry) or just taking the easy road by moving manufacturing capacity overseas. We need brakes on the military-industrial-congressional complex that pours scarce resources into unnecessary military projects just because they support individual companies or electoral districts.

The U.S. laissez-faire political-economic model has a very short-term focus. This served us reasonably well until close to the end of the twentieth century. It provided a fertile environment for enterprising individuals and businesses to be enormously productive, and it produced a very rich nation with a powerful military. But our nation's history is relatively short, and living in the moment probably cannot address successfully all the challenges this increasingly complex world will throw at us. Our previous challenges in the international arena came mostly from Europe and South America, whose cultural roots we shared. Our roots in Asia are fewer and shallower. We are going to have to cultivate ourselves assiduously just to stay even with those cultures.

NOTE

1. The Tartar City refers to the city originally built by the Mongol rulers of China during the Yuan Dynasty (1271–1368). It contains the Forbidden City, where the emperors of the Yuan and the succeeding Ming and Qing dynasties resided, and what is now Tiananmen Square. The Chinese City refers to the section that was added to the south of the Tartar City by the Han rulers of the Ming Dynasty (1368–1644).

Chapter Six

Where "the Dawn Comes Up like Thunder": Rangoon (August 1988–January 1990) [1]

In late 1987, I bid on the job of counselor for political and economic affairs at the embassy in Rangoon, Burma. I had been curious about Burma since my work at the United Nations in 1970, where I had met Aung San Suu Kyi, the daughter of the revered founder of modern Burma, Aung San. The job looked interesting, managing both the political and economic activities of the embassy, and I would be working again for Burt Levin, who was now ambassador in Rangoon. Burma seemed exotic and different. It had been very isolated and quiet for decades. While this might mean the professional challenges would be limited, we thought that might actually be a plus, as it would give us more time together as a family. Our son, Charles, was just two and a half, and the prospect of spending more time with him and Ginger seemed pretty attractive.

As it turned out, we flew right into the middle of a massive popular uprising against the twenty-six-year-old dictatorship of Ne Win. The professional challenges were extraordinary, and the time for family was very limited, at least in the beginning. Just two weeks after we arrived, the U.S. Embassy evacuated all dependents and nonessential personnel. They went to Bangkok, where they lived in hotels for six weeks until we judged it safe for them to return.

***

When we arrived in Burma on August 20, we were met by the deputy chief of mission (DCM) and his wife, a political officer at the embassy, both of whom we had known before. As we drove in from the airport, they pointed out to us several sites where demonstrations had been suppressed on August 8—an auspicious day on Asian calendars because it was all eights (8/8/88), and eights are related to prosperity and good fortune. There were still blood-stains on the streets, meaning it clearly had not been auspicious for some. Other than that, it was quiet and people seemed to be going about their business. Two days after we arrived, Aung San Suu Kyi gave her first public speech in Rangoon. It was an impromptu appearance on the steps of a building in downtown Rangoon. Suu Kyi was forty-three years old and had spent much of her life outside of Burma. She had been educated in England and Japan; was married to a British professor, Michael Aris; and had two teenage sons. When I knew her in New York she was serious, hard working, and very disciplined. She was devoted to and deeply concerned about her country, but at the time she was afraid the Ne Win regime would prevent her from leaving the country if she returned as a Burmese citizen. She therefore was careful only to visit using her United Nations laissez-passer (passport), though it was difficult for her to get a visa on that laissez-passer from the Burmese government.

I had not been in touch with her since 1971, and when I received my assignment to Rangoon in early 1988, I tried to locate her. During my prede-parture consultations in Washington, I had found no one who knew where she was. In fact, most seemed a little surprised that I even asked. This in itself was surprising, particularly since I later discovered that the embassy in Rangoon knew very well where she was. In my experience, that kind of disconnect between an embassy and Washington is quite rare.

When I arrived in Rangoon in mid-August, I put the same question to my senior Foreign Service National (FSN), and his answer was, "Here in Rangoon, sir." By coincidence, she had returned to Burma in the spring of 1988 to help her ailing mother, and she was still there when the first serious uprisings occurred in early August. On August 25, several days after she gave her first speech, she gave another one. This one was not impromptu, and it was at the Shwedagon Pagoda, Rangoon's central and most sacred loca-tion. Thousands of people came to the field just west of the temple to listen to her, and the excitement and unity of the onlookers was tremendous. I went with several of my embassy colleagues. The scene is well etched in my memory, in part because it was my first real introduction to the Burmese heat. We sat on the ground in the sun for what seemed like hours.

To an outsider, the Burmese people seemed to be getting to know each other again. There had been very little participation by the average Burmese in the body politic for almost thirty years. Government was something done by others more powerful. The average person had little or no say in it and therefore had taken little interest in it. Many were not happy with their lot, however, and when it began to look as though they might be able to have an impact, masses of people literally threw themselves into the process. The demonstrations grew rapidly, and by the end of August millions were marching through the streets of Rangoon.

Their enthusiasm and hope were exciting, but they had little practical understanding of how to contribute or what to expect. More importantly, the military elite had no intention of ushering in a substantially different political era or of allowing its preeminent position to be undermined.

***

As events began to unfold, I accompanied Ambassador Burt Levin on calls to senior members of the government. Ambassador Levin had been in Burma for more than a year by that time, and was used to the environment. I, however, was very surprised at how difficult it was to communicate with our hosts. Language was not the issue. We did have Burmese language officers at the embassy (I admit with some chagrin that I was not one of them), but these Burmese senior government officials all spoke English—good English. Some of them had been educated overseas; most of them, particularly the military, had been taught English in school in Burma—some of them while the British were still there. We both understood the words that each other spoke. The difficulty lay in the context, the perspective—and the restrictions.

Ambassador Levin, the DCM, and I had previously worked with officials from the People's Republic of China, and we were familiar with a fairly high level of official restriction on what they could say. What we encountered in Burma went far beyond that. In those first meetings with senior government officials, in a seriously deteriorating situation, I saw no dialogue. I thought I saw no effort to communicate to us any understanding of the current situation, and certainly no willingness to listen to our views. Most of the officials we called on were extremely gracious and pleasant. They were generous and considerate hosts—but that seemed in their minds to be sufficient. No substantive communication was offered.

Shortly after the ambassador's call on Acting Prime Minister Maung Maung, who had inherited at least nominal leadership of Ne Win's regime, the government withdrew to the sidelines and allowed the people to take to the streets. We did not know if the regime was disintegrating or just adopting another strategy. Ambassador Levin then expanded his calls to the most obvious popular leaders of the time: Aung San Suu Kyi, Tin Oo, Aung Gyi, and U Nu.

U Nu had been president of Burma in the early 1950s, taking over the reins of government when Suu Kyi's father, Aung San, was assassinated. When we met him he was more than ninety years old. In the years since being deposed by General Ne Win's 1962 coup he had often been critical of the regime. For a time he had led a resistance group from outside the country, but he had returned with amnesty in 1980. He lived in a very nice compound with his family and servants, where he received us. He was white-haired, well-dressed, and very dignified. His servants kneeled in front of him when they served him, something I thought was more a Thai than a Burmese custom. U Nu believed strongly that the military regime was responsible for Burma's lack of progress and much of its suffering, and that it needed to go. However, his age prevented him from playing a very active role.

Aung Gyi was a former military officer himself, a brigadier general. He once had been very close to Ne Win and was his second in command after the 1962 coup. However, he had fallen out with the regime early on, and he had actually been imprisoned for several years in the 1960s and 1970s. He was no longer part of the military regime but seemed to retain close ties to the military. In the spring of 1988, he had been one of the early voices of open criticism of the regime, and he became the first chairman of the opposition political party, National League for Democracy, which quickly became associated primarily with Aung San Suu Kyi. When Aung Gyi spoke with us, he believed that it was both necessary and possible to work with the military regime to bring change to Burma. In some ways he sounded similar to the government officials with whom we spoke. He never really attracted a wide personal following, and after a few months broke with both Aung San Suu Kyi and the National League for Democracy.

Tin Oo was a former military officer as well, but younger than Aung Gyi. He was a national hero who had been decorated for bravery and promoted to general and commander in chief of the armed forces in the early 1970s. However, in 1976 he had been accused and convicted of high treason and given a harsh prison sentence and hard labor. Many believed the real reason was that he was becoming too popular with the rank-and-file military and was seen by the leadership as a potential threat. He was released in 1980 and led a quiet, nonpolitical life until 1988. When we met with him, we were quite impressed. He was very softspoken, but frank, straightforward, and thoughtful. He was also profuse in his praise of Aung San Suu Kyi, while the others had been distinctly reserved. Shortly after our meeting Tin Oo publicly joined forces with Suu Kyi, and they remained loyal allies until their imprisonment the following year.

Aung San Suu Kyi was the most impressive of the four—at least to us westerners. She had a very broad and deep perspective on Burma, and she also brought an extensive knowledge of the outside world. She had lived in India when her mother was Burma's ambassador there; received her university education in Britain; did more study in Japan; worked at the United Nations in New York; and raised her family in London. She had a sophisticated understanding of international relations, and though she had lived outside of Burma for most of her adult life, she knew its history, its culture, and its traditions well. She admired democracy as a political system and believed it could be—and should be—exercised in Burma. She also showed herself to be a superb public speaker and someone who could connect on many levels with the population of Burma. She was aided in this effort by the mantle of her father, Aung San, who had led Burma to independence from the British before being assassinated when she was still a young child. Many of the older Burmese who had known her father expressed awe at how much she looked and sounded like him.

***

As the crowds marching through the streets of Rangoon and other major cities grew into the millions, anxiety began to grow about the fabric of law and order. The vast majority of demonstrators were peaceful and disciplined. However, with that number of people on the streets there were bound to be some incidents of violence, intended or unintended. When the regime pulled back from active management of government services, it also pulled the police back. Then it opened the prisons, releasing not only political prisoners but also criminals and other disturbed persons.

No one knew whether the regime was giving up or just biding its time, although the continued operation of the state-run television network was at least one clue. It broadcast continued stories about the violence being committed by the demonstrators. We at the embassy did not witness any such violence, even though we went out continually to monitor what was going on. We all knew there was a danger that at some point the crowds might become violent, but that did not appear imminent. We also believed it was highly unlikely that their anger would be directed at the U.S. Embassy or its people. In fact, the United States seemed to be the "good guy," and many of the demonstrators in Rangoon would march past the embassy cheering it and the United States as the example of democracy to which they aspired.

The government also closed the banks and stopped other economic services. We began to hear many reports of rice shortages, and of concern that the population would soon not have enough to eat. At the embassy, we considered bringing in PL-480 rice from the United States, but we decided that the problem was related to a shortage of money and hoarding rather than an actual shortage of rice. The ambassador had the authority to spend $25,000 as emergency assistance, but there were no banks open where we could purchase the Burmese currency. I went out and made contact with some of the more well-to-do (and often behind-the-scenes) businessmen to see if they would be able to make the exchange. Since there was no government and no law enforcement, we reasoned that changing money on the "open market" could not be considered illegal. Initially, I was concerned that our contacts would not be able to change such a large sum, but as it turned out they thought our proposal was almost insignificant. Nevertheless, when word got out that the American Embassy was planning to put money into the market to purchase rice, the hoarded rice came out so quickly that in fact we never had to spend anything.

Then, however, we began to hear rumors of divisions in the armed forces and a possibility that conflict might break out between different units. At that point, the ambassador called several of us into his office and asked our opinion on whether we should take the precaution of evacuating the families and nonessential personnel. All of us thought the time had come. While we still believed that extensive violence was unlikely, we also thought it might be impossible to get families out if things did break down. We informed the Foreign Ministry of the decision, and they were shocked. They insisted that there was no danger for foreigners and asked the ambassador to reconsider, but his decision was firm.

The embassy chartered a flight with Thai Airlines. However, on the day the families were to depart, the government withdrew all personnel at the airport, from ticket and baggage handlers to air traffic controllers. When the embassy convoy with the families arrived, the plane and the Thai Airlines crew were there, but the airport was empty and nonfunctional. Ambassador Levin's response was to put embassy personnel to the task of loading the plane and manning all the necessary stations. The assistant defense attaché, an Air Force colonel, ran the flight deck. It took longer than it would have with the regular staff, but the plane got off safely. The families had waited patiently in the hot terminal (no air conditioning, either).

The night after the families took off for Bangkok, there actually was some limited fighting between military units in and around Rangoon. I spent the night out at the DCM's residence and stood on his front porch with him and his wife watching tracers arching over the city and listening to the explosions of mortar shells. However, the fighting did not continue beyond that night, and the next day demonstrations resumed. Shortly thereafter, however, the regime reappeared on the scene, announced that no more demonstrations would be permitted, and ordered the population to stay home.

The morning after the regime's announcement, we went into the embassy as usual. The demonstrators were gathering again in spite of the government warnings, but this time the military moved in and took up positions throughout Rangoon and other cities. Troops set up positions about fifty yards down the street from the embassy and ordered everyone to go home. Most of the demonstrators were defiant and continued their chanting as in previous days.

However, at one point an older monk who spoke English knocked at the front door of the embassy. Speaking with the regional security officer, he said he was worried that something terrible was about to happen, and he asked if he could please bring several students for whom he felt responsible into the embassy for a short while. The security officer checked with the ambassador, who agreed. They came in just in time. Five minutes later the military opened fire on the demonstrators, and a number of them were killed. Those of us in the embassy lay on the floor away from the windows listening to the gunfire and commotion on the street below. At one point, an ambulance arrived to care for the injured, but the military would not allow it to enter the street. The dead and wounded were left on the street for several hours. We later estimated that several hundred people had been killed that day at different locations in the city. Many hours later we quietly let the monk and his charges out the back door of the embassy and hoped they managed to navigate their way home safely.

After that, all opposition was suppressed ruthlessly. The regime imposed a dusk-to-dawn curfew and threatened to shoot violators. There were no more demonstrations and no more marches.

***

When we were in Burma, from 1988 to 1990, the American Embassy was in downtown Rangoon, in an old building on a pretty square that was laid out in English fashion. It was a very nice setting. Rangoon had once been a very attractive city. It was still attractive but deteriorating seriously, as very little had been done to maintain it over the previous decades. There had been little new building (which aesthetically might actually have been a good thing), and there was moss or mold growing on many of the city's existing buildings. The embassy had been maintained a little better than surrounding buildings, but it was still badly in need of repair and renovation. It had been originally built for the tropics, with large windows and high ceilings. Misguided American attempts to modernize it with air conditioning and low false ceilings had created a kind of sealed mausoleum.

Most embassy employees lived on one of two compounds on one of the lakes nearby. This made for very comfortable living and pretty good security, but it also enhanced our residents' isolation from the local community. Some senior officials had houses that were separate. The ambassador and deputy chief of mission lived on another compound farther up the lake that was stunningly beautiful. While access to the compound was carefully controlled, the ambassador and DCM both maintained very active social and representational schedules that regularly brought Burmese guests and others from the diplomatic and business communities to their homes. Other senior officials in the political, economic, and military sections of the embassy had houses that were actually in the local communities, where access was not restricted. While access was not formally restricted, the local population had to be a little careful about visiting too often. Just across the street from our house was a house belonging to one of Burma's intelligence organizations, and all assumed that they kept a close watch on comings and goings.

We got to know some of our neighbors a little. They were friendly and extremely gracious. One invited us to dinner once and shared a very useful book on Burmese history and culture with us. I think he wanted us to understand that there was more to Burma's self-imposed isolation than simply a fear of the outside world. I would have liked to have spent more time with him, but I was reticent—perhaps more than I should have been. Our official relations with the Burmese government were very tense, and I was always concerned that any association with me would cause trouble to individuals who did not have an obvious official reason to associate with me. This attitude was influenced by my experience in Beijing, where the control had been pervasive.

Some of the older Burmese we met, particularly those who did not actively seek out association with foreigners, gently tried to warn against relying on our Western standards to understand and assess the Burmese political situation. They might admit to not liking the ruling regime and the state of affairs, but they pointed out in different ways that it was very Burmese. They even suggested that trying to change the situation might make things worse.

There was an element of truth, or at least a certain pragmatism, in those messages with which our neighbors and other interlocutors tried to educate us, but I tended to brush those messages off. They sounded quite similar to the statements of some of the government officials with whom we spoke—though perhaps more articulate. Most of us at the embassy thought that Burma was suffering under an unenlightened regime and would be far better off if it changed. We thought the "realism" of these interlocutors was pessimism or cynicism. We held out the hope that the extraordinary expression of popular demand for change would prevail, and that even some in the entrenched governing elite would conclude that such change was in the national interest. That did not happen.

***

Events of the first two months after our arrival had severely shaken our hopes of having more time together as a family. However, after the popular uprising was put down and families returned from their exile in Bangkok, we actually did get more time together. Not only were we back together, but the government imposed martial law and a strict curfew from 6 p.m. to 6 a.m., which mercifully avoided the normal evening socializing of diplomatic life.

Some of us needed that time to repair the damage of the evacuation. Our son, Charles, had been two years and two months old when Ginger and he were evacuated to Thailand. After they left, we didn't see each other for more than three weeks. We tried to talk on the telephone, but the lines were often down so communication was erratic. After three weeks, the embassy sent me to Bangkok to see my own family and to brief the other families on our views about when things would stabilize enough for them to return. Charles had been happy to see his father again, and the three of us had a wonderful weekend playing, going to the zoo, and being together. Then I left again. We tried to explain what was happening and that it was temporary, but it was not enough. When I next called from Burma, he refused to talk with me, and whenever Ginger mentioned me, he would turn and walk away.

He was quickly learning about the world around him, and after three weeks, the staff and many of the guests at the Imperial Hotel in Bangkok were familiar with this very active two-year-old and his mother. He enjoyed the pool and explored the hotel. He and Ginger would make frequent trips into the city to take him to a small day-care center where he could play with other children, or just to visit the busy shopping centers and ride the elevators. To get downtown they would ride the *tutus*, three-wheeled and very loudly motorized pedicabs. Not only were these immensely practical taxis economical, but they could whisk in and out of congested traffic getting to the desired destination much faster than other transportation options. Charles loved them, but looking back on it, they were a bit dangerous.

Charles was also beginning to assert himself, and one day he discovered a place in the hotel where his mother couldn't follow him—the men's room. When he was displeased with his mother, he could slip into the men's room, and for a while he was free. She would wait patiently outside, occasionally asking the male patrons to check and make sure he was all right. To escape his mother, he resorted to the men's room. To show disapproval for his father, he turned his back on the telephone. So when they returned to Burma, it was good to have some time to rebuild the relationship.

***

As head of the political and economic sections I was assigned a house in a community within walking distance of the Shwedagon Pagoda. The house was very large, with big rooms and high ceilings originally designed to handle the tropical heat without air conditioning. Although there was air conditioning in parts of the house, we still slept with mosquito nets. The high ceilings meant there was also a very large and long staircase, which was a little worrisome with a two-year-old. The house also had a substantial garden and its own tennis court.

We couldn't take care of it all ourselves and hired a cook, housekeeper, and gardener to help. This was Ginger's first experience in managing a staff, but coming from a very large extended Chinese family, it seemed to be second nature to her. She intuitively sized up the applicants, brought in an ethnic Indian woman to cook, her sister to clean the house, and an older ethnic Burman woman to help look after Charles—and she kept the gardener, who was so old that he may have come from a time before there were ethnic differences in Burma. Ginger was not just their manager. She played the matriarch, directing their work, making sure they got along with each other, advising them on their personal problems, and looking after their health. Not too long after we moved in, the gardener became terminally ill. He had no family, except for us and the rest of the staff who had adopted him. Ginger organized his care, eventually moved him to the hospital, and visited him in the hospital until he passed away. The hospital staff did their best, but the hospital was a bit of a scary experience—for me at least. It was a very old brick building and reminded me of old war movies where the hospitals are dark, dirty, and overcrowded.

Our cook and her sister brought their two children with them, a year-old boy and a four-year-old girl. Together with the two boys (aged two and five) of our assistant defense attaché, who lived in the house next door, we had a group of five children who kept the house humming. Inevitably, that activity reached the top of our long staircase, and Charles fell all the way down it. Somehow, he was not injured, but he has retained a wariness of stairs and steep hills to this day. Ginger augmented his playmates by discovering one of the local orphanages. She would take Charles there to play with the other children, and occasionally bring fifteen or twenty of them back to the house to play with Charles.

They played outside, too, having good-sized yards in both houses, and the tennis courts. The tropical vegetation was magnificent, including fruit trees I had never seen before, and all kinds of strange insects and animals. I was a little worried about snakes. Burma has cobras. Having read Rudyard Kipling's *Rikki-Tikki-Tavi* when I was little, I have always had a horror of cobras, and the submissiveness of the cobras in Taipei's snake alley had not eliminated it. Luckily, we only saw one snake in the yard the whole time we were there. One member of the local animal kingdom, however, paid us a visit that I won't forget. The three of us were getting ready for bed one evening when we heard an extraordinary loud noise somewhere in the garden. It was something between the bleat of a goat and the sound that an injured and frightened cow makes. We had occasionally seen cows on the streets, and we wondered if one had wandered into our yard and was in trouble. We could see nothing out of the ordinary from the window, so we went downstairs and out the front door. We could see nothing there, but then we all jumped when the sound trumpeted again right near us. Looking more carefully, we saw a small frog, no larger than a quarter, in the drainage ditch. Impossible!—but as we watched he puffed himself up very briefly and then brayed like a bull. To this day, I don't understand how something so small could make such a sound.

The embassy also had a compound just outside of the city that had a large swimming pool, and we would go there as often as we could. Ginger was not a swimmer, but Charles took to it very quickly. He could spend hours jumping into the pool from the side, and while he couldn't swim on top of the water, he was very happy swimming under the surface like a fish as long as someone would pull him out every once in a while to take a breath. I had at least as much fun as he did, playing the whale who would take him down to the bottom of the deep end and then let him bounce back to the surface on his own.

Ginger also got to know the food markets and the bazaars during the day. She would often go with Charles, and then the two of them would introduce me to them on the weekends.

***

Burma is an extraordinarily exotic place. Partially because of its history and culture, and partially because of its long isolation, it is perhaps as different from the West as any other country in the world. Much of Burma's difference from the West relates to Buddhism—or more accurately, a kind of cultural Buddhism that may be peculiar to Burma. Theravada (also known as Hinayana) Buddhism is central to Burmese culture. The people and the culture pay homage to many of the principles enunciated by Shakyamuni Buddha twenty-five hundred years ago. Monks, nuns, and the temple are a part of every individual's life. The monks and the nuns are very colorful. The monks wear saffron-colored robes, and one sees them often in both the city and the countryside. The nuns have pastel-colored garments and look like dainty butterflies when they walk down the streets in small groups with their parasols. The nuns in China, where Mahayana Buddhism is prevalent, wear gray like the monks. They are not permitted anything colorful. I was severely scolded by Ginger once when, influenced by my observations in Burma, I bought a pink umbrella for a nun in Hong Kong.

Most Burmese men become monks for a period of time—like men in other cultures become soldiers. To be irreverent, it looked a little like going off to summer camp. Most people taste it, hopefully learn from it, and then return to their normal lives. Occasionally, the monks depart from their normal routines of meditation and daily chores, detached from the affairs of society and politics, and wade into the political fray. This happened in 1988. The reasoning, as I understood it, was that they have an obligation not just to avoid harming others, but also to help others, and too many people had been suffering as a result of the country's leadership. However, while I strongly sympathized with the cause they were supporting, it seemed to me that some of the monks pursued this effort with the kind of emotion their religious discipline is supposed to help them let go of. Perhaps this was because those who are only in that practice for a relatively short period of time do not have the time to develop the discipline necessary for the extraordinarily difficult task of controlling those emotions. It is probably not possible to know how many of those who participated in the political events of 1988 were full-time monks and how many were "on sabbatical" from their normal secular lives.

We were fortunate enough to get to know two older monks quite well. When Ginger returned from Thailand, she and I stayed in touch with the old monk who had sought refuge in the embassy with his charges. He was a very polite and cultured man, leading a life that many in the West would consider quite bizarre. He meditated on human bones, death, and the transitory nature of human existence—probably good subjects in that time and place. Sometimes he would spend days at a time in the graveyard. In the beginning the police gave him a hard time, but eventually they let him stay when they became convinced it was not subversive. We learned he came from an old wealthy family. He even lived in and practiced his meditation in his own house in Rangoon. We visited once. It was a substantial house in a nice neighborhood. Like much in Rangoon, it was run down, but his house was particularly desolate. It had almost no furniture in it—just bones that he had collected from the graveyard. There is a Chinese meditation technique that involves meditating on one's own skeleton, but it uses visualization rather than the bones themselves, and it is directed at understanding and harnessing natural energy flows in the body.

The other monk was quite different. He had a senior position in a monastery. He too was quite serious about his religious practice, but he was not trying to live an ascetic life. To the contrary, he was very straightforward about his enjoyment of material things. His practice to a certain degree was focused on the manipulation of material phenomena—perhaps not unlike the Tibetan fascination with esoteric practices. Once, we invited him to lunch at our house (an early lunch, since monks are not supposed to eat after noon), along with a colleague from the Japanese embassy and his wife. During lunch he asked me if I had an alchemical stone yet. I don't know how prevalent these are in other cultures, but they are very popular in Burma. The stone is a small bead made out of several different kinds of metal and other substances in a complicated alchemical process. It is intended to bestow on the wearer special powers that protect him or her from harm or illness. Many Burmese have one, worn either as a ring or a pendant. It is often given to students or disciples by their spiritual teacher. When our friend asked me if I had one, I replied that I did not, and he said, "Very well, then I will ask my teacher to make one for you." I thanked him and turned back to the conversation with the rest of the table. A few minutes later, he asked me, "Is it there yet?" I asked him what he meant, and he asked again, "Is the stone there yet?" At that point I looked down at the table, and right in the middle of my place setting was a small ball of metal. To this day, I do not know how he managed to put it there. He was sitting at the head of the table and was not within arm's reach of me. He could not have placed it there without one of us noticing—unless he hypnotized us—and there were four others at the table. My wife then said in Chinese, "*Ketou, gang kuai ketou*" ("Kowtow"). She meant it figuratively, to show respect. However, I got up from the table and did it literally, putting my head on the floor in his direction. Later, my Japanese colleague expressed wonderment that a westerner would do that, and I replied that I thought what he did was pretty impressive and deserved a similar gesture.

Burma's cultural Buddhism includes many elements that seem remote from the core Buddhist teachings. Alchemy is one of them. It is supposed to have come to Burma from India in the fifth century and to have been nurtured at least partially by the accessibility of Burma's mineral wealth. Burmese historian Maung Htin Aung has explained that between the fifth and eleventh centuries it was closely tied to the philosophical and religious pursuit of spiritual cultivation. Alchemy was directed first at producing a "stone of living metal," which endowed whoever wore it with special powers. If the alchemist could perfect this metal compound, the next stage was to ingest it, which would give the body special powers and immortality—or at least longevity. However, this process was very dangerous. The practitioner had to die "temporarily" and be buried for seven days, because any contact with air would make the death permanent. Very few were successful. This description has elements in common with seekers of longevity through Taoism in China. One of China's most famous emperors, Wu Di of the Han Dynasty, is believed to have died after ingesting a longevity potion.

During that early period, Buddhism in Burma had many esoteric characteristics, similar to Tibetan Buddhism. However, after King Anawrahta made Theravada Buddhism the official religion in the mid-eleventh century, such esoteric elements were discouraged. Alchemy was practiced less by the monks. It was taken up by individuals who used it to make a living, and that seems to be how the production of protection amulets grew. I never put my amulet to the test, and—other than my friend's method of presentation—I cannot report any special powers or phenomena.

In Burma there is also a whole world of beings or spirits, called *nats*, to which the people appeal for various kinds of help in their daily lives. These existed before the eleventh century and were specifically incorporated into

Burma's Theravada Buddhism by King Anawrahta, in much the same way that the Catholic Church has given local deities the status of saints. Burma's *nats* contribute to a very colorful socioreligious fabric. There are beings associated with places, trees, and activities. When a new house is built thanks are given and appeals are made to one spirit; when a new car is purchased appeals are made to another. They are present in houses, stores, offices, and temples, though they are assigned to a lower level of the hierarchy than the Buddha, Bodhisattvas, and other traditional Buddhist figures.

***

Burma's political isolation over the previous thirty years had shielded its social customs, political relations, and economy from the global forces that were stimulating—or infecting—other peoples all over the world. The political elite may not have been quite so isolated, though. We heard many stories about the materialistic, even sybaritic lifestyle of Ne Win's daughter and her circle of friends. In the 1980s, parts of that shield of isolation were also beginning to be circumvented for other parts of society, not so much from the West, but from the East. Burma's largest neighbor, China, was initiating the economic policies that would soon move it toward superpower status on the global stage. In Burma's more limited world, those changes meant that the long China-Burma border that had been essentially closed for thirty years began to open. Chinese traders and goods began pouring into Burma. This was harder to control, both domestically and internationally, than contact with the West or even with India, and probably contributed to the destabilizing events that began in 1988.

Another important characteristic of Burma, which adds to its color and complicates its body politic, is the vast array of ethnic groups that inhabit this country. More than a hundred different ethnic groups have been officially recognized by the Burmese government at one time or another. Burmans make up close to 70 percent of the total, followed by Shan, Karen, Chinese, Indians, Kachin, Mon, and Wa, but these groups also have many tribal divisions within them that are so significant that the languages they speak are mutually unintelligible. The country is slightly smaller than Texas, but climate and topography keep many of these groups relatively isolated from the rest of their compatriots.

The military regime led by Ne Win from 1962 to 1988 waged constant war against these different groups. There was almost always a military campaign going on against one or another, punctuated by truces of varying kinds and lengths, and this has largely continued with the successor military regime. It almost looked a little like George Orwell's novel *1984*, in which the government used constant war to provide occupation for some elements of society and control over other elements. Orwell, in fact, did spend time in Burma with the Indian Imperial Police from 1922 to 1927; he wrote a book specifically about Burma, called *Burmese Days*. It described British society in pre–World War II Burma, and also Burmese society—not always in complimentary terms. This was well before Ne Win's takeover, but Orwell was a part of the British effort to control that ethnically diverse region. I wondered how much *1984* drew on his Burmese experience, and also how much Ne Win and the Burmese military drew from the British military's divide-and-conquer approach.

***

The physical appearance of the country is both magnificent and mysterious. We were restricted in our travels, but I managed three trips outside Rangoon and was awed with what I saw. One was to the hill station of Maymyo, where the climate was significantly cooler than the tropical lowlands. I wanted to go farther, up into the Shan States and to the border with China, but both of those were off-limits to Western diplomats. The area around Taunggyi, south of Maymyo, once had grown opium but had successfully switched to coffee, partially with encouragement from the United States and other Western nations. The substitution had been a great success, and the coffee was exquisite. Unfortunately, opium production had not stopped—it had just moved farther east into the Shan States.

Another trip was across the Irrawaddy River and down toward the delta region. We traveled there with the visiting agricultural attaché from the U.S. Embassy in Bangkok. He had regional responsibilities that covered Burma, and one of his jobs was to do an annual report on the rice harvests. It was a wonderful opportunity for me, because he knew a great deal about rice growing and had visited Burma many times in the past. We drove through villages, stopping to talk with the farmers and the merchants. There was plenty of rice, but the towns were not prosperous. Most did not have electricity, and sometimes one village would share a single gasoline or diesel generator to run a television and VCR to show movies for the population in the evenings. That trip impressed us with the size of the country. The roads were basic, and services were few and far between. On the way back, our embassy vehicle overheated. We spent hours on the edge of a small village resting in the shade, hoping that another vehicle would pass by with help. None came, and we eventually limped from village to village replenishing the radiator's water until we reached the river again; then we managed to hitchhike the remaining fifty miles or so back to Rangoon.

Our most interesting trip, however, was to Mandalay, Sagaing, Monywa, and Pagan. Mandalay has been an important center for Burmese life since it was founded as the capital of the last Burmese kingdom in the mid-nine-teenth century. After the British took over Burma and moved the capital to Rangoon, Mandalay remained an important cultural, educational, and commercial center. While it had been allowed, even encouraged, to deteriorate by the military regime since 1962, it was still influential. The United States used to have a working consulate there. It had been closed for some time when I was stationed in Burma, but we still had the property. During my year and a half in Burma, I only got to Mandalay once, not because it was not important, but because it was so difficult to get permission to travel. In most countries, the first thing on the agenda for our trip would have been to call on the local government, but by that time our relations were frosty, and my visit was confined to inspecting the property and calling on some Burmese and Chinese businesspeople. After Mandalay, we visited Sagaing, which is located just across the Irrawaddy River. It too, used to be a royal capital, but only for a short time in the eighteenth century. When we visited, it was primarily a religious city of temples, monks, and nuns. We called on the abbot of a temple there who was extraordinarily knowledgeable and equally extraordinarily willing to talk frankly. He was well-informed about the political events, but not political himself. His first concern was caring for his temple and the people who were a part of it, and he was very pragmatically inclined. We learned a lot from him. From Sagaing we headed northwest, and then drove to Po Win Taung, near the town of Monywa. This is an extraordinary set of shrines carved out of volcanic rock. There were lots of monkeys and almost no people when we wandered through the hundreds of small temples, each with one or more Buddhist statues. They range from small, individual cubbyholes to a whole temple carved into the hill. There is an energy there that is so strong you can literally feel it. In several of the shrines when I passed my hand over the head of the statue I would feel a tingling like a mild electric shock. The work dates back to the sixteenth century, but apparently some was done as recently as the mid-twentieth century. From Po Win Taung we turned south again, visiting Mount Popa between Mandalay and Pagan. This is a small mountain that used to be a volcano. It rises straight up from the valley floor, almost like a pillar. There is a narrow road that winds to a temple which is perched on top, with sheer cliffs dropping away. The whole mountain is covered with vegetation and infested with monkeys. Mount Popa is considered to be the home of the *nats*, and the temple is devoted to them.

When we visited Pagan, farther to the south, the impression was completely different. Both Po Win Taung and Mount Popa are limited to relatively confined spaces. Their creators developed every nook and cranny and filled them with meaning. Pagan is expansive, covering a huge area. It is flat, and the temples, stupas, and other structures (more than two thousand of them) stretch as far as the eye can see. It is an arid plain, very different from the humid climate of Rangoon and the lower delta. Pagan was first established in AD 800, but most of the temples and other structures date to the eleventh to thirteenth centuries, when it was the capital of the first Burman empire founded by King Anawrahta. The empire came to an end late in the thirteenth century, when it tried to resist the Yuan Dynasty's demand that it submit to tributary state status with the Chinese empire.

The site and the endless vista of temples are stunning, but even more stunning for us was the devastation. We expected to see the deterioration of centuries of weather and perhaps neglect, but we were not prepared for the vandalism. In virtually every temple that we visited, the heads of the Buddhist statues had been cut off. This was a country where all sectors of society, including the military, prided themselves on their adherence to Buddhist teachings and principles. Yet the authorities and the population had been unable or unwilling to prevent this desecration. The contradiction between what we were told about respect for the sacred and what we saw was breathtaking. The motive we assumed was not sheer vandalism but money. The heads were sold to whoever would buy them.

***

Now I must add another personal anecdote. I became a purchaser of one of those vandalized heads. One day, when we were at home in Rangoon, a man came to our door and offered to sell us a Buddha's head. We asked to see it, and he brought it in. It was a large bronze head, more than one cubic foot in size, and very heavy. It was also strikingly beautiful. It was very tempting just from an artistic point of view, but both Ginger and I were very reluctant to encourage this practice in any way.

I have to admit that I was willing to consider buying it just because it was so beautiful. However, Ginger's point was more important. "If we buy it, we will treat it with the respect that it deserves. If it goes to someone who is just interested in money, it will be abused." We did buy it, and we put it in our meditation room for the rest of the time that we were in Burma. When we left, we carried it with us as hand luggage (the heaviest hand luggage I have ever traveled with) and flew to Hong Kong, where we gave it to someone who undertook to recreate the body. He found a highly skilled and knowledgeable craftsman in central China to do the work. In the process, he learned that the original statue, in fact, had not been made in Burma. It had been created in China and sent to Burma during the Yuan Dynasty, probably as a gift (perhaps as part of the failed attempt to secure submission peacefully?). It is now back in China at a Buddhist meditation center. It has returned home.

Obviously, my job was fascinating. As counselor for economic and political affairs, I was responsible for analyzing and reporting to Washington on all aspects of Burma's political and economic environment. We had a good-sized section of Americans and Burmese to do this, and the information we presented made an important input to the policy decisions that governed our relations. Several of our Foreign Service officers had received Burmese language training and were enthusiastic observers. Our Burmese employees were very intelligent, competent, and devoted both to our work and to strengthening relations between our two countries. Some of them were quite distressed by the regime's actions, and some of them supported the regime. Some were very adept at maintaining their ties with all parties, regardless of how contradictory this effort might seem at any given moment.

My view was that in societies like Burma and China, our employees could not afford to burn their bridges with local authorities, and these relationships would always exist. We did not allow them access to classified information, and we naturally limited certain discussions with them. As long as we recognized that their environment placed certain demands on them that necessarily limited the degree to which we could count on them, we could work effectively together on common interests. Sometimes the ties and even obligations that they retained with their own authorities could be helpful to us all. Not all of my American colleagues agreed with me, and my successors eventually dismissed one of the employees I had considered to be most effective.

We had relatively little relationship with government officials. This was partially because they either didn't want any relationship with us or had to be very careful about getting close to us. It was also partially because after the regime's brutal crackdown on the demonstrators, we chose to maintain a certain distance in the relationship. This decision was reinforced by the regime's practice of using the official media (the only media) to exploit any such contact for its own propaganda purposes. It became very difficult for us to have quiet discussions, even when we wanted it.

We did try to develop contacts with other sectors of society: the opposition political parties (before they were banned or imprisoned), the business community, religious figures, and so on. Some were very interested in talking with us, others less so. We and they all had to be careful, as they could get into trouble with the regime if they were seen to become too close to us. That limited the depth of the relationships we could develop and the understanding of the environment that such relationships could give to us. The main opposition political party, the National League for Democracy, led by Aung San Suu Kyi, openly welcomed contact with us. I met relatively often with Suu Kyi and her colleagues both officially and personally. I was less worried about such contacts, because Aung San Suu Kyi and her colleagues were so high-profile that contact with us had less marginal impact on them than it would on others.

Some of my favorite memories of working the environment were wandering down alleyways in Rangoon, looking for the offices of businesspeople whose influence was in reverse proportion to the elegance of their working quarters. For people who reached a certain level of economic activity, it was sometimes better to remain very low-profile. They had to do business with the regime, but they didn't necessarily want to advertise that fact for any of their customers.

Others of my favorite memories were stopping by the roadside on trips outside Rangoon to talk with truck drivers or entrepreneurs. Their trucks were always breaking down because they were so old. We saw trucks made in the 1920s still on the road—their owners proficient in making parts from scratch. We would ask them about the scope of their business and their travels. Some of them made regular trips to the Chinese or Indian borders, places to which we were denied access. Two years later, when I was assigned to China, I encountered one of the Burmese businessmen I had talked with in Mandalay, in a border town on the Chinese side of the border. Both of us were astonished to see each other in that setting. It was as unexpected as meeting on the moon.

***

Of course, we also had the rest of the foreign community in Rangoon to talk with. They had far fewer concerns about spending time with us and sharing their views. Even the Chinese diplomats, who in China and some other overseas settings were still reticent about their contacts with us, kept an open door for us in Burma—and sometimes even sought us out. The British seemed to have the best understanding of Burma and the Burmese among the Western diplomats in Burma, probably due to their past relationship, and more depth of experience and language training. They were closely followed by the Australians, who made up for any lack of experience with tremendous energy and enthusiasm. Every Friday evening, the Australian Embassy held an open house for whatever Burmese or foreigners could manage to get there, and it was a very pleasant venue for relaxing and sharing views about what we were all experiencing.

I was particularly struck by the Chinese diplomacy in Rangoon at the time. All the Western governments were critical of Burma's ruling regime and openly supportive of the democracy movement. Even the Russians and the East Europeans were critical of the regime, at least in private. But the Chinese maintained their diplomatic support of the regime assiduously. They appeared not to communicate with the leading democratic candidates, though some believed Aung Gyi had made overtures to them, as he had some Chinese ancestry. With the exception of the British ambassador, the Chinese diplomats had had more experience in the country than most other diplomatic missions there, and they had strong Burmese language capability. The Chinese political counselor at the time had been a Burmese-Chinese language interpreter and was fluent in Burmese. I once introduced her to Aung San Suu Kyi at a party. The Chinese political counselor was polite, but it clearly made her extremely uncomfortable, and she moved away as quickly as she could.

The Chinese have successfully maintained their relationship with Burma. Of course, their goals are different. China seems to be treating Burma more as a traditional tributary state. This was an approach that China applied for centuries to the countries on its borders, all of which were smaller and most of which were less powerful than the Chinese empire. China would usually ignore all aspects of those countries' domestic politics as long as they did nothing that presented strategic problems for the empire. This approach worked pretty well for the governments of present-day China and Burma for several decades. Burma was a small country that could present very little threat to China on its own, and its self-enforced "hermit" status prevented other world powers from becoming involved. The upheavals that China went through between 1950 and 1979 were primarily internal and further limited any active Chinese interest in Burma.

However, China would have seen as much more problematic any Burmese regime experimenting with democratic forces and supported by foreign powers. I tried to argue to my Chinese counterparts that a democratic regime might be better able to peacefully incorporate all ethnic groups into the body politic, creating more long-term stability, and better able to reduce the narcotics trafficking that threatened to become a larger problem for southwest China. I don't think I made much impact. Interestingly enough, many of those in the Chinese embassy were as shaken by the violence with which the Burmese regime put down the demonstrations as we were. They told us both officially and personally that such an approach would never happen in China. I imagine they were even more shaken by the crackdown that took place less than one year later in Beijing, Chengdu, and other Chinese cities.

***

Even after the crackdown on the demonstrators and the resumption of power by the military regime, albeit under another name, there remained a great deal of hope within the nation that change could still be effected. The new regime, the State Law and Order Restoration Committee (SLORC), announced that elections would take place in six months and all major accredited political parties could participate. The next six months were a frenzy of political activity not experienced in Burma for more than thirty years. There were many parties and candidates, but there was never any question which party and which candidate was the most connected with the population. The National League for Democracy led from the start. Its leading light, Aung San Suu Kyi, drew enormous crowds wherever she spoke, and she spoke everywhere. Her campaign would have been considered a phenomenon in any country. In Burma, it was almost a miracle. She provided impressive leadership: always rational, articulate, and respectful of both her supporters and her opponents. She was critical of the regime, but with remarkably little rancor. She had tremendous faith in the ability of the will of the people and democracy to prevail. She had long been an admirer of Mahatma Gandhi, and that showed in her perseverance. When the National League for Democracy won a resounding victory at the polls, no one was surprised. When the military regime then refused to recognize the results, there was tremendous disappointment. When the regime then arrested the main opposition politicians and put Aung San Suu Kyi under house arrest, everyone was shocked—but not really surprised.

Sadly, neither the people of Burma nor the United States nor the international community was able effectively to call the military regime to account. Just before she was confined to house arrest, Suu Kyi told me that she did not know whether the regime intended to arrest her or kill her. She was afraid, but she said she was prepared for either. I told her then that I thought there was very little the United States could do at that point to make a difference. The United States was committed to diplomacy and never seriously considered military action. We did distance ourselves further from the regime, and we led the international effort to impose sanctions, but sanctions had no noticeable effect on the regime and its policies.

The people of Burma have continued to suffer. The country's economy remains stagnant, and what little productive energy exists is directed to the ruling elite. The educational system has never recovered. The political system is oppressive, and none of the interethnic divisions have been addressed in any long-term way. Narcotics are still a significant export, and Burma is considered a pariah nation by most of the world. In addition, both the people of Burma and the rest of the world have been denied the talents of a very remarkable woman. Aung San Suu Kyi could probably have negotiated her release from house arrest at several points in the last seventeen years, if she had been willing to accept voluntary exile from her country. I, for one, would have encouraged her to do so. However, she had ruled out that possibility after she returned to Burma in 1988. She told me that she had given two decades of her life to her husband and her two sons. She said her sons were then old enough to understand and take responsibility for themselves, and she had told the three of them that it was then time for her to give the rest of her life to her country—in whatever form that might take.

***

For more than twenty years after the 1989 crackdown, the United States continued to treat Burma as a pariah nation and encouraged the rest of the world to do so as well. The decision to take this approach—after the military regime first cracked down on demonstrators for democracy and then canceled the results of the election they held and imprisoned Aung San Suu Kyi—was reasonable at the time.

After Burt Levin departed the USG proposed a replacement, who was rejected by the military regime. The State Department tried again, nominating a career Foreign Service officer I had known in a previous post. We had a chance to talk when he was in Washington studying Burmese and waiting for his confirmation process to work through. I congratulated him on the assignment but told him that I personally believed we should not send an ambassador to Burma at that time. I thought that it would be a stamp of approval for the SLORC and that we should continue to maintain our distance. Apparently some members of Congress had the same sentiments, and they let it be known that no ambassadorial nominee would be approved. So we started down our road of sanction diplomacy—and eventually paralysis.

In retrospect, I believe we did the wrong thing. The formal distance that we maintained from the Burmese regime or State Law and Order Restoration Council (SLORC)—later called the State Peace and Development Council— made very little real difference. Once you start holding people or governments at arm's length, it becomes increasingly difficult to communicate with them, understand them, influence them, or have any real impact. Worse, in the United States, once we start down a road of sanctions it becomes very hard to turn around. It becomes irrational foreign policy frozen in place by domestic politics.

In 1995, when the SLORC first released Aung San Suu Kyi from house arrest, I sent a letter to the assistant secretary for East Asian and Pacific affairs, arguing that the time had come to change our policy and reestablish ambassadorial representation in Rangoon. I argued we could do it as recognition of the first reasonable step the regime had made since arresting Aung San Suu Kyi. We could claim for ourselves that our policy had been successful. We could put ourselves in a better position to promote continued change—and if things went the other way we would then have something to withdraw again to show our displeasure. When I talked with him about it, the assistant secretary laughed and teased me about having someone specific in mind for the position of ambassador (meaning myself). He agreed that there was some logic to the proposal, but said there was no possibility in the current (U.S.) political climate that it would be considered.

Many elements of American foreign policy have supporters or detractors outside of the foreign affairs agencies and outside of the government. Some are in the business community, which may seek better access to foreign markets or resources, or may promote policies that will provide them opportunities for greater sales to the U.S. government—such as weapons. Some are in the political community, where various ethnic or religious groups seek support for associated communities in other countries—such as American Jews, Greeks, Armenians, Georgians, Vietnamese, Chinese, and so on. Some, such as human rights groups, have more generic interests that strike a chord with the American electorate in support of communities in other countries that are suffering from one form of persecution or another—such as Tibetans, Sudanese, Kurds, or Burmese. The Clinton administration was both ideologically attuned to the latter concerns and politically mortgaged to ethnic interest groups. For whatever reasons, the State Department and the administration chose to stick with the Burma policy's inertia rather than try to take back control of it.

It took more than 15 years before the Burmese regime began another more substantial relaxation. Would things have been different if we had had the flexibility to act differently? I believe there was at least a chance, but we did not try it then.

There was at least one opportunity to take direct action to bring about change in the short term that we did not take. In the early weeks of the government meltdown in 1988, we talked with an elderly Burmese man who was well-educated, experienced, and highly respected in Burma. After very few formalities, he shocked us by saying, "I will tell you how to set things right here. I can give you five or ten targets for your F-15s to bomb. Do that and everything will be OK." We replied (in what was perhaps just as predictable and boring a response as given to us by Burmese officials) that the United States did not intend to interfere in Burma's internal affairs. At the time we wondered if perhaps he was so old that he had become senile—but in retrospect, he was probably right. The military leadership had determined it would not allow any progress in the direction of democracy, and preventing the military's intervention would have been the only way to allow the process of popular self-determination to take place.

However, the United States was probably right in not following his advice. It would have been a very serious departure from American foreign policy at the time. It certainly would have resulted in more loss of life in Burma, and it might have made things worse there. It would also have impacted our relations with both the Soviet Union and China, and probably would have put our relations with China on a more negative trajectory.

Aung San Suu Kyi's approach was the opposite of this man's recommendation. She too believed the military regime needed to go. However, she believed it needed to be replaced by a government of the people, a democracy. She also continually argued against all forms of violence—either for acquiring power or for maintaining it. She had tremendous faith in democracy and the idea that the people of a nation can embody wisdom in the affairs of men and bring that wisdom to bear to govern effectively. Through her years of imprisonment she appears never to have relinquished that faith.

She has so far been unsuccessful in bring about a change of regime. However, because of her example she is still revered by much of the population. Perhaps through that example she will give birth to change in the population that will in turn bring change over a longer period of time. It would be nice if that period of time were short enough to allow her to see it in her lifetime.

NOTE

1. "The dawn comes up like thunder" is from Rudyard Kipling's poem "Mandalay."

Chapter Seven

Flower Pepper and Buttered Tea: Chengdu (February 1990—July 1992)

A famous Tang Dynasty poet, Li Bai, wrote that "the road to Shu[1] is hard, harder than climbing to Heaven." He was, I think, referring to the fact that Sichuan (四川) is surrounded by a protective wall of mountains. It was definitely hard for me to get there, but it had nothing to do with mountains. I first sought an assignment to the U.S. Consulate General in Chengdu, Sichuan, when I was stationed in Beijing and the United States was still negotiating with China about opening more posts in China's interior. It looked like a dream assignment: the world's most populous consular district; Sichuan, China's most populous province; Yunnan, the other end of World War II's fabled "Burma Road"; Guizhou; and of course, Tibet. Like many Americans, I knew little about Sichuan and other Chinese provinces, but I was fascinated with the exotic and mysterious land of Tibet and concerned about the destruction it had suffered since the armies of the People's Republic moved into it in 1950. I was not successful in my efforts to get the assignment then. There were too many more senior and better-connected colleagues in the China field. The first two consuls general in Chengdu were longtime "China hands" who had studied Chinese before I even joined the Foreign Service.

However, my chance came in 1989, while I was still stationed in Rangoon, Burma. The second person assigned to Chengdu as consul general had returned to the United States for health reasons. By late fall, the Department of State had decided that it could not leave the post unfilled any longer during that sensitive period in our relations. The regular personnel cycle had finished, so the China Office had to recruit outside the normal procedures. The deputy director responsible for personnel remembered my interest and called me in Rangoon, asking if I would be willing to leave Rangoon before my assignment was over and transfer directly to Chengdu. Rangoon was quiet. The 1988 uprising had been crushed; the 1989 election of Aung San Suu Kyi and her party had been overturned, and she had been put under house arrest by the military regime. There was nothing that I could do to affect those things, and very little was happening, so Ambassador Levin agreed to let me leave early.

***

Sichuan is a very special place in China, though not well known beyond China's borders. Many Americans have heard of "Chungking" (now written Chongqing), China's twentieth-century wartime capital where the allied nations (primarily the United States) helped China resist the Japanese during World War II. Most in the West who have some familiarity with China know that Sichuan has long been the country's most populous province.[2] Some know that Sichuan is where the giant pandas come from. Sichuan's spicy cuisine is world famous, but in most places outside of Sichuan what is served is substantially different from what the people of Sichuan are fond of.

The province sits in the western middle of China. If China were a human body, Sichuan would be the stomach—if not the heart. Topographically, it is a bowl, surrounded by mountains—the Himalayas in the west, the Qinling and Daba in the north, and the mountains of Yunnan in the south. In this bowl is a fertile plain, often called the Chengdu Plain, fed by the Min River (Minjiang), which has supported Sichuan's vast population for centuries.

The surrounding mountains keep the climate fairly stable and mild. They also tend to hold in the water vapor and the clouds, making Sichuan more humid and somewhat misty or hazy. Satellite pictures show a perpetual sea of clouds hovering over the basin, and the province to the south is appropriately named Yunnan, or "south of the clouds." Bright blue skies in most of Sichuan are a rarity, but so are storms and violent weather.

One of the products of this humid and hazy climate is the Sichuan cuisine. It is very spicy, and the most important spice is *huajiao* (花 椒), which translates as "flower pepper." This pepper can be found in other parts of Asia but is uniquely popular in Sichuan. It is rare in the United States, because from 1968 to 2005 its import was banned by the U.S. Food and Drug Administration out of concern that it might carry a fungus dangerous to other plants. It has a pungent flavor and is not just hot and spicy, but has a mild numbing effect on the mouth and lips. The first time that Ginger and I experienced it was in the dining room of Chengdu's Jin Jiang hotel on our way to Tibet in 1985. It was not an unpleasant sensation, but it took us some time to understand that it was coming from the food, and that it was intentional! Like the tiny green peppers in Thai food and the peppers in some Latin American food, *huajiao* has a purpose beyond just making the food taste better. It is medicinal, being particularly effective in getting rid of excess moisture from the body and counteracting the sluggishness that can result from excessive humidity. Neither of us had heard of this before, and for an instant we wondered if someone had decided to poison the foreigners!

The mountains that hold the clouds in have also kept invading armies out. There is a very famous pass in the mountains that separates Sichuan from Shanxi called Jianmenguan (劍門關 Sword Gate Pass). It is so narrow that only a few persons can pass through abreast. We visited it on a trip to the Jiuzhaigou National Park, and it is quite formidable. There is a Chinese saying that "one man at the pass keeps 10,000 at bay" (一夫當關, 萬夫莫開—yi fu dang guan, wan fu mo kai).

Shu (蜀) became a place where people fleeing the collapse of dynasties or foreign invasions could find refuge. Over the centuries, layer after layer of human cultural sediment has been deposited in this area. It's a little like a Chinese medicine bowl. In Chinese medicine, the doctor will select a collection of herbs and medicinal products to deal with a particular affliction. He will then place them in a large pot of water and boil them down over an extended period of time until it becomes a thick and potent brew. Sichuan is like a medicine bowl where centuries of Chinese culture and tradition have been boiled down and concentrated unlike anywhere else. The population of the bowl itself is predominantly Han, but it is surrounded by many different minorities, including the Tibetans who inhabit most of the mountainous region west of the Chengdu plain—which used to be part of Tibet.

However, Sichuan's population growth and cultural concentration were not due solely to topography, but to what its people did with the topography. The province is home to one of the world's oldest irrigation projects, Dujiangyan (都江堰). In the third century BC, during China's Warring States period, the Qin governor of Shu conceived and directed an extraordinary engineering project that put an end to the annual flooding of the Min River and diverted water into the vast Chengdu plain. To do this he had to cut a channel through a small mountain. This was before explosives, since gunpowder (a Chinese invention) was not developed until at least five hundred years later. Shu's governor therefore directed his people to alternate hot and cold water to crack the rocks. It took them eight years to get through, but this project turned Sichuan into one of the breadbaskets of China.

It also contributed to something with which we Americans are much more familiar. Shortly after the project's completion, a man named Ying Zheng acceded to the Qin throne. The rapid growth of food production in the Chengdu plain enabled Ying to accelerate Qin's military growth and finally gain supremacy over its two rivals, bringing the Warring States period to a close. In 221 BC, Ying Zheng became Qin Shi Huang (秦始皇), the first emperor of a unified Chinese state. Qin Shi Huang, among other things, began construction of the Great Wall and created the Terracotta Warrior Army for his extraordinary tomb in Xian, just north of Sichuan.

***

This region has also been a source of support, pleasure, and anguish for generations of Chinese rulers. It is famous for beautiful and intelligent women. The only woman in China's five thousand years of recorded history to serve as emperor, Wu Zetian (武则天), was from Sichuan.[3] Her rise was quite extraordinary, starting as a concubine of the Tang Dynasty emperor Taizong, then becoming his successor's (and son's) concubine, and finally graduating to empress. She gradually took over official duties as Emperor Gaozong became progressively ill (some believe of her doing). After Gaozong died, she ruled for several years in the name of two of her sons, removing the first when he tried to be independent. Then she took over the throne herself, ruling as the first emperor of a new Zhou Dynasty—which ended when she was deposed fifteen years later. She is generally recognized to have been a competent administrator, though extremely ruthless.

China's most famous imperial concubine and legendary beauty, the eighth-century Tang Dynasty consort Yang Guifei, was also born in Sichuan. Both women used their feminine talents to attain influence and power—and in both cases the courts and imperial administration around them were corrupted by that influence and eventually overthrown.

Sichuan is a province where China's traditional male chauvinism is tempered by cooking and housework. It is common in Sichuan for the principal cook in the family to be the husband/father. It seemed like everyone in Sichuan was proud of Sichuan cuisine and interested in it. This is justifiably so, as the cuisine is extraordinary. Many of the men we met in Sichuan saw cooking not as a duty, but as a calling.

***

Personally and politically, the Sichuan people are as volatile as any in China. Perhaps it is the food. Perhaps it is compensation for the mild and unexciting climate. Perhaps it is the concentration of centuries of human culture. Perhaps that volatility was part of what made Yang Guifei so attractive to Emperor Xuanzang. It may have helped to make the area less hospitable to outside invaders, like the Japanese.

It has also made the area and its people problematic to successive Chinese governments. One of the central figures in the creation of the Communist Party and its eventual defeat of Chiang Kai-shek's Nationalists was Deng Xiaoping, a native of Sichuan. Later, Deng became a challenge to Mao

Zedong's control. He was suppressed and persecuted until he in turn rose to power and revolutionized Mao's revolution.

In 1989, China's communist rulers were surprised by the uprising in Beijing's Tiananmen Square. I was told by several people, however, that the leadership had not been surprised by the unrest itself. They were expecting it; but they had expected it to happen first in Sichuan! In fact, Sichuan's capital city, Chengdu, did experience serious unrest during that period, but it was overshadowed by Beijing. Ten years later, when the United States accidentally destroyed the Chinese embassy in Belgrade during its bombing of Serbia, the Western press sent out pictures of crowds breaking the windows of the U.S. Embassy in Beijing—but paid less attention to the crowd in Chengdu burning the residence of the U.S. consul general.

***

Ginger, Charles, and I arrived in Chengdu in the winter of 1990, only seven months after the "Tiananmen Square massacre"—known in China more colloquially as 6/4, (六 四 liu si), for June 4. All of China was still very tense, and Sichuan particularly so. Chinese officials believed they had to be very careful with everything they did. Dealing with foreigners could be personally risky even if (and sometimes particularly if) it was one's business.

The Tiananmen demonstration—which began in mid-April and ended with the military crackdown on June 4, 1989—had been both disturbing and confusing to many in and associated with government. It had been a clear challenge to the autocratic rule of the Communist Party, and many were surprised by how rapid was the mushrooming of popular sentiment in favor of increased political freedoms. While many were disturbed by the crushing force used against the demonstrators in Beijing and elsewhere, many were also disturbed by the popular challenge to government control.

What was particularly surprising to me was that the ambivalence of perception was not limited to those in officialdom. Memories of the Cultural Revolution were still very strong in the minds of those who had gone through it. During the Cultural Revolution nothing was safe, nothing was sacred. Any deviation from the official line could be fatal. One had to be nimble as well, because the official line itself could change at a moment's notice. Even more than usual in China, one had to work hard to stay in the good graces of those who wielded power—of any kind—and be very careful not to make enemies. Although the Cultural Revolution had been started by the country's leadership, it had gotten out of hand at all levels, and the extent of the destruction had been unimaginable.

A number of people in different parts of southwest China told us that when the demonstrations in Tiananmen Square in Beijing began, their biggest concern was that social and political disruption on the order of a second Cultural Revolution might be in the making. Even some of the most liberal thinkers I met expressed relief about the crackdown, while simultaneously being distressed about the loss of life, because it reassured them that the central government was still in charge and that a repeat of the excesses of the Cultural Revolution was less likely. While I had read about China's deep-seated historical concern about chaos (乱 luan), I had always associated it with war. This was the first time I saw some of the sociocultural underpinnings of that fear.

***

The U.S. Consulate General in Chengdu was opened in 1985. When I arrived in 1990, it was one of two foreign diplomatic missions in Chengdu. The other one was the consul from Nepal, but he was in Chengdu only part-time. The U.S. Consulate did not have its own building but maintained offices and apartments in the Jin Jiang Hotel, a massive Soviet-style hotel that for years had been the main place for visitors to stay. While few people were aware of the Nepali consulate, many knew the Americans were there. There were more of us (five American officials plus family members), we were representatives of a superpower, and we gave visas to visit the United States.

In Sichuan, public perceptions of the United States were ambivalent. For more than twenty years, from the establishment of the PRC in 1949 to the visit of President Nixon in 1972, the two countries had been enemies. Official propaganda in China had stressed this heavily. During the Cultural Revolution, the discovery of personal ties to the United States would likely have resulted in considerable persecution or even death for an individual and his family.

The province of Sichuan had also become more leery of foreigners in general since the founding of the PRC. During the 1960s, as Mao became increasingly worried about the possibility of war with the USSR, he ordered the removal of vast industrial infrastructure from coastal and other more vulnerable areas and sent them inland. Much of it landed in Sichuan. In that period there were virtually no foreigners in the area, but as China began to open up, foreigners began to return. This was disquieting to some.

However, there was also a history of friendly U.S.-China relations and mutual cooperation, particularly in Sichuan. U.S. General Joseph Stilwell spent several years in Chongqing, Sichuan, supporting Chiang Kai-shek's resistance to the Japanese invasion;[4] and airfields outside Chengdu were used to conduct B-29 bombing missions against Japan in the early 1940s. On numerous occasions we were approached by older Chinese, sometimes quietly and sometimes defiantly, who would proclaim their gratitude for what

America had done to help them at that time. Some described the excitement and the happiness they felt when they heard and saw the B-29s or the "Flying Tiger" aircraft in the skies, knowing they were not alone in that time of distress.

America was also Ronald Reagan's "city on the hill," the "golden mountain" (the Chinese name for San Francisco) of economic opportunity, a prominent reservoir of higher education, and the source of pop culture. Young people would stop us on the street or in the park to try to practice their English or just to see what Americans were like. In those cases, I was the one who was ambivalent, because I worried their association with me might get them into trouble.

***

The reception given to us by Chinese officials varied widely. I found that many officials were reluctant to meet with me, or to talk very long or too openly when we did meet. I found that frustrating, but I tried to accept that they had to be careful. Some were friendly; some were not. Some were open, or seemed to be, and some were very formal and distant. This seemed to be partly personality and partly position.

Those in primarily political positions (e.g., governor, mayor, party leaders) tended to be more distant. Ironically this also included the individual who had direct responsibility for dealing with the consulate, the head of the Foreign Affairs Office, or *waiban* (外办). He always had a beaming smile on his face but would never answer questions with any depth, and he seemed distinctly uncomfortable with encounters of any length. He could certainly have been in a vulnerable position, particularly if he were held responsible for whatever we did. I may have made his job more difficult sometimes, as I tended to be less diplomatic than some of my colleagues, perhaps giving controversial subjects more attention than was strictly necessary.

One example was the occasion of the second July 4 reception that our consulate hosted. The first had taken place just one year after Tiananmen, and official participation was limited. However, on the second year the governor replied that he would attend. It was an unusual and welcome step. Unfortunately, I spoiled it when I put a mention of human rights into my welcoming statement. It was a very gentle mention, simply stating that this was something important to Americans and would continue to be a subject of our relations. The mere mention of the term, however, was enough to cause the governor to withdraw his participation when he saw the advance copy that I sent over as a courtesy.

***

Officials in economic positions tended to be more comfortable in their association with us. Their charge was to develop opportunities. Officials in the business of developing trade and investment, as well as those running government or private businesses, were open to contact with official Americans and sometimes aggressively sought us out. One particularly impressive man was the director of the province's Office of Foreign Trade, with whom the consulate's economic officer had developed an excellent working relationship. He was young, well educated, spoke very good English, and seemed to have limitless energy and imagination. The ministry for which he worked, the Ministry of Foreign Economic Relations and Trade, had been given a central government mandate to establish and develop relations with foreign governments and companies—and they evidenced far less hesitation in their dealings with us than did those from other government organizations.

Before I arrived in Sichuan, the consulate had arranged to send this individual to the United States on a "leadership grant" managed by the U.S. Information Service. This took him to Washington, DC, and a variety of other cities in the United States of interest to him and to Sichuan Province. When he returned, he invited us to dinner to talk about his trip and to share his impressions of the United States. He had enjoyed his trip, and he told us with some amusement that there were three striking differences between the United States and China that had surprised him. I still remember them clearly:

- In China, which for a long time has been relatively poor, to be plump or corpulent is a mark of success and distinction. It is only the rich who can achieve that distinction. In the United States, to the contrary, it is the poor who seem to be very overweight, while the rich go to great lengths to be slim, dieting, and exercising ferociously!
- In China, the poor ride bicycles, and the rich drive cars. In America, the rich take pride in riding bicycles, and the poor drive enormous and colorful automobiles!
- In China, the poor work outside in the sun and their skin gets dark, whereas the rich do everything they can to shield themselves from the sun and maintain a pale complexion. In America, the poor have pale complexions, but the rich take every opportunity to darken their skin by exercising out-of-doors and sunbathing—even going to tanning salons in the winter.

***

One of the government organizations with which we had the most active relationship was the Foreign Affairs Services Office or Waishiban (外事办). This organization provided the consulate with our Chinese staff and therefore had a practical working relationship with us—as contrasted with the *waiban*, whose relationship was primarily political. The consulate had a staff of about thirty Chinese employees. These included drivers, secretaries, clerks, bookkeepers, and managerial assistants for the different sections. These employees were not hired or chosen by us directly. Our staff had two masters, which is always a tricky situation. However, the Waishiban did everything they could to be helpful. They worked hard to find the right people to work in the consulate, and were willing to change people who didn't work out.

On one occasion, they most generously took all of the consulate employees on a trip to the Jiuzhaigou National Park in northwestern Sichuan. This is one of the most beautiful wilderness areas that I have seen anywhere. The trip up and back was also spectacular as the mountain roads were susceptible to landslides, one of which just missed our bus. Our common adventures on that trip—including a snowball fight high in the mountains (for several of our staff the first time they had ever seen snow) also helped bring us closer to our Chinese staff.

As we got to know them better, they taught us more about how things worked in Chengdu and beyond, and even served as an informal link to other less accessible parts of the government. I would go by occasionally to discuss issues with them. Ginger went more often, sometimes for rather sensitive reasons. Some American businessmen and officials came to Sichuan without their families. They were alone and attractive targets for the single Sichuan women—who were also attractive targets. That was problematic enough for the families, but it could have other implications if either government was involved. On a couple of occasions, Ginger dropped by the Waishiban to ask for their "advice" on how to address specific situations to protect the families. Sometimes the advice was helpful. Perhaps just as important, it made clear that we were aware of the situations and were watching them closely.

***

Building teams that can work synergistically to achieve common goals is a challenge for U.S. embassies and consulates all over the world. We are often separated from our local staff by language, custom, and perspective. The language, cultural, and historical differences for Americans in China are as great as anywhere in the world. Add to these the fact that sometimes our staff might be getting different instructions from their other bosses, and the difficulty is increased significantly.

I encouraged the American staff to give as much responsibility as possible to their Chinese employees. I tried to include my Chinese staff in most of my activities setting up meetings and activities, and discussing the results of them afterward. We were restricted in the kinds of things we could do with officials and businesspeople. They had to be careful about spending too much time with us in their offices or at social events. However, we discovered that lunches or dinners at restaurants were considered to be fairly safe. Also, many of the people we depended on for all kinds of services, from hiring staff to customs to purchasing airline tickets, did not have many opportunities to go to some of the more prestigious restaurants in Chengdu, because most government salaries in China were still too low. So we used that venue as often as we could afford it. We got to know them a little better, and they got to know us. We included our staff. It gave them more stature, and it enormously increased our understanding of the way things worked.

There was still more of a formality gap, however, between the American and Chinese staff than I was comfortable with. For most people that was a given, but Ginger and I talked often about how to shrink it. Then one day our son Charles found an unorthodox approach for us.

He and Ginger would go regularly to the People's Park (Renmin Gongyuan), where they could walk along the pathways, watch men playing chess on stone tables, and feed the fish in the ponds. They would have tea in the little restaurants. The hot tea was poured from teapots with long spouts and would arch steaming through the air before splashing into the cups. He was also introduced to the Sichuan snacks, which included boiled peanuts, steamed bread, and tiny boiled snails that you dig out of the shell with toothpicks. However, what caught his eye that day was something very Western and a little out of place in that ancient Chinese park. A small carnival had been set up, and in it was a rink with bumper cars.

He showed it to me a few days later. It was the first time that I had seen anything like that in China, and people seemed to be enjoying it. My birthday was coming up soon, and we decided to invite the whole consulate during a long lunch hour to ride the bumper cars. It was a totally undiplomatic and unbureaucratic thing to do. The Chinese staff did not know quite what to make of it, but they went along with it. Most of them had never ridden bumper cars before, but it did not take long for them to catch on, and there was great hilarity as everyone careened around smashing into each other without regard for race, creed, or cultural background. It was silly, but it was fun—and it did shrink that gap.

As in Hong Kong, I came to value highly the knowledge and judgment of some of our Chinese staff. They were well educated and well informed about the region—and about us. Some of them had worked at the consulate for several years and had a pretty good understanding of how we operated and what was important to us.

***

One of the consulate's most difficult jobs was responding to the large and growing demand from the population of the region for visas to visit the United States. For more than two hundred years most Americans have been proud of the fact that our country welcomes immigration from all over the world. The Statue of Liberty in New York Harbor is engraved with the words, "Give me your tired, your poor, your huddled masses yearning to breathe free. . . ." We champion the ability of people to move freely, and encourage (also browbeat and threaten) other nations to accord that freedom. However, even before 9/11 we were becoming increasingly restrictive ourselves about who we allow to our shores. In 1979, Deng Xiaoping, meeting with President Carter gently pointed this out when Carter expressed concern over the right of the Chinese people to emigrate. He asked President Carter just how many Chinese he wanted—ten million, twenty million, thirty million?

All non-U.S. citizens must have a visa to enter the United States, unless their country has been granted a waiver to that requirement. China was not one of those countries in 1990 and still is not. The United States has essentially two categories of visas: immigrant visas for those coming to the United States to reside permanently; and nonimmigrant visas for temporary stays. Immigrant visas are very limited in number, and in many countries they are only issued by U.S. embassies and not by consulates. In Chengdu, we issued only nonimmigrant visas. U.S. immigration law states that such visas can only be issued if the applicant can demonstrate that he or she does not intend to reside in the United States. Consular officers are taught that one of the most important ways of demonstrating such intent is the existence of strong economic ties to home that a person would not want to give up by remaining in the United States. In China in 1990—where for the previous four decades at least most of the population had no property and questionable economic prospects—making such a demonstration to an American consular officer was very difficult. Most applicants were judged to be "intending immigrants" and denied visas.

This was very difficult to understand for the Chinese applicants—particularly those who honestly did not want to stay in the United States but could not prove it to the consular officer. It was very disappointing to many who wished to visit relatives, study, or just see the United States. It was emotionally devastating to some who thought that for the first time in more than forty years they had a chance to see long-lost family members (some of whom were still uneasy about visiting "communist" China). It was also very stressful to the American consular officers, who were doing their best to abide by the requirements of U.S. law—and who also wanted to respond to the endless appeals for help.

U.S. embassy officials at all levels, including American ambassadors, are strictly proscribed from interfering in the visa process beyond providing whatever information they have about an individual's ties that might be useful to the consular officer. The responsibility for visa issuance lies solely with the consular officer—which is both a substantial power and a great burden—and supervisors may not pressure them in any way. A consular supervisor may review a decision, decide it was incorrect, and issue a new visa in his or her own name, but only if the supervisor has a consular commission issued by the Department of State for that particular time and place. As consul general in Chengdu, I had such a commission, and on very rare occasions used it to issue a visa previously denied if I thought the circumstances and U.S. interests warranted it.

We had one instance in which a businessman from Guizhou Province, whom I had met on an earlier visit there, brought a relative of his to Chengdu to apply for a student visa for the United States. He called on me with his relative, and he also brought thirty bottles of Guizhou's famous Maotai liquor. I told him that we could not accept the Maotai liquor because the visas had to be adjudicated absolutely objectively. He insisted profusely that the Maotai had nothing to do with the visa application but was a cultural gift from his province that he wanted to share. After a while neither of us could prevail, so I said that I would accept the Maotai for the consulate, but that it would not affect the visa application and he needed to recognize that. He agreed. I then distributed the Maotai to all of our Chinese employees. The businessman's relative made his application, had his interview with the consular officer—and was denied a visa on the grounds that he could not prove his intention to return to China. They were naturally disappointed. After that, I don't think anyone arrived at the consulate bearing gifts for the rest of my tour.

At the time, I really did not know what else I could do, because refusing to accept the Maotai seemed impolite, particularly in light of the visitor's protestations. The lesson to future applicants was certainly useful, but in retrospect, I should have taken it one step further by finding a way to compensate the man for the expense of the Maotai—by giving him a similar gift or taking him and his family to dinner or something. That at least would have balanced the scale a little.

***

One of the most frustrating problems we had was the restriction on our travel within the province of Sichuan. When the consulate was established in 1985, consulate officials were allowed to travel on only a few roads out of the city, and only for a limited distance, unless we obtained special permission—which was done through the *waiban*. Getting special permission was a slow process, and often the answer was no. The consulate had tried several times without success to get the area accessible to us expanded. When I reviewed the past efforts, which were largely focused on the local Sichuan authorities with some appeals to the Foreign Ministry in Beijing, I concluded that the main problem was inertia. There did not seem to be real security concerns for the Chinese. However, there were numerous actors involved (political, economic, and security), and most of them saw no clear benefit to themselves of allowing us to travel around and complicate their lives.

We thought that there were in fact many benefits to the province in general. There were many Chinese who for legitimate reasons wanted more contact with Americans, and the Sichuan area was one that could make good use of foreign business interest and capital. However, achieving consensus was just too difficult for the Foreign Affairs agencies with whom we dealt to commit their resources and risk their reputations by seriously going to bat for us. I could not offer them the kind of immediate benefits that would overcome that inertia. However, I could lobby to level the playing field, which at the time was decidedly tilted in favor of our Chinese diplomatic colleagues.

It was completely natural for the Chinese to restrict the movement of foreigners on their territory. They had been doing it for hundreds of years, not just under the People's Republic. It was equally natural for the Americans not to put restrictions on the movement of Chinese diplomats in the United States. Since the establishment of relations in 1979, both sides had taken both conditions for granted. I asked the embassy and the Department of State to change that by applying the principle of "reciprocity" or equal treatment and restricting the movement of Chinese diplomats. I argued to both our embassy and to the Office of Foreign Missions in the Department of State that this was not a punitive action, but that establishing conditions for Chinese diplomats in the United States similar to ours in China was both fair and would provide the incentive for the Chinese to overcome their own internal inertia. After some time the American bureaucracy began to soften, and we then made the decision easier for them by providing detailed proposals for what to do in the United States.

For this purpose, I specifically included our Chinese staff. They had a responsibility to report back to their other bosses, and I wanted them to understand the reasons for this course and our objectives. I wanted the Chinese authorities to understand, and I wanted them not to be surprised. The best way to ensure that was to have their own people actually involved in the project. Our staff could not refuse, because they did work for us; but I tried not to put them in a position that would compromise them. We pulled out maps of China and the United States, and I chose the Chinese consulate general in Houston as comparable in size and importance to ours in Chengdu. We marked off the roads accessible to us (there were only about five), and then I chose similar ones leading out of Houston. Then we applied the same distances the Chinese authorities allowed our consulate, which as I recall now was about twenty to seventy-five kilometers, depending on the road. We sent in our proposal and the Department of State applied it immediately. Less than two weeks after the Chinese Embassy in Washington was informed of the new restrictions, the territory accessible to our consulate in Chengdu was vastly expanded, and we were able to relax the restrictions on Houston. Expanding access in Sichuan benefited both countries. We had been able to generate enough energy to break the inertia in China, and did so, I think, without hurting or embarrassing anyone.

***

My other project on removing bureaucratic obstacles was directed at the U.S. government, and it concerned the stalled construction of a new office building and residence for the consulate general. Living in the hotel was certainly not unbearable, but it did constrain both our work and our lives. The city of Chengdu had provided land for a new consulate compound not far from the hotel, and a Chinese construction company had actually built several buildings on it. They had tried to coordinate their work with the Foreign Buildings Office (FBO) in Washington, which was responsible for all nonmilitary official U.S. construction overseas, but that relationship had not developed productively. Before I left Washington, I was told by the FBO that the construction was below standard, and they believed the compound could never meet U.S. standards. It was clearly very low on their list of priorities. When I arrived in Chengdu, I visited the site and met with officials from the local government and the construction company. The buildings looked reasonable to me. The Chinese officials said they had tried very hard to work with the FBO and thought that they had done everything that the FBO told them to do. However, they found it very difficult to get replies from the FBO, and when they did the replies were unclear. I concluded that completing the compound would not be difficult, and that whatever obstacles lay on the Chinese side would not be difficult to overcome. Our own bureaucracy, however, was not about to be moved.

When in Washington, I had also called on the State Department's undersecretary for management—who oversaw the FBO—and raised the issue with him. He was a political appointee rather than a career Foreign Service or Civil Service officer, and he was less entangled in the spiderweb of relationships and conventional wisdom that so many bureaucracies nurture. He expressed support in principle for the idea of completing the consulate compound. He also made the mistake of politely inviting me to stay in touch. For the first year of my tour in Chengdu, I sent him telegrams almost every two weeks updating him on discussions in Chengdu, ideas and proposals for addressing problems—and a running tabulation of how much it was costing the U.S. government to keep us in the hotel. It took about a year, but the FBO finally assigned an architect and a building manager to the project. Once that happened, the project began to move forward. The architect was enthusiastic and creative, and the project manager was a competent engineer who established excellent relations with all his Chinese counterparts. I watched the project take off, but I never got to see the final result. My successor moved in, and I have not been back to Chengdu since we departed in 1992.

My understanding from talking with some of my successors is that the compound has made an important contribution to our work in southwest China and to our relationship with that region. I was very proud of what we as a consulate were able to accomplish in breaking the logjam that had kept the project frozen for five years.

***

Part of the mandate of our diplomatic posts is to promote American business—to the degree that it is possible and desirable. I thought that having more American businesses involved in southwest China would be desirable—both for American businesses and for the region. Things were changing. I thought that the trend would continue and that it would be good for American companies to get into the area sooner rather than later. There were plenty of Chinese who wanted to see them come in, but convincing the Americans was difficult. Sichuan was an inland province. It had tremendous potential for development, but it was also difficult to access.

At one point I made a trip down to Hong Kong and asked the American Chamber of Commerce there, with whom I had worked closely years before, to set up a meeting for me with American companies interested in China. Only about fifteen or twenty people showed up. I talked about Sichuan and offered the consulate's services, but there were no takers, not even for a visit. One of the more honest representatives remarked to me, "You give us a guarantee of sales with a 25 percent profit margin and we'll come." I thought, "No wonder the Japanese and Taiwanese have the trade surplus, and the Americans the trade deficit."

To be fair, there were a few adventurous companies in the region. One was working at a combined military-civilian airfield outside of Chengdu, and one was working at the Xichang Satellite Launch Base in western Sichuan. Both were on the cutting edge of technology and of the U.S.-China relationship—and both had to be very careful about not crossing the line in sharing technology that was proscribed by the U.S. government with the Chinese companies and government.

Only one American company responded enthusiastically to our efforts to entice them to Sichuan, and the circumstances were unique. Toward the end of our tour in Chengdu, the consulate received word that the Seattle-based American mountaineer, Jim Whittaker, would be leading an assault on Mount Everest from Tibet with a combined American-Chinese-Russian team. They planned to stop in Chengdu on their way in and on their way out. I had met Jim's twin brother, Lou, in Beijing six years earlier when he had led a different team to the same mountain, which had not been successful. We were all very excited and anxious to meet the people who had embarked on this new adventure. When they arrived in Chengdu, we met them and talked about what they planned to accomplish and how the consulate might be supportive. When they moved on to Tibet, I asked Jim what he would most like to have when they stopped in Chengdu on their way out. His answer jokingly was, "Some Big Macs." We all laughed, because McDonald's in China was still in its infancy. However, I said I would see what we could do.

After they took off, I called the manager of McDonald's in Hong Kong, explained the situation, and asked if they might be interested in catering an event to welcome the international team in Chengdu when they returned. He saw the possibilities immediately and got to work on it. McDonald's Hong Kong put together a team, filled up a plane with the necessary materials, and came up to Chengdu to cater a party for three hundred Chinese officials, businessmen, and local Americans. We called the team in Tibet and told them what was waiting for them. When they came back triumphant, they had a reception such as Chengdu had not seen in many years. In the car on the way to the reception, I told Jim that I and the mayor of Chengdu would say a few words, and then invite him to take the first bite. He asked me if I wanted him to say anything. I replied that he was most welcome to, but that this was for him and the team's enjoyment, and we were not putting any obligations on him. He said in that case he would rather just eat. The party was a big success. The team members enjoyed it, and they liked the Big Macs. The locals enjoyed both seeing the team and getting the introduction to McDonald's. The only one not happy was ironically another American at one of the local universities, who sent me a letter saying how disgusted he was at the crass business promotion and the failure to invite Jim Whittaker to speak.

***

Life in Chengdu for us and for our American colleagues was quite unique. Living in the hotel for two and a half years was a little constraining. That was particularly true for my colleagues. Since the hotel didn't actually have suites, these were created by connecting two rooms together. Ginger, Charles, and I had a larger apartment for representational purposes. In our case, the hotel had blocked off a section of a hallway, giving us about six rooms and the central hallway. The "kitchens" were bathrooms with the toilet and bathtubs covered by makeshift countertops, with hotplates and toaster ovens. When we arrived, the entrance to our apartment was a small makeshift door in the obviously temporary wall the hotel had built to cordon off our apartment. It looked like something one might see in a back alley somewhere—something that Dr. Jekyll would furtively slip into to change into Mr. Hyde. Since entranceways are important in Chinese culture, one of the first things we did after arriving was to have large double doors installed and paint them red.

Being in the hotel did have some advantages. We could just walk downstairs to the hotel dining room when we got tired of cooking meals in the toaster oven, and it was only a two-floor commute to the office, which was also in the hotel just below us.

The downside was a lack of privacy. Although the hotel staff tried hard to respect it, we were pretty much always on display. It was worst for our consular officers, who were the most sought-after individuals in the consulate. Both working and living in the hotel, which was basically a public place, meant there was almost never any respite from that pressure.

As in Beijing, there was also the ever-present surveillance. About six months into our tour, I ordered a device from a mail order company in the United States designed to detect electronic eavesdropping. It had a screen that showed the presence of a bug and measured how strong its presence was, with between one and four bars. Ginger and I had great fun wandering through the apartment testing the signals. Some of the rooms, such as Charles's room, had no signal. In the living room and front hallway near the entrance, the signal was fairly strong. Perhaps predictably, the strongest was in our bedroom.

***

Life for a four-year-old was pretty good. Charles was three and a half when we arrived and six when we left. He learned to ride a bicycle first with trainer wheels in the hallway of our apartment, then on the paths of the hotel's rose garden, and finally on the sidewalks of Chengdu. There was a basketball court in a corner of the hotel property, and he took an early interest in it. He could barely lift a basketball above his head when we arrived, but he would spend hours at a time heaving it toward the net. By the time we left he could manage a few baskets.

He and Ginger explored the city in ways that I could not. There were many pedicabs (bicycle taxis) near the hotel, and they made friends with one driver who was very strong and could take them just about anywhere they wanted to go. He was quite a curiosity for Charles because he had two thumbs on one of his hands. When they went out on their own they could do so without calling much attention to themselves. Those who looked closely could tell that Charles was part foreigner, but then they tended to assume that Ginger was the nanny so they would talk freely with her.

Ginger took Charles to one of the local primary schools to see if he might be enrolled there. It was pretty basic, a little like summer camp with latrines instead of bathrooms, but the people were very friendly and welcoming. Ginger decided not to send him there, primarily because most instruction was in the Chengdu dialect—which even she could not understand. We ordered a long-distance learning program from the Calvert School in Maryland and tutored him ourselves for the time we were there. We also hired a young woman who spoke some English to take care of him. After two years, we liked her so much that Ginger introduced her to her brother in Taiwan. The two are now happily married in Taiwan with two children of their own, and forging family and business ties between Taiwan and the mainland.

TIBET (西藏)

Many Americans are intrigued by Tibet—its art, its religion, its culture, and its sheer exoticness. We are attracted by the allure of the mythical "Shangri-La," by the mystery of a culture so different from our own, by a location that seems almost impossible to reach. We are also energized by the idea of a small, weak, but colorful people resisting occupation and absorption by a much larger culture. We find common cause with them, as many of us consider that our immigrant ancestors came to the New World to escape oppression themselves. We also tend to miss the irony that our ancestors were significantly less sympathetic to the Native Americans, whom they quickly outnumbered and overwhelmed.

I had been fascinated for many years by the phenomenon of Tibet, and at one time I had even planned a sabbatical from the diplomatic service to study with a Tibetan lama. My assignment later to the U.S. Consulate General in Chengdu, which has as part of its consular district the Autonomous Region of Tibet, was a dream come true. Over a period of two years in southwest China, I talked with Tibetans, Chinese, and foreigners in and around Tibet. I watched, to the degree that I could, their lives and their relations, and I tried to understand their different aspirations. The experience did not diminish my fascination with Tibet. However, my perspective changed substantially.

***

As mentioned earlier, my first visit to Tibet was actually in September 1985, while still stationed at the embassy in Beijing. Ginger and I were there for ten days, visiting Lhasa and the Zedang area in the southeast. It was a spectacular introduction to Tibet, both its past traditions and its current reality of Chinese rule. We were fortunate to be able to visit so early as well, before the PRC-managed tourist industry really took over, and before things began being built up. I was impressed with the stark beauty of the place, as I expected to be. We were impressed by the Potala Palace and Jokhang Temple, their mysterious statues and paintings of deities and former Dalai Lamas, and the physical impact of the light and smell of the butter candles. We were also struck by the vast destruction of the old temples and monasteries. We had taken an old (1930s) guidebook with us, and we were able to chronicle the changes—in some cases the complete disappearance of significant edifices. I was prepared to see the Tibetans and the Chinese as oppressed and oppressors. That was certainly a reality, but at the same time I was impressed and touched by how nice, hard-working, and helpful many of our Chinese interlocutors were.

In 1985 the contrasts between Tibet and the China that we had seen in major cities like Beijing, Xian, and Shanghai were more marked than when we visited in the early 1990s. By 1990 color had returned to the streets of China proper, and Lhasa had more Chinese people, more Chinese architecture, and more Chinese business influence.

The altitude had not changed, though, and the difficulty that I had with it on that first trip never really went away on my subsequent seven visits to Tibet. However, I eventually developed several rules that permitted me to function reasonably well. They included: drink more water than you believe humanly possible; eat as little as possible; never drink alcohol (though tea and coffee are okay because they help keep your system going); avoid excessive physical effort (which in the beginning may mean anything other than walking to the bathroom); and talk as little as possible (listening is okay). I also found that chewing on dried ginseng root helped. Ginger insisted that drinking the Tibetan buttered tea made all the difference for her, but it didn't work for me. I admit to having felt very embarrassed and inadequate in the beginning by my weakness and apparent inability to cope. However, I learned that the altitude was quite unpredictable in its effect. When my eighty-year-old father and 66-year-old mother met us in Tibet in 1992, the altitude didn't bother either of them. When our five-year-old son arrived on that same trip, he turned gray an hour after arrival and had to go to the hospital. After a short rest he was back to normal and was not bothered for the rest of the week. However, what finally reassured me that I was not just a hopeless wimp was being told by my hosts that Harrison Ford, who was visiting Tibet at the same time as one of my visits, actually had to leave the region after only a short time, because his reaction was deemed too dangerous for him to remain. Outlasting Indiana Jones had to be good for something.

***

Tibet is a nation like many others, whose borders have changed dramatically over the centuries of its existence. The term "nation" here is controversial. I use it in the original sense of the word—a grouping of human beings with a common racial, cultural, and political heritage—rather than in the current sense of a state whose borders and sovereignty are formally recognized by the international community.

Tibet has existed in one form or another for more than a thousand years. Located in the Himalayan Mountains on one of the highest inhabitable plateaus of the planet, it has been naturally protected and isolated from its neighbors and the rest of the world. In the twentieth century it caught the interest and stimulated the imagination of peoples and countries far removed from the Asian landscape as a mysterious and exotic utopia, the embodiment of the Shangri-La described in Hilton's book *Lost Horizon*. Many cultures have myths or stories that hold up the possibility of a society, or a heaven, where all kinds of human aspirations, impossible to realize at home, are actually possible. These are romantic concepts—impractical but not altogether impossible. Tibetan culture and the former Tibetan political state actually pursued with some discipline and accomplishment things that most of the Western world considers impossible. They also did so in ways that many in the West and the East would consider reprehensible.

The government of the People's Republic of China teaches its citizens that Tibet before the central government's military intervention in the 1950s was a feudal society that enslaved its people and needed to be liberated. That assertion is rejected as propaganda by most of the West, as well as by much of Asia, but some of it is true. Tibet was a feudal state. The population was stratified, and portions of the population did in fact have the status of slaves. Unlike the feudal cultures of Europe and Asia that many of us are familiar with, however, Tibet's structure was directed not just at human survival, but at something more akin to human evolution. The Tibetan state was organized with one purpose: to make it possible for a small group of people to practice a specific spiritual discipline based on esoteric Buddhist and Taoist teachings.

What most of the world knows as Buddhism today originated on the Indian subcontinent in the sixth century BC from the experience and teaching of Siddhartha Gautama, better known as Shakyamuni Buddha or the Buddha of the current age. In the ensuing centuries it spread through most of the rest of Asia. It is practiced by laypeople in the course of their daily lives and also by monks, who in varying degrees isolate themselves from the demands and temptations of daily life to concentrate on certain specific aspects of the Buddhist teachings. Buddhism first reached Tibet in the seventh century AD and grew rapidly in importance. The setting and isolation of the Tibetan plateau permitted the development of a political state that was in effect a large monastery sustained by a population whose place was carefully defined and controlled. In this setting Tibetan Buddhism also developed its own characteristics, influenced by mystics like Padmasambhava and Taoist physical disciplines that were first developed and practiced in China, then made their way into Tibet via India.

Over the centuries, Tibetans experimented and developed their practices in relative isolation. The esoteric Buddhism developed in Tibet is different from most of the Buddhism practiced in China, India, and Southeast Asia. Many of the practices focus on transforming the body to enable the practitioner to more quickly attain spiritual enlightenment. The most powerful of these are the tantric sexual practices. They are also the most dangerous for the serious cultivator. My understanding is that these practices were not taught by Shakyamuni Buddha, because they carry with them the danger of becoming more attached to the world of desire rather than becoming free of it.[5]

A few hardy and determined foreigners made their way into Tibet to learn from individual teachers or schools, and some of them returned to their own cultures to teach in turn. The Mongolians developed a particular affinity for Tibetan "lamaism" and maintained relatively close ties. But for most, Tibet was far away and hard to reach. European cultures were largely unaware of its existence. Elements of the Chinese and Indian cultures and states were aware of and sometimes quite familiar with Tibet. Neither was particularly interested in what Tibetan culture might offer. Both China and India hosted extensive populations engaged in the teaching and practice of Buddhism and Taoism, and Tibet was viewed by many Chinese in earlier dynasties as a barbarian region.

However, China did recognize Tibet as a threat or potential threat. During the Tang Dynasty, Tibet was aggressively expansionist. For more than a hundred years its forces encroached on Tang borders and fought with the Tang armies. In the middle of the eighth century they actually invaded and occupied the Tang capital of Changan (Xian) for a few weeks. Although after the eighth century Tibet itself was no longer a real threat to the Chinese empire, the shock of that eighth-century occupation kept the Chinese state sensitive to the potential for danger from that area for the next thousand years. Specifically, it was seen as a potential base for other powers that threatened the empire—most notably various Central Asian tribes in the seventeenth and eighteenth centuries and the British in the nineteenth and twentieth centuries. In the late twentieth century the potential danger appeared to come from India and the United States.

For the most part, at least before the Yuan Dynasty, the Chinese empire viewed Tibet as it viewed most of the other countries, tribes, or groupings on and around its borders—as a *gongguo* (貢國 tributary state), one that paid regular tribute to the emperor as symbolic recognition of the emperor's superior position).[6] These states were considered separate and independent (culturally, racially, or whatever) and free to govern themselves as they wished—as long as they did not threaten or interfere with China and its interests. The groups were expected to recognize China's central position of dominance, but for the most part they were left to their own devices. There were two ways in which they could change the relationship—and diminish that independence. Tibet did both.

One way was to become a direct threat to the empire, in which case the emperor would punish them and take whatever other action was deemed necessary to prevent the threat from recurring. As mentioned above, Tibet was periodically a threat to the Tang; it later also threatened the Mongols, who first conquered it and then incorporated it into the Yuan Dynasty. The second way was to appeal directly to the emperor for assistance in one form or another. During the Tang Dynasty Tibet appealed to China to share the core of its civilization, the Chinese writing system. That appeal was rejected by Emperor Taizong, whose prime minister advised that sharing such knowledge with a barbarian population might be dangerous for China. Taizong did eventually send one of his nieces, the Chinese princess Wencheng (文成公主), to marry the Tibetan king Songtsen Gampo, and many believe that she made a important contribution to the transmission of Buddhism to Tibet. Later, during the Qing Dynasty, Tibet appealed to China for intervention in its own civil wars.

The use of military force to assert control over Tibet by the People's Republic of China in the 1950s was widely condemned by the international community. Many people at that time saw that action as the invasion of a sovereign nation. However, by that time most governments had already accepted China's claim to sovereignty over Tibet. Although Tibet did exercise what many have called "de facto independence" during the period 1912 to 1949 when China was torn by warlordism, the war with Japan, and civil war, China maintained its claim to sovereignty and most nations continued to accept that claim. When the United Nations was created in 1945, Tibet was not a member.

***

In spite of the formal positions taken by national governments accepting China's sovereignty over Tibet, many westerners continue to reject China's claim and to believe that Tibet has a right to be an independent state. Given the political chaos that reigned on the Asian continent for most of the twentieth century, the assertion by Chinese, both in the People's Republic and on Taiwan, that Tibet is historically and currently an integral part of China makes little sense to many westerners. I have to admit that it seemed very contrived to me, and I said so in quite a few discussions with Chinese friends and officials in Taiwan, Hong Kong, and Beijing. In that regard, I was perhaps less diplomatic or politically correct than some of my colleagues who more carefully (and correctly) toed the line that the United States recognized Tibet as a "part of China." I also exposed myself to an effective rejoinder. The view, particularly as expressed by many Americans, that China has illegally invaded, occupied, and suppressed an independent nation seems absurd to many Chinese who look at the conquest of North America by Europeans as a very recent occurrence—two hundred to six hundred years ago at the most. China's documented relationship with Tibet goes back more than a thousand years. Compared to the virtual eradication of Native American peoples and cultures by the Europeans, many Chinese consider China's relationship with Tibetans and Tibetan culture to be a model of respect and restraint.

I could understand the point about the treatment of Native Americans, but it took me longer to see the other perspective, and I didn't do so by myself. Rather, it was a series of conversations over several years with Professor Nan Huai-Chin about Chinese culture and history in general, with occasional digressions to Tibet, which helped me see this part of the human condition more through the lens of Chinese experience. In other words, I had to get off the horse, get closer to the flowers, and see them as the gardener of that area saw them.

During the Tang Dynasty, Tibet was at the height of its expansionist power and at times presented a serious threat to the Chinese empire. The Tibetan threat diminished toward the end of the Tang Dynasty and through the Song Dynasty as the Tibetan political structure fractured, and China viewed and treated Tibet as a tributary state. In the thirteenth century, however, Tibet was incorporated into the Mongol-dominated Yuan Dynasty. It was no longer a tributary state but part of the Chinese empire. The Chinese maintain that status continued through the Ming and Qing dynasties and the

Republican period, and that therefore Tibet has been an integral part of China for more than seven hundred years. Many non-Chinese scholars argue that even though the Ming continued the political structures designed to manage Tibet, it was unable to assert real authority there, and, therefore, at best China maintained sporadic suzerainty.

However, the subsequent Qing Dynasty does appear to have been more successful. In the early to mid-seventeenth century, as the Manchu forces led by Huang Taiji (first emperor of the Qing) were moving on the crumbling Ming Dynasty, Tibet was also going through significant changes. The fifth Dalai Lama, then leader of the Gelugpa sect, was seeking to wrest power from other religious sects and the Tsangpa kings. He sought help both from the Qing and from one of the Mongol khans. Gusri Khan responded by invading Tibet, deposing the king, and installing himself as secular leader and the fifth Dalai Lama as spiritual leader. During Gusri Khan's reign, the fifth Dalai Lama traveled to Beijing and met with Emperor Shunzhi, Huang Taiji's successor. The Chinese position is that during that visit, Emperor Shunzhi and the fifth Dalai Lama essentially reestablished the patron-priest relationship that existed between Tibet and the Yuan Dynasty emperors, in which the emperor recognized the Dalai Lama as spiritual leader, and the Dalai Lama in turn accepted the sovereignty of emperor in Beijing. Whatever formal agreement was or wasn't made, neither player considered the other a threat. After Gusri Khan's death, the fifth Dalai Lama moved to assume the king's secular powers, but he was careful not to disturb his relationship with the Qing. In particular, he exercised a restraining influence on the Dzungar Mongols, who at the time were the Qing's most serious enemy.

That balance was acceptable to the Qing, but when the fifth Dalai Lama died, Sangye Gyatso, who ruled Tibet as Regent while the sixth Dalai Lama was growing to maturity, was not so careful. His efforts to build a stronger relationship with the Dzungar Mongols were perceived as a major threat to the Qing and led Emperor Kangxi to intervene, at first indirectly to depose the regent and later directly to repel invading Dzungars and to install the recently recognized seventh Dalai Lama.[7] This reestablished the practice of more active intervention in Tibetan affairs, and Qing troops were then stationed in Lhasa. They were removed once by Kangxi's successor Yongzheng, but quickly returned as civil war broke out and both sides appealed to Yongzheng for intervention. The emperor then invited (summoned) the seventh Dalai Lama to Beijing, where a number of changes were made. Permanent imperial representatives were established in Lhasa, and the Panchen Lama was given sovereignty over Tashilumpo, setting up an alternative to the Dalai. Finally, the seventh Dalai Lama swore fealty to the emperor, and the emperor recognized him as his spiritual advisor. This set the tone of the relationship for the future. Under Emperor Qianlong the administrative machinery became more formalized, and though the Qing weakened in the nineteenth century, the basic relationship remained the same. By that time, China's biggest external worry was the British Empire, which had humiliated it in the Opium Wars and was expanding northward from the Indian subcontinent. The British invaded Tibet in 1904, sending the thirteenth Dalai Lama fleeing, first to Mongolia and later to Beijing. The Qing sent its armies into Tibet one last time in 1908 to help repel the British, before collapsing itself in 1911.

Many in the West do not accept that this history establishes historical Chinese sovereignty over Tibet. By Chinese standards, including particularly the relationship established between the seventh Dalai Lama and the emperor Yongzheng, it is determinative.

***

If one adds to that historical perspective the strategic imperative of the latter part of the twentieth century, it becomes very difficult to envisage anything other than the assertion of complete Chinese authority over Tibet.

After Mao Zedong won the civil war, established the People's Republic of China, and forced the government of the Republic of China to flee to Taiwan, the Chinese mainland was more secure than it had been for many years. However, the strategic danger in Tibet must have appeared to be increasing. The Chinese (in both the PRC and ROC governments) considered that throughout the Yuan, Ming, and Qing dynasties, Tibet's position as part of China was clear. There were disputes and conflicts, but the Tibetan government did not assert independence. However, in 1950, the Chinese government in Beijing at least believed that elements in the Dalai Lama's circle were not advocating just a hard negotiating line, but separation. Those elements were appealing to outside forces for help, and the international community was becoming more hostile toward the PRC.

The new PRC regime devoted some effort to negotiating with the Dalai Lama's government in the spring and summer of 1950, seeking agreement and cooperation to control any strategic threat. However, once conflict with the United States in Korea became a reality, the regime probably concluded it could wait no longer to secure its back door, and it dispatched its military forces to the Tibetan plateau. Later, reports of CIA support to Tibetan resistance fighters probably confirmed for the PRC the wisdom of that choice and increased the pressure for more active intervention in Tibet's internal autonomy.

The global advance of the Western nation-state system in the nineteenth and twentieth centuries has probably also enhanced the starkness of China's strategic choice. Until the early 1900s, China was truly the Middle Kingdom in Asia. It dominated the region culturally, economically, politically, and militarily. It defined the relations between states, and the states on its borders accepted certain obligations to the emperor that China was ready and able to enforce. The impact of British expansion in the nineteenth century, the advance of Japan, and the weakening and eventual collapse of the Qing Dynasty in the twentieth century all made that system of relationships dysfunctional, though it continued to exist in the philosophy and approach of successive Chinese governments. The PRC might have been willing to continue the more loosely defined suzerain relationship China had had at times with Tibet in the past. However, the United Nations Charter, the new emphasis on self-determination of peoples, and even the post–World War II decolonization movement made that more difficult. China could not accept anything less than complete strategic control of the Tibetan plateau, and the only way to ensure that was to continue to insist that Tibet was an integral part of China. There could be no in-between.

Sadly, the advent of the Cultural Revolution—which devastated all of China—wreaked incredible damage on Tibet[8] and made much more difficult any restoration of social and cultural autonomy for the Tibetan people there. In spite of constitutional protections for religion, significant Chinese government investment in Tibetan cultural sites, and political support for religious figures such as the Panchen Lama, the Tibetan people have continued to suffer culturally, psychologically, and sometimes physically from their growing assimilation into the Chinese nation.

Ironically, the escalation of direct Chinese intervention in Tibetan affairs also did something that the communist regime could not possibly have intended. It spread Tibetan religion, philosophy, and culture to the four corners of the world. Like a pretty yellow dandelion it had grown for centuries alone and untouchable. Only when part of it died was it able to spread. Today the whole world is familiar with, and enchanted by, Tibetan culture. There are monasteries and Tibetan communities popping up all over the United States and in Europe. The Dalai Lama has become an internationally admired cultural and religious figure who shares his heritage not just with a small elite group of Tibetan monks and nobles, but with the whole world. The politicization of Tibetan culture and religion has also spread. A clear "separation of church and state" might help, but politics and religion have been intertwined in Tibet for centuries. It is very difficult for most people to distinguish where one leaves off and the other begins.

***

Most of my work on Tibetan issues was actually done in Tibet rather than from the consulate in Chengdu. There were some officials in Chengdu with various kinds of responsibilities relating to Tibet, but there was not much incentive for them to be too forthcoming with official Americans. There were Tibetans who lived and worked in Chengdu, and Tibetans who regularly traveled to and through Chengdu. Some of them were interested in talking with American diplomats. However, we were all watched closely, and too much of that kind of contact could put those individuals in a difficult situation with the local or national authorities.

On my visits to Tibet as the accredited U.S. representative to the area, my host was the Foreign Affairs Office of the Tibet Autonomous Region (TAR). In contrast to my experience in Chengdu, I found the director of that office to be very helpful. Perhaps this was because he, too, was a professional diplomat. He had been stationed overseas in China's diplomatic service, and he understood both my situation and the opportunities that working cooperatively might offer. We were able to have frank discussions about the situation in Tibet and how it related to relations between the United States and China. Naturally, we disagreed often, but I think we were both able to impact the other's perspective. He did his best to provide me access to officials in Lhasa, including several meetings with the governor of the TAR, as well as permission to visit locations outside of Lhasa. Those were not easy tasks during that period of time.

I would visit monasteries or temples and try to talk with both senior and junior monks. Sometimes I had more luck than others. I didn't speak Tibetan, so my access was limited to those who could speak Chinese—both of us speaking a foreign tongue to try to understand or be understood. I don't remember speaking with any monks who were happy with the Chinese presence, though some were less hostile than others. The younger monks just didn't want the Chinese around. They were more emotional and more overtly nationalistic. The older monks were more concerned with the deterioration of their religious practices. Some explained that the decline was not the direct result of suppression, because the Chinese government in principle allowed the practice of religion. Rather, it was because the best teachers had left Tibet or were dying off. The younger monks suffered from lack of instruction and guidance. Experienced and wise teachers are essential. They help the aspirants over the many obstacles along the cultivation path, and they protect them from being sidelined by temptations, misunderstandings, fears, and so on.

One thing the Foreign Affairs director was not able to arrange was a meeting for me with the man who was the Communist Party secretary of the TAR. That man was Hu Jintao, who is now the national party secretary and leader of the People's Republic of China. I asked every time I visited Tibet, but he was never available. I think the director of the Foreign Affairs Office did try, but it probably was never in the cards. I did not begrudge the party secretary that. For a man in his shoes at that time, there was probably little to be gained by meeting with the American consul general or even with the

American ambassador, and potentially much to lose. His tenure in Tibet covered a potentially dangerous time, coming on the heels of Tiananmen, but Tibet remained relatively quiet. I'm sure that the party secretary deserved a great deal of credit for that, and I assume that it contributed to his subsequent rapid rise to the pinnacle of Chinese power.

The United States has paid a lot of attention to Tibet. That has been a source of irritation for the Chinese government. It has also been a source of hope for the Tibetan people—but it has not always helped them. Popular demonstrations in the United States and statements by public figures (government or otherwise) get back to the Chinese government and to the people of Tibet pretty quickly. The U.S. Embassy in Beijing and the U.S. Consulate in Chengdu make diplomatic demarches regularly requesting information about Tibetan prisoners or commenting on various aspects of human rights in Tibet. Every time that I made an official trip to Tibet, I would take a list of names that we had from Washington, Amnesty International, or other sources of Tibetans who had been arrested or disappeared. I would usually be told that this was an internal affair of China, and it was none of our business. I, in turn, would recognize that China had a different opinion on the propriety of U.S. government interest, but I would explain this was important to Americans in general, and the responsiveness of the Chinese government or lack thereof would have an impact on the development of bilateral relations that were important to both sides. Sometimes I was given specific information on individuals that helped reassure those concerned about their welfare. On one occasion I was able to accompany the American ambassador on a visit to the main prison in Lhasa to look at the conditions and to meet with some of the prisoners. What we saw was spartan but adequate, and the prisoners we saw were in good health.

I think the official U.S. approach to human rights in Tibet has been appropriate, and it has had some positive impact. The public expressions of concern in the United States, while natural to the American political system, have perhaps been less so. In an ironic kind of way, they may have actually hurt the people they were trying to help. Over the two and a half years that I was in Chengdu, I saw a pattern in this relationship. Demonstrations or statements would occur in the United States. The news would filter back to Tibet. People would get excited and feel encouraged that they were being supported, and they would take to the streets in their own demonstrations. If they got out of hand, the government would crack down. More people would be arrested, hurt, or sometimes killed.

We cannot ask people in the United States not to exercise their First Amendment rights, particularly if they are strongly felt. We should be proud of the concern and compassion Americans feel for those far away from our own land. However, we do need to try to understand, and to help each other understand, how our best intentions can sometimes make the plight of those people worse than it would normally be. I did not know how to do that when I was in Chengdu. I still don't.

YUNNAN (雲 南)

Yunnan means "south of the clouds." It lies just south of the perpetual haze that covers the Sichuan basin, and it forms the southwest corner of mainland China. Bordering on Burma, Laos, Cambodia, and Vietnam, it is also a kind of back door to China. During World War II, the "Burma Road" that ran from Mandalay to Kunming was a major supply route for the Chinese government in Chongqing (Chungking), holding out against the Japanese army. My uncle, Jack Huyler, had been stationed with U.S. forces in Kunming during that period, and was, I believe, the first in our large extended family to learn the Chinese language.

The Mekong River runs through Yunnan on its way from the Tibetan plateau to Southeast Asia. The province is predominantly high plateau and the altitude (6,200 feet) compensates beautifully for its more southern latitude. The capital city of Kunming is called the city of eternal spring because the temperatures average 50–70°F. Summers are cool and winters are mild. From Yunnan the land slopes downward west into Burma and south into Laos and Vietnam. Thailand is just a few miles across Laos from the Yunnan region of Xishuangbanna, and when we first visited there was talk of organizing a road rally from Xishuangbanna to Chiang Mai.

Yunnan's climate gives it a decidedly different appearance from many other Chinese provinces. Its proximity to these other nations and its large minority populations give it a decidedly different character. There is a wide variety of non-Han minority peoples.

Yunnan's political climate was also different. Its long borders with Southeast Asian nations both enhanced its influence beyond China and caused it to be influenced. It did not have the luxury of ignoring the outside world, and many of its officials were able to see the challenges of those borders as opportunities.

***

One of the foreign policy issues that the United States was most concerned with in the early 1990s was narcotics. The Golden Triangle, which produced a significant amount of the world's heroin, spreads across the borders of Burma, Thailand, China, Laos, and Vietnam. Some of that heroin went out from Burma and Thailand; and some of it moved across the Chinese border into Yunnan and then down to Hong Kong, from where it could be smuggled to all corners of the world. The U.S. Drug Enforcement Agency (DEA) had an office at the U.S. Consulate General in Hong Kong and was very interested in getting into China. However, at that time the Chinese government was holding them at arm's length. There were regular visits by DEA officials to Beijing to talk with their Public Security Bureau (PSB) counterparts, but it was harder to get out into the rest of the country.

On my first trip to Kunming, when I met with the province's Foreign Affairs Office, I told the director that I was interested in visiting the Burmese border region—because I had just come from Burma—and that I would like to promote cooperation between DEA and Yunnan narcotics agencies. The director was an extraordinary man, who was interested not only in taking care of his foreign charges but also in promoting any contacts that might be beneficial to the development of Yunnan Province.

He arranged for me and one of the DEA representatives in Hong Kong first to visit Kunming and then to travel to the Yunnan-Burma border. We visited the town of Ruili and went to the customs area where trucks were inspected coming in and going out of China. We visited a drug treatment center and talked with both staff and patients. It was particularly poignant for me, because I had been unable to visit the border from the Burmese side. Now I was on the Chinese side, watching the Burmese move back and forth and make their deals with the Chinese merchants. On that first trip, by coincidence, I actually encountered a Burmese whom I had met previously in Mandalay. It was quite a surprise for both of us. I did not know that he was traveling to China, and he was not expecting to see any Americans in that area, much less me.

There were no other westerners there. We were the first official Americans to visit the area since 1949, and unofficial Americans in that region were very rare also. This was a trailblazing event. A year later, we were able to arrange a similar trip for the assistant secretary of state responsible for international narcotics policy, and that time we also visited several other villages along the border and talked with people about the fallout of the narcotics trade. The Chinese government was very strict about narcotics abuse. When Mao Zedong won the civil war back in 1949, the narcotics trade and opium addiction were extensive and serious problems. The Nationalist government had been either unable or unwilling to conquer it. The communist government, shortly after taking over, made trade or use of narcotics an offense punishable by death. Enforcement was brutal—thousands were executed—and it was successful. China's narcotics problem was negligible until China began to open again in the late 1970s. By the 1990s, China had become a transit route for narcotics from the Golden Triangle, and the social impact was worrying officials in southwest China and Beijing. We hoped by expanding contacts between DEA and Chinese authorities that we could also increase information sharing and the efficacy of enforcement.

Just before I left China in 1992, I made a farewell trip to Yunnan, and the same DEA agent who accompanied me on that first trip came along. The director of the Public Security Bureau, who, with the director of the Foreign Affairs Office, had made the border trips possible, invited us to lunch. Toward the end of the meal, he leaned across the table and told us that just three years earlier, he could never have imagined he would even meet an American official, much less share a meal as we were doing that day. He thanked us for our efforts and toasted a future of cooperative effort. Looking back on it now, I realize that during my introductory two years in Beijing, the idea that I would be on such friendly terms with a provincial public security official would have seemed equally unlikely. We had all come a long way in a short time.

Part of it was the inexorable changes that were taking place in China with the blessing of the senior leadership in Beijing. However, part of it was also the willingness of individual officials to take initiatives that required foresight and courage. The Foreign Affairs director in Yunnan arranged our unprecedented visit to the Burma border and later took us down to the Xishuangbanna region next to Laos. He also opened doors for us to many senior officials. I was able to call on the governor of the province, and even the party secretary. The latter was unusual. I only met one other senior party secretary. That was the party secretary for the city of Chongqing. Those for Sichuan, Tibet, and Guizhou were not available.

***

Yunnan also treated me to another perspective-altering experience. Many of us who went to China in the 1980s when it was just beginning to open its doors were endlessly frustrated by the constant supervision we received and the restrictions on movement and association imposed upon us. We saw them as designed to control us and protect China and the Chinese from any insidious influence that we might carry with us. I, for one, did not understand—or chose not to understand—that there was another side to this attention. That was that officials—of many different ranks and responsibilities—were charged with the responsibility of ensuring that no harm befell us, from any quarter.

On one of my trips to Yunnan, I decided to take the train back from Kunming to Chengdu. It was a long, overnight journey, but the scenery was supposed to be quite spectacular. My hosts in Kunming had escorted me to the train station. They introduced me to the conductor of the "soft class"[9] train car, who then showed me to my compartment. It looked like I had the entire six-seat compartment to myself, but shortly after we left the station three military personnel joined me. They were very pleasant, but their accents made it a little difficult for me to talk with them. I was tired from my trip and just wanted to rest anyway. However, they began smoking, and when the compartment filled up with smoke, I left for cleaner air. After trying several times to go back in and get used to it, I finally gave up and found a fold-down seat in the hallway next to the restroom. It was uncomfortable and a little cold, but at least I could breathe. At one point my companions came out and tried to get me to go back inside, where they said it was much more comfortable. I said I really preferred the view and the cold air—and stayed there until long after the sun went down. I returned to the compartment when the conductor came around and pulled down the beds. We all got ready for bed and turned out the lights. When one of my companions started to smoke again, I begged him to wait until morning, and we finally got to sleep.

The next morning when I went to the dining car for breakfast, the conductor sat down at my table and engaged me in conversation, asking how the trip was and how I liked the train. He was very personable and soon shared with me that when I got on the train he had been quite worried. He had never had a foreign official in his car before, and the officials who had escorted me to the train had admonished him to take extra good care of me. He did not know how to do this. What if something bad happened to me on his watch? Fortunately, he had then found these three senior military officers in the "hard class" car who were willing to come and sit with me. After that he was reassured that I would be safe! I nodded and thanked him, as sincerely as I could, for going to so much trouble on my behalf. I was relieved to be breathing fresh air *and* sitting on a comfortable seat, and he was obviously even more relieved that I had escaped harm from whatever dangers were lurking on his train. We had a very pleasant breakfast, and after that I never saw my "handlers" in quite the same light again.

***

While we were in Chengdu, during the last decade of the twentieth century, an event took place that had nothing to do with China directly, but which in my belief had a profound impact on future U.S.-China relations. Saddam Hussein invaded Kuwait, and the United States made a fateful decision to intervene and restore the status quo with the first Gulf War.

Our reasons for taking this action were defensible. One nation had, without provocation, invaded and conquered another, contrary to accepted rules of international behavior. That invasion also threatened U.S. strategic interests, because the United States was so heavily dependent on Middle Eastern oil. The United States was careful to seek international approval for this action in the United Nations. Then, when Saddam was evicted from Kuwait, and the country's original government reinstated, the United States returned its forces—most of them—to the United States. The reaction from most of the world was favorable.

The impact in China was mixed. The display of force and technical brilliance was vividly displayed by the American broadcasting company CNN. Technically, CNN was restricted to major hotels and other selected institutions. In reality, it was accessible to many Chinese. It was certainly available to the government and the military. We in the consulate were awed by the display and proud of our nation's accomplishments. Many of our Chinese friends and associates were impressed and complimentary. However, even our friends were somewhat ambivalent. They saw that the United States had capabilities and powers beyond what they had imagined. Even more significantly, it was willing to use those powers far beyond its borders with very little advance notice. Some people saw this as a good thing. Others saw it as a warning and concluded that China must prepare to meet a potential U.S. threat in the future.

As in virtually every nation, in China there are differences of opinions about policy among different factions in government and society. "China watchers" in various agencies of the U.S. government often focus on the give-and-take between these factions—who is up, who is down—to predict China's future courses of action. The display of American might thousands of miles from American borders on behalf of a tiny nation against another nation (with which the United States had had close relations only a few years earlier) had to strengthen the voices within China's ruling elites inclined to position China toward a hostile rather than a benign or friendly America. This impact could only have been reinforced by the U.S. bombing of Serbia in 1999 and the resultant destruction of the Chinese Embassy there, as well as later by the massive U.S. invasions of Iraq and Afghanistan in the early twenty-first century.

China's extraordinary military buildup has its roots in Deng Xiaoping's political and economic decisions of the 1970s. However, a perception within China's elite leadership and within its population that the United States is a growing threat to China would make it more difficult to argue caution with that buildup and to constrain the influence of the military.

Today, twenty years later, we are seeing signs of a military not only more overtly hostile to the United States but also speaking out internationally with a tone noticeably more strident than the civilian authorities. Did policies we espoused and actions we took—which our leadership believed had little to do with China—influence or accelerate this phenomenon?

Shortly after the first Gulf War, when the U.S. presidential election campaign of 1992 was under way, a very wise Chinese observer, who has advised the highest levels of the Chinese government, told me that the next U.S. president should reduce the American presence overseas and turn its attention inward rather than outward. I argued the opposite: that the United States as the world's only remaining superpower had a responsibility to play a prominent role on the international stage. His point, though, was that with all of the changes then taking place, America needed to regroup, get its own house in order, and stabilize its own identity before extending its attention beyond its borders. Interestingly, he had a similar concern about China—that the country's phenomenal economic progress was setting China on a trajectory for which it was politically and socially unprepared, and that it needed to keep the brakes on long enough to reestablish its culturally rooted identity in order to lessen the destabilizing impact of its forward momentum.

He seems to have been right. Almost twenty years later the United States became bogged down in two wars in the Middle East that seriously depleted its treasury and weakened rather than strengthened American influence in the region. The full impact of those adventures on American society may not become fully apparent for years to come. However, the U.S. political system is perhaps more divided and antagonistic than at any time since the Civil War. We are having extreme difficulty dealing effectively with the destabilizing impact of a severe financial crisis as well as natural and man-made disasters, and our population is becoming increasingly xenophobic in the face of very unpredictable terrorism and very predictable immigration. Could these problems of the twenty-first century's first decade have been prevented or diminished if we had paid more attention to putting our house in order in the twentieth century's last decade?

NOTES

1. Shu (蜀) is the ancient name for Sichuan.

2. Technically, Sichuan is now the third largest, because in 1997 Chongqing was made an independent provincial-level municipality and took about thirty million people with it. However, when we were there Chongqing was still a part of Sichuan, and the province's population stood at about 110 million people. That would have made it about the world's eleventh largest country, very close in size to Japan.

3. The female ruler of China better known to the West, the Qing Dynasty Empress Dowager Cixi, was never the sovereign in her own right, but ruled in the name of two successive sons.

4. It should be noted that while relations between the two countries were friendly, relations between Stilwell and Chiang were notoriously stressful.

5. The different emphasis of the two approaches has been described as follows: Taoism considers that without the body, the Tao cannot be attained; Buddhism warns that with the body, truth can never be realized.

6. Sometimes, if the bordering states became particularly strong, the tributary relationship might be reversed, with China paying the tribute.

7. The interregnum between the fifth and seventh Dalai Lamas, and the short reign of the sixth Dalai Lama is another story altogether, which some believe challenges the legitimacy of all the subsequent Dalai Lamas. It is complicated, and there is not room here to give it the attention it deserves.

8. The Chinese argue that in fact most of the damage to temples and Tibetan culture was actually inflicted by Tibetans.

9. First class—the only class that official foreigners were allowed to travel in at the time.

Chapter Eight

Old War: Tuzla (September 2002–June 2003)

In the mid 1990s the United States, led by Assistant Secretary of State for European Affairs Richard C. Holbrooke, managed to bring all of the warring parties of the former Yugoslavia, as well as many of the concerned (and meddling) spectators, to the negotiating table. In Dayton, Ohio, the parties signed a General Framework Agreement for Peace, which ended the conflict and provided for an international effort to stabilize the area over time. In the end, success was sealed by the commitment of tens of thousands of NATO forces, heavily American, to ensure that the negotiated peace was honored by all parties.

I had been peripherally involved in the effort that led to the Dayton Accords as office director for southern European affairs in the mid-1990s, helping to resolve a festering dispute between Greece and the Former Yugoslav Republic of Macedonia, just to the south. However, when Holbrooke asked me to move into the position of deputy assistant secretary, replacing Ambassador Robert Frasure, who had been killed on the last of his many missions to Bosnia, he reorganized the portfolio and gave Bosnia to someone else. I traveled with Holbrooke in the region, but when he went into Bosnia, I would peel off and head for other destinations. For me, therefore, it was more than a little ironic to be assigned to Bosnia five years later as a foreign policy advisor to the American peacekeeping forces there.

***

The role of the political advisor—or POLAD in political-military lingo—was different from anything I had done before in the Foreign Service. Normally, a

Foreign Service officer assigned overseas concentrates first and foremost on the local environment and population. FSOs are charged with getting to know their environment and as much as possible becoming a part of that environment. We learn the language, live on the economy, and work with host government officials, politicians, and businesspeople. We take our instructions from, report what we learn to, and make policy recommendations to the Department of State.

The POLAD, on the other hand, is assigned to the senior American military commander for the area or function concerned. In my case, I was to work for the American general leading a multinational NATO force in the northeastern section of Bosnia. The POLAD's first responsibility is to serve the military commander. He or she advises the commander on all foreign policy aspects of the commander's mission and serves as a liaison between the commander, the Department of State, U.S. diplomatic missions, and local authorities. As POLAD, therefore, my first job was to get to know the personalities, the culture, and the needs of the U.S. military. My contacts with local officials and the local environment were supportive of that first responsibility.

In addition, as POLAD, I did not live on the local economy but instead on "Eagle Base," a military installation and airfield built originally as part of Yugoslavia's defense establishment. It had been taken over by NATO and was being managed by the American military and its contractors. The base was several kilometers from the city of Tuzla, the largest city in the region and the seat of the Tuzla Canton. Eagle Base was populated primarily by American and European military personnel (mostly American). With the exception of Bosnians who worked in the mess halls or managed some of the concessions, it was pretty isolated from the rest of Bosnia.

***

For the first time in my life, I was to actually live and work on an American military base in a foreign country. The base phenomenon was not unfamiliar to me. In the 1950s, when we were living in Brussels, as a seven-year-old I visited an American military base in Germany for our family physical. While there my mother was diagnosed with cancer and immediately flown back to the United States for surgery—not a good memory. Later, living in Paris in the early 1960s, my mother would take me to the American base in Garches to shop at the commissary. That was a better memory—they had American ice cream. We visited friends at another base in Germany during that period, where I pulled my first all-nighter playing football in the street with other American teenagers. That was surreal. I knew we were in Germany. I had always been taught to respect and try to get to know the different cultures in which we lived. But my teenage companions knew almost nothing about Germany—and didn't want to. They were derisive about the people, the language, and the culture. Even later, when we were posted to Panama, I experienced the Panama Canal Zone, which was in essence a mega–military base acting like a mini-country. Many of its inhabitants also had very little interest in and very little to do with the host country. These places seemed like hermetically sealed capsules that offered very little cultural cross-fertilization.

In retrospect, there was of course cross-fertilization going on. Men and women will always find ways to overcome barriers—cultural or otherwise—placed between them. The bases also influence the economies around them through employment and commerce, and they influence social perceptions just by their presence.

It was all very different from the diplomatic presence, which has among its primary objectives getting to know and interacting with the host country's society and culture. Diplomats are concerned with influences—both intentional and unintentional. Soldiers are more concerned with getting a specific job done. Soldiers are often better in that category than are diplomats, but give less attention to the other ways in which their presence and activity might impact the host country and its people.

***

NATO's sixty thousand strong multinational Implementation Force (IFOR) was created in December 1995 and moved in across Bosnia's northern border in early 1996 with great fanfare and media attention. After one year it was cut in half and reestablished as the Stabilization Force (SFOR). NATO was charged with implementing the military part of the General Framework Agreement, which was essentially to provide a secure environment in which reforms could be enacted and provide the foundation for a long-term peace. The civilian effort promoting political and security reform was to be led by the Office of the High Representative with an international staff spread around the country.

The initial military forces were predominantly American. Contingents from other NATO members arrived later and eventually took up their duties in three different parts of the country. When I was there, the UK and the Netherlands had responsibility for the northwest of Bosnia and were stationed in the Republika Srpska[1] city of Banja Luka. The French, Germans, Italians, and Spanish had the southeastern section, centered on the city of Mostar (and also containing the coveted Adriatic coast with the city of Dubrovnik). The Americans had responsibility for central and northeastern Bosnia. This sector had about half of the Republika Srpska, and the town of

Srebrenica where the terrible massacre had taken place. America also had the command role at the NATO headquarters in Sarajevo. My unit was called Multinational Brigade—North, or MNB-N. (The military—and many government bureaucracies—tend to reduce most names to acronyms, which can sometimes make ordinary conversations almost incomprehensible to the uninitiated.)

Before I arrived, there had been ten changes of command at Eagle Base, near Tuzla. Each contingent would stay for six months only. The first ten units had been divisions, led by major generals (two-star). They had been mostly active duty. Only two of the first ten had been National Guard units. By the time I arrived, the decision had been made to reduce the size of the unit to a brigade and to rely primarily, if not solely, on National Guard units. Both units with which I served were Guard, from Pennsylvania's Twenty-Eighth Division and from Kansas's Thirty-Fifth Division. Most of the soldiers, both men and women, had very little overseas experience. Many had not been outside the United States at all. All of them seemed to be very enthusiastic about this particular adventure. These were, for the most part, not professional soldiers. They were businesspeople, doctors, lawyers, ministers, teachers, civil servants, laborers, and so on. They loved their part-time work with the National Guard, and they loved the idea that by doing it they were supporting their country. They were very excited about going to Bosnia and actually putting into practice their years of training.

***

I first met the officers of the Twenty-Eighth Division at a training session in Fort Leavenworth, Kansas. I really did not know what to expect. I had worked with plenty of colonels and lieutenant colonels assigned to Defense attaché offices at embassies overseas. I had worked with one-, two-, and three-star generals in Washington in and around the Pentagon. However, they had usually been on my turf—the foreign policy arena. Now, I was going to live and work with them on a military base. At Leavenworth, I watched as the leaders of the division were briefed on their exercise, as they practiced their roles and received feedback from the trainers. I was uncomfortable with the whole process. It seemed very artificial and shallow to me, and I really did not understand what kind of role I could usefully play in the exercise. However, I did at least get the chance to meet some of the individuals with whom I would be working. My first impression of them was good, and during the six months that I would spend with them in Bosnia that impression would be reinforced many times over.

We had our second meeting in Hohenfels, Germany, where the brigade was going through its final preparations for deployment to Bosnia. The brigade was spending several weeks at the U.S. Army's Combat Maneuver Training Center there, "pretending" it was in Bosnia. It operated with its regular schedule of intelligence briefings, patrols, and daily reviews. The "patrols" were able to drive around the extensive grounds of the base, practicing their security measures, and meeting with "Bosnian officials" located in small "towns" that had been set up to simulate different environments for different exercises. The physical plant was really quite impressive, and it must have cost a fortune to build and maintain. Each day the soldiers and their leadership would be challenged by situations and events created and orchestrated by the trainers. Some of them were not very realistic, but some of them were brilliant. There was one trainer in particular who had a stable of individuals, mostly real Bosnians, who would role-play different officials or personalities that the brigade might encounter. The trainer would give role-players their basic instructions for the meetings, and then he would attend the meetings as an observer. He would stand behind the soldiers facing the role-players and give them silent instructions on how to move the encounter, depending on how the soldiers were performing. It was very realistic and quite effective. On occasion, he would escalate the tensions, even making the problems virtually impossible to resolve, to drive home the lesson. During my first session in the fall of 2002, I watched him nail the brigade's commander, making him so angry that it took all of the commander's considerable self-discipline to keep from walking out. He didn't walk out but afterward declared that he would not subject himself again to such a "waste of time."

While that particular exercise was definitely not a waste of time, I sympathized with the commander. I personally found the whole process tedious and often shallow, in spite of the competent and interesting trainers. During my career, virtually all of my training was on the job. My Foreign Service colleagues and I would learn our environment in real time and with real people, absorbing the uniqueness of each place into our cognitive and decision-making background. Of course, most of us had come into the diplomatic service with education, experience, and even languages that gave us some preparation for those unfamiliar environments. At least in the beginning of our careers, our imperative was more to observe than to act, and, therefore, our ability to do harm was naturally constrained. The military, however, was different. It could arrive, in places like Bosnia, in large numbers, armed to the teeth, and capable of doing a lot of damage. With the exception of the Defense attachés assigned to embassies—trained and in small numbers—it had far less background, education, or language to direct or cushion its impact. So the training, as tedious as it was for me, was essential. If we could have afforded it, even more might have been helpful. As for that first commander, to give him credit, he showed himself to be significantly more sensitive and adept at dealing with his Bosnian counterparts than our training exercise had suggested.

My first meeting with the men and women of the Thirty-Fifth Division took place during my second visit to the training center at Hohenfels. That time, I was one of the briefers, having already spent six months in Bosnia and being a newly crafted "expert." The two units were quite different, reflecting in part their different geographic homes. The Twenty-Eighth Division was from the "old" colonial East. One of its units claimed to have participated in every one of America's major conflicts since the Revolutionary War. It was steeped in tradition and very proud. The Thirty-Fifth was created in 1917 for World War I and drew its people from the Midwest. It was open and flexible. Both performed very well.

***

Nevertheless, in a strange sort of way, both brigades focused more on themselves than on Bosnia. Part of the reason was just the need to keep so many soldiers—most of whom had no overseas experience—focused, busy, and out of trouble. They had their daily routines that kept them busy during the day. Their mealtimes were set. There were limited entertainment opportunities on the base, and they were not permitted off the base except for official duties. No alcohol was permitted, under "General Rule #1," except for one or two beers on special occasions. This particular rule only applied to Americans. The other NATO and non-NATO participating countries were not so restrictive. For the most part, all American soldiers were confined to the base, and recreational fraternization off-base with Bosnians was not permitted. Local authorities repeatedly appealed to the base commanders to allow the soldiers to come into the towns to socialize. There was a strong economic interest on the part of local businesses, but many of them also wanted to get to know better those who had brought peace to the area. Again, the other peacekeeping nations were more flexible in this regard than the Americans.

Patrols went out every day. At the time SFOR 12 and 13 were there, the importance of just showing the military presence to keep the peace was less important, though reminders to some elements of the local society were still useful. Part of the job of the patrols was to talk with local officials and others and bring back information about current issues. The patrols dutifully made their reports at the daily meetings, but they rarely seemed to bring back significant insights about what was going on. Full battle gear does not seem to be conducive to candid or thoughtful conversation.

Sometimes the biggest difficulty the patrols faced was getting back onto their own base. The security was extraordinary. All vehicles were checked and rechecked for bombs before being allowed back on the base. Sometimes the process could take twenty minutes or more. On base, all soldiers were required to carry their weapons and ammunition, though the weapons were not supposed to be loaded. Each time an individual entered a building—like the mess hall—he or she had to fire the weapon into a can of sand to make absolutely sure there was no live ammunition in the chamber. The requirement to carry weapons at all times seemed to make almost no sense in Bosnia in 2002, but it was probably a good service discipline for the deployed forces.

Each day would begin with an intelligence briefing of information picked up by patrols and coming in from other sources. The intelligence people worked hard and did a pretty good job with what they had. A few of them were very impressive, not just hard-working and smart but intuitive as well. None were what I would call experts on Bosnia or the region, not even the contract people, though some had been in and around the region for several years. However, most of them knew more about Bosnia than I did, at least when I arrived. I was embarrassed by my lack of expertise in the region, and it took me some time to find how I could actually help them. In the beginning, I would question how they got their information, warn them about drawing significant conclusions from sketchy information or questionable sources, and encourage them to expand and deepen their sources. As time went on, and I got out and met more local officials, I was able to add insights into personal and community relations and motivations.

***

On Eagle Base we also had a small brigade of soldiers from Finland. They were devoted exclusively to Civil-Military Cooperation (CIMIC). This meant that their primary responsibility was to establish and maintain relations with national and local authorities, the civilian population, and international and nongovernmental organizations in the area. They spent more of their time off the base working and talking with the local population. On Eagle Base they had their own mini-base, and access to it was restricted for most of the American military population because of the availability of alcohol. One of the other things they had on their mini-base was a sauna to which they would occasionally invite us. They definitely knew how to make the most of their overseas posting.

The other significant congregation of non-American troops in MNB-N was the Russian brigade. This was a historically significant presence, as it was the first instance of Russian troops serving together with NATO and actually under the command of an American general. The Russian brigade, known as RUSBDE, arrived in Bosnia in 1996 as part of IFOR and remained until 2006, leaving just before my own tour of duty in Bosnia ended. They were assigned to MNB-N, reporting to the American general in charge, but they were not put on Eagle Base. Instead, they had their own small base, named Camp Ugljevik (nicknamed "Camp Ugly" by the Americans) located in the ethnic Serbian part of the area. By the time I arrived in Bosnia their numbers had dropped to 350 soldiers. Their responsibilities were similar to the other peacekeeping forces. They went out on patrols and worked with local officials. They had an advantage over most of the NATO forces in that Russian is a Slavic language and quite similar to Serbo-Croatian, so communication was nominally easier for them. Having a related language, a common religion (Eastern Orthodoxy), and a historically common enemy in the Muslim Ottoman Empire resulted in a certain mutual sympathy with the ethnic Serbs, which also supported better communication—though it created some discomfort for the ethnic Bosnians, or Bosniacs. In addition, this was the first time at least in modern times that the Russian soldiers were playing a peacekeeping role, and they had little experience or training for it. Nevertheless, they did their job, and they made a contribution.

The Russian troops were quite interesting in some ways. They were very tough, particularly their special forces contingent (Spetsnaz) and loved to put on demonstrations of their physical prowess, including breaking bottles and boards with their heads and smashing stones held on the stomachs of their comrades with sledgehammers. There was not much fraternization between the American and Russian troops, if for no other reason than the language difference. The American commander, of course, had regular communication with the Russian commander. I found one Russian officer who spoke passable French, and we were able to communicate some, though my American military colleagues were a little uncomfortable as they assumed he was an intelligence officer. Perhaps he was. I imagine the Russians assumed I was, and we never managed to develop our discussions into broader cooperation.

***

One of the things that bothered me the most was the priority the military command had been given. After 9/11, terrorism was the primary foreign policy focus of the U.S. government, and this was applied very quickly to Bosnia. During the war, volunteers had traveled to Bosnia from many parts of the Muslim world to help the Bosnian forces in their struggle with the Serbs. After the war, some of those fighters had remained in Bosnia and made it their home. Some of those who remained were radical Islamists who supported jihad against the West, and the military was charged with keeping track of them. I soon found out that this was true for much of our embassy in Sarajevo as well. There was correspondingly less focus on some of the key issues left by the Dayton Accords, specifically the reestablishment of a balanced civil society and the apprehension of war criminals.

The latter was important, because as long as those individuals who had done so much to poison the relations between different ethnic groups were at large, ordinary citizens could not fully believe in or commit themselves to a new order and new rules. In talking with some of my predecessor POLADs, with the U.S. military, and with the Bosnian interpreters and others working for the NATO forces, it became clear to me that at least some of the military assigned to Bosnia—from the time of their first arrival in 1996—had intentionally avoided efforts to apprehend war criminals. The first brigade with which I worked in Bosnia gave a low priority to apprehending war criminals. In fact, some of them believed that they had been specifically instructed to avoid such actions. The second division, on the other hand, worked hard on the issue, though with little success.

***

I tried to get off the base and into the community as much as possible. My preference would have been every day, but sometimes I had to settle for several times a week. Whereas the military had to travel with a minimum of two vehicles everywhere they went, I had an exception. I would go out with the one Toyota Land Cruiser assigned to me with my deputy, a major with the unit, and an interpreter. One of them would drive. The deputy had several jobs, to help me with my work and interaction with the rest of the division (an invaluable service), to protect me when we were outside the base (not so necessary), and presumably to keep an eye on me for the division (perhaps a good precaution). It was a somewhat peculiar job for the two deputies I had that year because it was not really military. There was no command responsibility in it, and so the credit they would receive was somewhat questionable. It seemed to me that to some degree they were making a personal sacrifice in career terms (the National Guard is a parallel career and personal advancement is important), so I tried to include them in everything I did and make it as interesting as possible for them.

We went out and called on community leaders in the Tuzla area and in as many towns and other administrative areas as possible. This included provincial governors, city mayors, security personnel, religious leaders, business leaders, professionals, and so on. We would sit down with them and discuss their relations with the American military, progress or lack thereof in implementation of the Dayton Accords, current economic and political issues, and whatever else was appropriate at the time. I was looking for information that would help me better understand the situation in Bosnia and better assist my military colleagues in focusing their resources in the best possible way to support implementation of Dayton.

***

Sometimes the commanding general would call on community leaders and I would go with him. More often I would go by myself. I was freer to go more often and slightly less formally. There was, not surprisingly, a marked difference in the reception we received from Bosniac and Serbian officials. The Bosniac community leaders were usually glad to see us. They viewed us in a cooperative and facilitating role. The Serb leaders were less happy to see us. To many of them, we were the occupiers, the enemy. Interestingly, we got a similar reception from some of the more radical Islamists. Some of the Muslim fighters who went to Bosnia to help during the war decided to remain in Bosnia-Herzegovina, married, and established themselves in the community. They, too, were very suspicious of the NATO forces, perhaps because the NATO forces were suspicious of them.

However, there was one Serb mayor in our area who was a little different, or at least I thought so. He was the mayor of Bijeljina, one of the largest—and most hard-line—cities in the Republika Srpska. It was one of the first places in Bosnia where ethnic cleansing was carried out. In 1992 perhaps a thousand civilians were killed, and the non-Serb population was driven out. The mayor was considered one of the most resistant Serb leaders to the High Commissioner's efforts to reform the structure of government and society in that area; specifically to permit the return of refugees, their right to retrieve confiscated property, and their right to live in their former neighborhoods with guaranteed security, freedom from discrimination, and equal rights with their Serb neighbors.

Progress in Bijeljina was very difficult, and the mayor as leader of the community was blamed by the international community for obstructing progress. He certainly bore significant responsibility, but it was unclear to me whether he was actually leading the resistance or just representing the resistance of his community. Bijeljina was also where the Orthodox bishop for the region lived. I never met him, because he was never available to meet with us when we came to town; but he was reported to be a very hard-line anti-Muslim who had played a role inciting anti-Muslim activity during and after the war. I imagined it was probably pretty difficult for any mayor to deal with that kind of a figure, particularly given the importance of the Orthodox Church in that culture. I met with the mayor on several occasions, sometimes carrying messages from the international community or the NATO command. It was very difficult to get him to commit to anything or to be forthcoming in discussions. I did not succeed in moving him, but I enjoyed our conversations and verbal sparring matches. Not long after I left Bosnia, the high commissioner exercised his authority and removed that mayor from his position. I don't know if his successors were more coopera-tive.

***

I tried to coordinate my work in the local communities with the international community in Tuzla. There was another American Foreign Service officer in Tuzla who was working for the high representative, and there were represen-tatives of a variety of government and nongovernmental assistance organiza-tions as well. We would meet at least once a month to share our experiences and information and to look for ways in which we could help each other. There were many reasons why local communities could fall behind in their obligations to implement the accords, ranging from lack of resources to unforeseen complications to just plain resistance. Sometimes the military could provide resources, both men and money, to help out. NATO was also still the eight-hundred-pound gorilla in Bosnia, and sometimes just a call from the military's representative was enough to overcome resistance to required changes (at least temporarily).

When I was in Bosnia, the Office of the High Representative in Sarajevo was led by Sir Paddy Ashdown, a very experienced, wise, and active British official. He may have been the most active of the four high representatives in Bosnia up to that time, and he tried very hard to set the reform process on a self-sustaining track before the NATO military effort came to an end. Ash-down was ably supported by an American Foreign Service officer, Ambassa-dor Don Hays, who had worked closely with Richard Holbrooke during and after the negotiation of the Dayton Accords. They, along with the United Nations, the Organization for Security and Co-operation in Europe (OSCE), and the embassies of supporting nations worked hard to make a difference. Cooperation and coordination were pretty good, but unfortunately that coop-eration was exceptional compared to the previous seven years. Judging from the comments of those in the community who had been there longer than I, the international civilian effort in Bosnia, unlike the military effort, had been characterized by confusion, petty personal rivalries, and paralysis.

That is not to say that the individuals were not dedicated and hard-work-ing. Certainly when I was there those in the field were doing yeoman's work under some difficult conditions. The representatives of international and non-governmental organizations lived in cities throughout Bosnia dealing with a myriad of social, economic, and political problems left over from the war. Those in ethnic Bosnian areas tended to be welcomed and supported. How-ever, those in ethnic Serb areas were looked on with suspicion and often hostility. It required real courage and personal fortitude to remain in place and do their job.

***

The city of Srebrenica, where the horrific massacre of Bosnian Muslims by the Serb army took place, was only about an hour's drive from Tuzla. A Bosnian enclave there had held out for several years surrounded by the Serb army. It was nominally protected by a small contingent of UN peacekeeping troops from the Netherlands. However, in July 1995, the Serbs, led by General Ratko Mladic, pressured the Dutch UN peacekeeping troops to leave. As soon as his forces moved in, they separated the female and male populations. They sent twenty-five thousand women, small male children, and elderly off to Tuzla and then massacred their Bosnian male captives, numbering about eight thousand, and buried them in mass graves. When I was in Bosnia new graves were still being found, scattered around the territory previously held by Serb forces. I visited one in a field tucked away on a hill surrounded by forest, shortly after its discovery and again after excavators had been at work for several days. It was very macabre. Several pits had been excavated, and the remains taken back to Tuzla for identification, but much of the field had not yet been dug up. We walked around the field, and there were many places where the land was sunken and spongy, often a sign of where bodies had been dumped and covered. The decomposing bodies would shrink, and the land would sink over them.

When remains were discovered they would be carefully exhumed and sent to Tuzla, where the International Commission on Missing Persons (ICMP) was addressing the monumental task of identifying the remains. They were sent to a morgue at the bottom of a small valley on the edge of the city. The morgue was simply overwhelmed. The staff there did the best they could, but they simply didn't have sufficient space or refrigeration capacity to cope. The smell of decomposing bodies hung over the morgue and the entrance to that small valley like a cloud, and it was hard for those of us who visited to spend much time there. This was seven years after the massacre. I don't know how those working there coped, but they did. There was a charming little restaurant at the end of the valley about a mile up the road from the morgue. It had a deck where one could eat outside and look out over the valley and the town. We ate there a couple of times, but it was too close. It seemed as though the smell would reach across that distance to remind us that the past was not so far away either.

Many of the women who had survived Srebrenica had made their homes in Tuzla—either permanently or hoping eventually to return. There was an organization in Tuzla established by some of those women to help their fellow refugees survive—both financially and psychologically—by providing them with work knitting and weaving the wool from the ubiquitous sheep. I purchased several sweaters and commissioned a knitted blanket from them. We advertised for them at Eagle Base and purchased rugs and sweaters for some of our colleagues who were not able to go into town.

The women working there were so nice. All of them had lost their husbands, fathers, and sons to the executioners. Some tried to be philosophical about it, and some would not talk about it at all. One woman with whom we spoke had a wrenching sequel to her tragedy. She had mentioned that she and her daughter were going to Srebrenica for the weekend, and I expressed surprise. She explained that they were trying to retrieve their house, which had been commandeered by the Serb forces. When I asked how that process was going she said it was very difficult. It was not just the bureaucracy. She discovered when she made her application that the person in charge of the process was the same individual—a Serbian soldier—who had separated her from her husband when Srebrenica fell. That revelation and the ensuing process for her were devastating. In a different way it was devastating for me as well. This was a process of rehabilitation and restoration supervised by the international community, of which I was a part. How could the people of this land possibly have faith in such a process if it was run like that? I passed on the story to the high commissioner's office—but never succeeded in understanding it better.

We visited Srebrenica quite a few times in the period I was in Bosnia. The first time I saw it I was shocked. It was an inhabited ghost town. The destruction of the war was still evident; very little had been repaired. There were almost no signs of the vibrancy of life—no decorations, no maintenance, no children playing in the streets, few people on the streets, no signs of social congregation. The population was almost entirely Serb, and the atmosphere was depressed, sullen, and resentful. I was struck by the impression that this was in some ways how I would envision Hell. The inhabitants had committed terrible crimes that had secured them a place in this city. But now they were prisoners here, forced to live in the spoils of war—and these spoils were truly spoiled. The coup de grâce was the memorial then being built on the main road into the city—a memorial and graveyard for the men and boys who had been put to death in their own town by, in some cases, their own neighbors.

***

Islam was obviously an important part of the environment in Bosnia. From the time that the Ottoman Empire conquered the territory in 1463 until its departure in 1878, Islam was the official religion, and the social structure was heavily influenced by it. After the Ottomans left Islam continued to be the religion of a majority of Bosnians, but it had no official role in government. Prior to the Bosnian War, the Islam practiced in Bosnia was socially and politically conservative. It was a far cry from the fundamentalist, radical interpretation of Islam found in some parts of the Middle East that tries to inspire widespread jihad today.

Since the war, however, Islam in some circles of Bosnia has been taking on a different character and role. To some degree the fighters who came to help brought a more activist approach to religion. Saudi Arabia was influential, because the Saudis helped finance much of the military assistance as well as the postwar relief. The Islam of Saudi Arabia is the more extremist variety, Wahhabism. Part of the Saudi reconstruction assistance came in the form of mosques—large and ornate with tall minarets—very different from the very simple box-like mosques that had been in Bosnia-Herzegovina for centuries. Many people welcomed the Saudi money and influence. They liked the community centers and the social and other services that came with the mosques.

Tuzla did not have a newly built mosque, and it showed little evidence of "outside" Islamic influence. There was a mufti, or Islamic scholar, who had been sent from Sarajevo as the senior authority on Islamic law and custom. He was well educated, very smooth, and reputed to be more fundamentalist and extreme in his views. When I first called on him we were concerned that he might refuse to include my deputy, who was a woman, in the meeting. However, at least in that meeting he did not live up to the reputation given him. He was welcoming, reasonable, tolerant—and well, liberal. But he was still very "official."

The imam, or congregational leader, of Tuzla was quite different. He was local and had been a member of the community in Tuzla for many years. I first arranged to meet with him in an outdoor café where we had coffee together. He expressed gratitude for the chance to meet with official Americans, and he explained that none of my predecessors had ever sought him out. The imam was a very devout and kind person. He was a model of tolerance, not just for people and ethnicities, but for ideas and philosophies. He was working closely with the local Orthodox priest on social projects in Tuzla to help bring the youth of the community together more. Later he invited the senior command of Eagle Base to his home for dinner, and we all went. We sat down with his family, ate together, prayed together, and told stories. It was one of the warmest and most personal experiences of my time in Bosnia.

***

The city of Tuzla is rather special. It is the third-largest city in Bosnia-Herzegovina, and the seat of the canton. Its history goes back more than a thousand years, when it was a center for salt mining. It is charming in its layout and its architecture. Everything is on a small scale. The main streets are only two lanes, and sometimes the sidewalks seem more important than the streets. There are many squares, small parks, and small openings where streets suddenly come together in an apparently unplanned way. These are all places to congregate and socialize.

In the warmer months they hosted a café-culture that was warm and vibrant. The favorite pastime seemed to be gathering and visiting with friends in this environment. Sometimes I wondered when they ever worked. Part of the answer to that was that there was a paucity of jobs and serious unemployment. Nevertheless, people seemed to have sufficient resources to be able to spend many hours there. Then again, it was not very expensive. Coffee (Turkish coffee, of course), beer and wine (the Muslim admonition against alcohol was viewed philosophically), and many different things to eat were wonderfully reasonable in price.

Sadly, there was also tragedy associated with this social congregation. One of the larger squares in town was often the site of community events. On May 25, 1995, it hosted a graduation ceremony for the town's high school children. On that sunny morning when the square was full, the surrounding Serb army shelled the city, apparently specifically targeting the square. Seventy-one people died, most of them between eighteen and twenty-five, and 240 were injured.

Tuzla's population at the time was not exclusively Bosniac Muslims. Like most of Bosnia-Herzegovina, the population was a mixture of Bosnian, Croatian, and Serbian, all of whom for one reason or another considered Bosnia-Herzegovina their home. As the war progressed in much of Bosnia-Herzegovina (and the former Yugoslavia in general), these populations segregated. The different ethnic and religious groups pulled (or were pushed) back to the safety or familiarity of their "own kind." Tuzla appears to have been an exception. When the city was besieged, the Serb army called on the Serb population of Tuzla to leave. Some did, but most stayed. Tuzla was their home. They chose to remain with their neighbors and friends. As the siege continued and hardships and fear increased, those relationships were severely tested. But the leadership of the city, which included all ethnic groups, was determined, and it succeeded in holding the community together. Tuzla survived physically. It did not fall to the siege. It survived socially and psychologically. It appears to have held as a community, and when we were there we saw plenty of evidence of people working to strengthen the ties between the different groups.

This is not to say that its behavior was impeccable. No one in that region appears to have been entirely without blame for the events that transpired. At the beginning of the war, the Yugoslav army garrison in Tuzla was forced to leave the city. An agreement was negotiated that permitted it to leave peacefully, but as the forces were leaving in convoy on May 15, 1992, they were ambushed—in violation of the agreement and the Geneva Convention—and many soldiers died. Perhaps it was not entirely by coincidence that the shelling of the high school graduation ceremony took place so close to the anniversary of that ambush three years later. In 2007 a Serb army officer was arrested and sentenced by the Court of Bosnia and Herzegovina to twenty-five years in prison for the shelling of the graduation ceremony. I don't think anyone has been arrested yet for the ambush of the Serb forces leaving Tuzla.

***

To assist me in my work, the command provided me with two interpreters. One was a Bosnian Muslim, and the other was part Bosnian and part Serb. They were well-educated and thoughtful people. They had learned English partly in school and partly from watching English or American soap operas on television. They were effective interpreters. They were also very good interlocutors on Bosnia and how NATO was doing there. I relied heavily on them for introduction to Bosnian history, culture, and politics, as well as for language interpretation. Together, we tried to develop approaches to several civil-military issues facing both the military and civilian efforts to implement the Dayton Accords.

The first was the terrible issue of mines left over from the war. Bosnia was absolutely infested with mines. The U.S. Department of State estimated that during the 1991–1995 war as many as one million mines had been spread throughout Bosnia. Close to 4 percent of the country's landmass was mined. Some of the minefields were known, but many were not. When I was there new minefields were still being discovered, and it seemed like at least every week there was a report of another person injured or killed by mines—many were children.

This effectively meant that much of the country was off-limits. If an area had not been inspected and declared safe, one best assumed it was dangerous. Even when minefields were discovered, they could sit for years before being cleared. The clearing process was slow and tedious. Funding for the effort was insufficient, and the government's organization was questionable. There were many stories of fields being cleared several times by commercial organizations seeking to make easy money. Some estimated that if the rate of clearance at the time continued, Bosnia would not be cleared of mines before 2050.

Some of us at Eagle Base thought that the process could be accelerated if a different approach were taken. We proposed that NATO encourage the Bosnian government to reorganize its military forces, creating a dedicated De-Mining Brigade that would eventually become a major part of the Bosnian Armed Forces. In this way military resources might be directed away from conflict and toward a direct contribution to the well-being of the entire nation. We suggested furthermore that after Bosnia had been cleared, this De-Mining Brigade could be deployed elsewhere in the world, independently or under NATO auspices to assist other infected nations. Our proposal was accepted by the NATO commander, Maj. Gen. Kip Ward. However, it never bore fruit. The American military units redeployed too often to keep the proposal in motion, and the U.S. Embassy and the Department of State were cool to the idea from the start.

Another issue was the environmental impact of the NATO forces on the country they were sent to protect. The first problem we had to deal with arose during the drawdown of the Russian brigade. As the Russians prepared to depart, reports began to come in from Bosnian communities in their area of illnesses, crop failures, and livestock deaths surrounding a weapons disposal area. The Russians insisted that they had followed all established procedures and there should be no danger to the surrounding population. However, we needed to be responsive to the population and, if there were a problem, take appropriate measures to address it.

We carefully interviewed farmers and villagers and pinpointed the alleged problem areas. Members of the military medical teams then took samples of the water and soil in these areas and sent them back to commercial laboratories in the United States for analysis. The results of the tests all came back clear. This was a great relief for both NATO and the local authorities, and afterward the reports subsided.

The second environmental problem was Eagle Base's trash disposal. The base was trucking all of its trash and garbage to local dumpsites. In the early days of the deployment the population had simply accepted additional burdens or inconveniences as unavoidable or a small price to pay for ending the hostilities. However, as the years of deployment mounted, so did the complaints. Dump managers began complaining that the base was overwhelming the dumps' capacity, and locals in the area were complaining about the endless smoke from the dumps' incinerators. Again, we talked with as many concerned parties as possible, and working with a waste management expert from one of the contractors, developed a plan to substantially reduce Eagle Base's trash. A major component of the plan was to eliminate reliance on drinking water in disposable plastic bottles, replacing it with bulk purification on the base. These efforts seemed to satisfy local concerns, and they may even have provided some longer-term guidance and help to the local communities.

***

Altogether, it was a year well spent. The two National Guard units did an excellent job with their primary responsibility of maintaining security in the region. They sustained good working relations with the community, and they made some valiant efforts to address a variety of ongoing and immediate issues that manifested during our time there.

By the end of the year, I was more familiar with the environment and the people, and I had a better understanding of how to address problems when they arose. However, I was still a very long way away from being an effective interlocutor and player in the broader effort to help Bosnia on to a sustainable path to long-term political and economic stability. Part of the reason was my separation from the community, which was enforced by living on and working from the military base. Another important part was—once again—language.

No training in Serbo-Croatian language was available to me before I left for Bosnia. I tried briefly to start language lessons when I arrived, but I didn't have the personal discipline to make it work with the rest of my schedule. Perhaps by then I also didn't have the brainpower to make it work. Serbo-Croatian is not a difficult language, but as we get older most of us find that our brains provide less receptive and less fertile soil for the seeds of new languages. Rather than settling and taking root, they rest for a brief moment and then blow on to some unknown destination. I was most frustrated and embarrassed that I learned so little Serbo-Croatian while there. The best interpreter in the world is no substitute for being able to listen to and talk directly with someone in their own language. I felt like I was in a bubble, watching but not connecting with the people and culture of that land. It was difficult to descend from my rather imposing horse to get close to the flowers. Even when I did, the lack of language made it impossible to experience those flowers except in the shallowest way.

***

Stopping the conflict in the Balkans made a real contribution to Europe, and possibly to the world. The alternative would have been to let the conflict continue with far more loss of life and even possibly expand to other countries. When Ambassador Richard Holbrooke initiated the U.S. mediation effort, the Serbs had the upper hand in the conflict. Had they continued to succeed, it seems possible there would have been more Srebrenicas.

Some have argued that the Bosnian forces could have turned the tide with the assistance they were receiving from the Muslim world, but even if true that would have taken time. The toll in lives would have been significant, and atrocities might have been inflicted on the other side. That kind of shift would have brought different problems. Serb appeals to other Orthodox Christian populations could have brought others into the conflict—the Russians, or even the Greeks. It is difficult to predict how those possibilities might have developed.

Nevertheless, the American diplomatic success, made possible with the employment of vast military power, had several unintended—if not totally unforeseeable—consequences.

- First, it created within Europe a long-term vulnerability to both internal and external destructive forces.
- Second, it removed the remaining taboo on the large-scale use of American military force as an active tool of diplomacy; and that contributed directly to the next administration's fiasco in Iraq.

***

America and Europe failed to follow up on the negotiating success of Dayton. NATO, mostly America, had the military force to make peace possible. However, for a variety of reasons, the NATO allies found it easier to deploy military forces than to mount a serious effort at economic reconstruction and political reform. This was a failure emanating from the weakness of our respective political systems and the body of political thought on which they are based.

We spent many millions of dollars maintaining military forces in Bosnia for eight to nine years. The military forces conducted exercises, drove around in patrols, and communicated with the local governments and peoples—in descending order of attention and effort. The civilian effort was less robust, less generous, and less effective. The military leadership was American, and that leadership was reasonably clear. The military task was easily definable, and it was limited. Unfortunately, the military leadership chose to limit its role even more than intended by the political leadership that negotiated Dayton—in particular by choosing not to pursue actively the apprehension of designated war criminals. That was an important decision, taken apparently without the engagement of the political leadership, and it further weakened the civilian effort.

The civilian role in Dayton implementation was not clearly defined. In fact, the task was so undefined that it was virtually unlimited. In addition, the leadership was neither clear, nor active, nor effective. The leadership was European, which meant that the candidates were chosen by compromise. From the beginning, that leadership had a limited ability to direct the U.S.-led military effort. None of the early high representatives worked closely

with the NATO leadership, even though the deputy was always American—
and at least one high representative was overtly hostile to the American
leadership. Not until Paddy Ashdown, from the UK, took over was there a
serious effort to push the different factions in Bosnia-Herzegovina to fulfill
their obligations and to promote political and economic reform. By then, it
was almost too late. Had the NATO allies been willing to keep the forces
there longer, it might have been possible even at that late date to promote
reform. However, once again, the military leadership took the lead by beginning to plan for withdrawal. The civilian leadership in Brussels and in Washington either did nothing or went along with the military planning initiative.
The withdrawal timetable was set, and all those forces in Bosnia that opposed
significant reform were essentially assured by that process that if they held
out long enough they would be home free.

This vulnerability is real. It will cause Europe problems for many years to
come, and as it weakens and distracts Europe, it will have a corresponding
impact on America.

- The weakness in governmental authority, governance, and the economy
  all provide fertile ground for organized crime, dealing in drugs, arms, and
  other contraband—including people. It will be a tempting target for these
  forces in the former Soviet Union and elsewhere. This will provide an
  open doorway into Europe, undermining both law and order and possibly
  the integrity of the European Union.
- The weakness in central government control will continue to allow sanctuary to forces of international terrorism, particularly Muslim extremists.
  These forces are abhorred and rejected by most of Bosnia's Muslim population, but without a strong central government and reliable law enforcement authorities to rely upon, extremism and the threat of violence will
  prevail over moderation.
- The ineffectiveness of government and the weakness in the economy will
  leave Bosnia's borders porous—with its neighbors and with the rest of
  Europe. This will either prevent Bosnia from developing closer integration
  with the EU, or it will damage the EU's internal integrity.
- The inability of the central government to enforce the laws and to maintain reasonable stability and predictability will allow, even encourage,
  extralegal economic activity. That in turn will prevent the development of
  a healthy and transparent economy, which will hold back all other political
  and social progress.
- The continued weakness of the central government will encourage continued ethnic divisions and tensions. If these cannot be healed or subsumed
  in a flourishing economy, Bosnia—and the entire Balkan region—will
  never be stable.

• If the Balkans continue to be unstable and unpredictable, this will influence politics and decision making in the rest of southeastern Europe (i.e., Greece, Turkey, and Cyprus). It could also undermine the progress of nearby Eastern European neighbors such as Bulgaria, Romania, and even Hungary.

***

The use of American military forces on the scale required by the Dayton Accords, and in a theater as central as Europe, also removed the last taboo on American military adventurism that had been set in place by the experience of the Vietnam War. That taboo was not entirely rational—no taboo is. However, the American political system is not entirely rational, either—and it needed that taboo to counterbalance the interests of a military-industrial complex that has continued to grow in spite of the end of the Soviet threat. For fifty years the world lived with a bipolar balance that essentially prohibited serious conflict. America had pressed those restraints to the limit in Vietnam in the 1970s and had failed. The Soviet Union pushed those restraints with its invasion of Afghanistan in the 1980s, and it failed too. The shock of failure in Vietnam held the forces of American adventurism in check for another twenty-five years, beyond the collapse of the USSR and the emergence of the United States as the planet's single superpower. Restraint was evident even in the first Gulf War, with open political opposition and the prompt withdrawal of military forces after the military victory. Dayton, however, unwittingly restored military adventurism to prominence—not in the Clinton administration, but in the subsequent Bush administration, led by a man who had none of his father's experience or moderation.

The new Bush administration had at its core a group of people who not only wanted to reinstate war as an active element of aggressive American foreign policy, but had a specific target in mind: the Middle East—beginning with Saddam Hussein and Iraq. The removal of the taboo empowered these people, ironically some of the same people who objected to an American role in Bosnia in the first place, to pursue their agenda. America—and Americans, who through most of the twentieth century thought of themselves as the world's peacekeepers—slipped all too easily into the role of military aggressors.

***

Why did this well-meaning, desperately needed, and brilliantly executed piece of American diplomacy fail to go the distance? I believe there are several reasons.

First, the individual who made the whole thing happen left too early. The Dayton Accords happened essentially because one man made them happen. Richard Holbrooke introduced vision and discipline into the foreign policy of an administration that had tremendous brainpower but little pragmatic direction. The administration wanted to stop the war but could not pull its disparate political pieces together to do it. Holbrooke made it happen by marshaling the various domestic forces and talents, matching what those various political components wanted with what he needed, and bringing all of it to bear on the international scene. However, after performing that yeoman task, he did not stay to ensure that discipline was maintained in the implementation stage.

Had he remained, even in the relatively low position of assistant secretary of state, the military-civilian and American-European gaps might have been kept under control. Had he been chosen as secretary of state when Warren Christopher stepped down in 1997, I believe his perspective and talents would have made significant contributions not only to the Balkans, but to other intractable problem areas such as Cyprus and Israel-Palestine. Richard Holbrooke was not always a pleasant person to work with, and many of us who worked for him had the bruises (figurative) to show for it. He had plenty of faults, but no one else that I saw, in that time period or since, had the combination of vision, energy, and talent to direct and manage the disparate resources and competing goals within the government and the American political system.

Second, the American system is not prepared to implement the kind of reform envisaged by the Dayton Accords. The United States does not yet have the administrative capability to govern and coach another nation to democratic maturity. We saw that in Bosnia, and we are seeing it now in Iraq and in Afghanistan. During the late nineteenth and early twentieth centuries, the European colonial powers developed whole bureaucracies devoted to at least some of those tasks with varying degrees of resources, emphasis, and success. The United States has nothing like it. The department of state is one of the U.S. government's smallest departments. The U.S. Agency for International Development can barely manage the small amount of assistance resources it now has, much less take on other tasks, which if done right would require resources far beyond what has been allocated to foreign assistance for the last three decades or more.

We are not prepared as a nation to allocate the kind of resources necessary to pay for these kinds of efforts. The defense budget is between ten and twenty times as large as the civilian foreign affairs budget of the United States, depending on how they are calculated. We, the people of the United States of America, are willing to put far more of our tax (or borrowed) dollars into our ability to wage war than into our ability to build peace.

Our democratic political system does not have the political attention span necessary to engage effectively in this kind of endeavor. It has the ability to tap into and realize the will of the majority, to keep abuses of power to a minimum, and many other strengths. However, the ability to pursue a complex task, far removed from the immediate experience of the American body politic, for an extended period of time in the face of competing demands is not one of them.

Finally, the Bush administration did not want to take it on. To some degree the administration of George W. Bush inherited the James Baker attitude of "We don't have a dog in this fight." For all its talk about setting clear priorities in foreign policy, when it came to exercising power it did not have many clear ideas of how it wanted to act on the international stage. It did appear to have some negative guidelines such as not wasting any time or resources carrying out something the Clinton administration had started. And it had a core of activists who wanted to use those resources in a very specific place: in the Middle East, on Iraq.

***

About halfway through my tour in Bosnia, Eagle Base received a visit from a senior Department of Defense official who was making a tour of the region. I had known him previously, and when we had breakfast together in the mess hall before he left he asked me my impressions of Bosnia. One of the things I held forth on was my view that many government officials and community leaders, both Serb and Bosniac, were using their positions to reinforce power relationships that had been developed during and after the collapse of Yugoslavia. In many cases these officials were the same people who had contributed to the outbreak of hostilities in the first place. I thought that the international community should have cleaned house at all levels of government when it had the ability to do so—in the months immediately following the Dayton Accords.

He then said that seemed to have some similarity to the situation in Iraq, and that perhaps the United States should clean house there before moving on to other reconstruction efforts. I replied that if it was anything like Bosnia, we probably should do that. Today, I hope very much that his mind had already been made up, and that what I said played no role in the way we proceeded in Iraq. As well-intentioned as it may have been, the decision to purge the Iraqi government and the military of Baathist party members was probably a huge mistake. Perhaps I was wrong about Bosnia-Herzegovina as well. The actions taken by outsiders arriving on horseback with imperfect information can sometimes do more harm than good.

NOTE

1. The Republika Srpska (Serb Republic) is one of two primary political-territorial divisions of Bosnia and Herzegovina, recognized by the General Framework Agreement for Peace in Bosnia and Herzegovina (Dayton Accords). The other is the Federation of Bosnia and Herzegovina.

Chapter Nine

New War: Special Operations Command, MacDill Air Force Base, Florida (August 2003–July 2006)

After a one-year tour in Bosnia, I was once again eligible to return to the United States. The Political Military Bureau asked me if I would be interested in interviewing for the position of Political Advisor to the Special Operations Command, located at MacDill Air Force Base in Tampa, Florida. I checked with my family; they agreed, and we went ahead. I was accepted, and we moved to Florida—our only U.S. assignment outside of Washington—two weeks after I returned from Bosnia.

***

The Special Operations Command, or SOCOM, is one of the U.S. military's most recently established Unified Combatant Commands (UCCs), which are led by four-star generals or admirals. They include six geographic commands and four functional commands. SOCOM is a functional command, and it was set up in 1987 by the Goldwater-Nichols Act. It is special in a number of ways. It is made up of elite personnel from the four branches of the armed forces: Army, Navy, Air Force, and Marines.[1] It has broader authorities than most of the other UCCs, such as its own budget authority, and since 2005 it has responsibility within the military to lead planning and operations against international terrorism.

For many years the Department of State has posted a senior Foreign Service officer, usually an ambassador, to SOCOM as Political Advisor (Foreign Policy Advisor) to the command. The Political Advisor's job is to provide foreign policy advice to the commander and a diplomatic perspective to command discussions and decisions. During my time at SOCOM the commander was Army General Bryan D. Brown, a remarkable man who had begun his career as an enlisted man several decades earlier. The "POLAD" also serves as a direct link to the Department of State and to ambassadors overseas. When I left the European Bureau in the late 1990s, I had been offered the opportunity of an ambassadorial assignment, but I chose to decline for family reasons. The subsequent lack of the title was a minor disadvantage when I got to SOCOM, because it can help open doors and it adds some prestige to the command. However, everyone was very courteous, and having the equivalent rank of a two-star general helped overcome bureaucratic obstacles. It was not an obstacle to coordinating with ambassadors, since I already knew most of them, having crossed paths with them in one way or another over the past thirty years.

The timing of my assignment was particularly interesting, because SOCOM had recently been given expanded operational responsibilities and authorities. After the terrorist attacks of September 11, 2001, the administration of President George W. Bush chose to declare a "War on Terror" and tended to view the military as its primary tool to deal with the terrorist threat.

***

Within the Department of Defense, the secretary of defense gave the lead for the War on Terror to the Special Operations Command. It became an operational command that could conduct and manage operations within and across the boundaries of the military's existing geographic commands. This raised the specter of turf battles between SOCOM and those geographic commands, and it also raised questions about how SOCOM would work with ambassadors in the field.

American ambassadors are sent to other nations as the president's personal representative. As such, they are the senior U.S. government officials in those countries, with responsibility for and authority over all other U.S. government officials, including the military. For decades there have been only a few exceptions. These have included those on the staff of international organizations, Voice of America correspondents, and those under the command of a "United States area military commander." The latter refers to the four-star geographic UCCs in circumstances where forces under a commander are stationed in a particular country, or may be sent to a country for a particular purpose.

If a geographic commander wished to send his forces into a new area, he had to first obtain the permission of the resident U.S. ambassador there. The two were then responsible for establishing the parameters of the mission and the effective chain of command. If there was any confusion about whose authority prevailed in any particular circumstance, the ambassador's authority would generally prevail unless overruled by Washington.

It was difficult enough when there were only two principals involved. However, the designation of SOCOM as an operational commander in the War on Terror made the situation more complicated. It added a third principal, but did not set clear guidelines for the respective authorities. The War on Terror was a work in progress. There was little formal guidance from Washington, because there was little consensus in Washington. The Department of State maintained that the ambassadors' authority remained intact. Within the Department of Defense, however, the secretary of defense made clear on a number of occasions his view that ambassadors were obstacles rather than authorities to be respected.

I don't think the senior leadership of the special operations forces (SOF) that I worked with was comfortable with this view. While most were frustrated at one time or another by ambassadorial resistance, they subscribed to the principle of ambassadorial authority. Fortunately, the professionals in the field, the ambassadors and the generals, were willing and able to work things out themselves and there were no serious incidents. Without guidance from Washington, however, resolution of disagreements could be considerably more time-consuming—and stressful. Part of my job was to help the command and the ambassadors communicate more effectively with each other for the benefit of the country as a whole.

SOCOM had a well-established program for taking newly appointed ambassadors to Fort Bragg, North Carolina, and giving them a thorough introduction to the mission and capabilities of special operations forces. It also gave them a chance to talk directly with the SOCOM commander before they went to post. Prior to those visits, someone from the State Department's counterterrorism office and I would brief the ambassadors on the dynamics and parameters of relations between ambassadors and SOCOM. This process helped reduce misunderstandings, but there was still a need for coordination. I traveled with the commander when he visited countries on every continent (except Antarctica), and we would always meet with the resident U.S. ambassador. I also visited some countries on my own to coordinate existing programs or to encourage ambassadors to consider ways to work more closely with SOCOM. We were able to reassure most ambassadors that in spite of some of the rhetoric and rumors from Washington, the command fully respected their authority. We were able to encourage some ambassadors to step up their own efforts to address real or perceived threats. The improved communication also enabled us on several occasions to find alternatives to military action that I believe would have been very damaging to broader U.S. interests and even to the War on Terror itself.

I had some familiarity with the dynamic of tension between military commanders and ambassadors, because I had watched my father deal with it when he was ambassador to Panama in the 1960s. At that time the U.S. Southern Command was located in the Panama Canal Zone and led by a four-star area commander.[2] The area commander had authority within the Canal Zone, but the ambassador insisted that the commander needed to have the ambassador's permission for any movement into the Republic of Panama. The general disagreed, and in contravention of the ambassador's guidelines flew a military aircraft into Panama without permission. This was a very sensitive time in U.S.-Panama relations. There had been serious anti-American riots in the mid-sixties, and the political environment was still volatile. It was also the era of the Vietnam War, and the Department of Defense was growing in power and influence. In Washington, the Departments of State and Defense apparently were not able to resolve this dispute. The ambassador, therefore, asked that both he and the general be called to Washington to meet with the president. They met with President Johnson, who listened to both sides and then unequivocally stated that the ambassador's authority prevailed. That authority does not appear to have been seriously questioned again until the G. W. Bush administration's War on Terror. Fortunately, it seems to have survived the initial pressures of that period.

***

International terrorism, of course, had not started with the attack on September 11, 2001. I had some personal familiarity with this phenomenon as well, since after Panama, my father had been ambassador to Uruguay between 1969 and 1972 during the height of the urban terrorism perpetuated by the Tupamaros,[3] an organization concentrated in the city of Montevideo and directed toward "national liberation." They carried out attacks on law enforcement personnel and kidnappings of high-profile government and diplomatic personnel. Unlike the terrorist groups today, they left women and children alone.

The U.S. ambassador was target number one, and the Department of State did its best to protect him and other members of the mission. My father told me he had the first armored sedan provided to a U.S. ambassador overseas.[4] His routes and the timing of his movements were constantly changed, and he was followed at all times by another car filled with guards carrying automatic weapons. When I visited Montevideo I rode in that follow-car from the airport. I was horrified by the distinctly undiplomatic driving protocol it exercised to stay close to its charge, until I belatedly realized its purpose.

The tactics succeeded in protecting the ambassador, though several other members of the embassy were not so lucky.[5] Neither was the British ambassador, Sir Geoffrey Jackson, who didn't change his route as often and as a result spent eight months in captivity.[6] I still remember lying in bed late at night in my room at the front of the ambassador's residence listening to the occasional car pull up to the front door—which was then not blocked—and wondering if this would be the time they tried to come in. The only guards at the residence were Uruguayan police. My father would not allow the Marines to be posted in the house, reasoning they would only be killed by a determined attack, while he would be taken alive.

During that visit, I attended a party with a number of young Uruguayans of different political persuasions, and we talked, among other things, about the Tupamaro phenomenon. I made the comment that it might be sort of interesting to be kidnapped. One of the guests smiled and averred that might be arranged. That was my last trip to Montevideo. The Tupamaros' prohibition on taking women and children did not extend to curious twenty-one-year-old men, and my father decided I should not return.

***

U.S. embassies, military installations, and American citizens had been attacked by terrorists for decades before 9/11, and all the U.S. foreign affairs agencies—civilian and military—had been seized with the problem to some degree. The best-known attacks were against the U.S. Embassy in Beirut in 1983 and against the embassies in Nairobi and Dar es Salaam in 1998.

After the latter, a commission was put together to study the preparedness of U.S. diplomatic offices overseas to withstand terrorist attacks. Led by retired Admiral William J. Crowe Jr., it made detailed recommendations for strengthening protection. Our government was slow to respond. In 1999 and 2000, as president of the American Foreign Service Association (AFSA), I spent a good deal of time arguing to both the Department of State and to Congress that neither had come close to implementing Admiral Crowe's recommendations. In spite of the tragedy of those losses, we did not have an operational consensus even about how to protect our embassies—much less about how to deal with the broad and growing threat of international terrorism in general.

There existed a body of knowledge of what measures worked against popular insurgencies, built up over the last century by the United States and European nations in response to challenges in places like Africa and Southeast Asia. Since the 1960s many nations had also developed capabilities to address and contain individual terrorist acts. However, as sophisticated as some of those measures were, they were inadequate to address a threat coming from people hidden in populations all over the world, driven by hatred that was sanctioned and encouraged by elements of a major world religion, and focused on killing anyone and everyone associated with the United States and other Western governments.

Some argued that it must be treated like an insurgency—that it was essential to understand the roots of this phenomenon and address whatever environmental factors supported it, so that it would not spread. That made sense, but no one came to the fore with convincing ways of actually doing that. This era had no equivalent of George Kennan, who predicted and defined the Cold War.

In the absence of that, it was easier intellectually, emotionally, and politically to "declare war" on this threat and to marshal our war-fighting resources to carry that war to the "enemy," whoever they were—and wherever we might think they were. In essence, the U.S. leadership decided to reply to the terrorist attacks in kind. To do this, the administration of George W. Bush relied overwhelmingly on the military and the intelligence services. Other agencies were pushed to the side and told to take supporting roles.

The Department of State did not seem to have alternatives to offer. It was not given the mandate to seek them, and it certainly was not given the resources to do so. The secretary of state, Colin Powell, with a distinguished military career behind him and the potential to be one of America's most outstanding secretaries of state, was forced into the position of supporting to the United Nations the invasion of a country that had virtually nothing to do with the terrorism threat.

The intelligence community had not been successful over the previous several decades in developing effective windows into the terrorist population. This was partly because it was a very different kind of phenomenon from the threat posed by national governments. It was also partially because successive political leaderships had not charged the intelligence community with this as a top priority. The Department of State had had an office dealing with terrorism since 1972, and an ambassadorial-level coordinator for counterterrorism since 1985, but it was a relatively small office with frequent staffing turnover. In 2001, it was not a significant repository either of understanding of the phenomenon or of wisdom for how to deal with it. Nor was the NSC's national coordinator for counterterrorism,[7] a position established in 1998.

This shortcoming was not limited to the U.S. government. During my tenure at SOCOM, the command made an impressive effort to reach out to European, Middle Eastern, and Asian counterparts. There was widespread commitment to work together, but beyond better coordination of intelligence and military operations directed at the immediate threat, I did not see many ideas about how to do so. The British in particular made no secret of their concern that the U.S. approach lacked dimension—i.e., it was not addressing the roots of the phenomenon—and I agreed with them. However, to the great frustration of my military colleagues, the Brits (and I) were rather short on specific alternatives.

With little policy guidance, SOCOM did its best to respond to the pressure put on it to produce results in this War on Terror—and they did very well. The soldiers of the special operations community are incredibly capable war fighters. They are intelligent, well trained, and extremely dedicated. They were most effective in the areas where there were military operations under way: in Afghanistan and Iraq, where they provided military commanders with extraordinary search-and-destroy capability. They also worked very well with ambassadors and other agencies in places like the Philippines where there were existing insurgencies (which had some relation to international terrorism) threatening the national government, and where the national government welcomed American assistance.

***

I have tremendous respect for those Americans who at various times in our history have taken an unequivocal stand against the use of force—war—to achieve national goals or defend national interests. I believe that our nation's willingness and ability to allow a place for conscientious objection to war is admirable and practical. I also believe that there are dangers against which our nation can only be protected by a substantial military force. The United States has been extraordinarily successful over the last two hundred years at creating and maintaining a powerful military capable of defending our nation against any military force on this planet.

Nevertheless, President Dwight D. Eisenhower's warning to the nation back in 1961 about the dangers posed by the growing military-industrial complex was justified and prescient, and we have not taken it seriously enough. When I was president of AFSA[8] from 1999 to 2001, I traveled around the country speaking to groups of retired Foreign Service officers and other foreign affairs groups to call attention to the State Department's serious budgetary deficiency that was constraining its ability to hire, train, and even protect its foreign affairs personnel. One of the points I made was that at that time the military budget of the United States was more than fourteen times the size of the entire civilian foreign affairs appropriation. The latter included not only the Department of State's budget, but all economic development assistance, trade and export promotion, and so on. Ten years later, the ratio appears to be about the same.

Certainly, we needed to counter the Soviet threat during the Cold War, but the growth of the military budget and the disparity between military and civilian elements is not solely—or even perhaps primarily—a rational response to a determined threat. It has come about because our defense budget has become a cash cow for an ever-growing sector of American business. Over the years, I have watched—and sometimes been a part of—the Department of State's efforts to get congressional committees and members to support increases for personnel or even counterterrorism security measures. The reception has generally been lukewarm to cold. On the other hand, when I was at SOCOM, I watched congressional delegations visit every several months not just asking patriotically what they could do to help, but even pressing SOCOM to accept budget increases for the purchase of equipment, systems, and even property. The military leadership for whom I worked would privately express exasperation that they were being constantly pressured to spend money (large amounts of money) for things they did not need. I should note here, however, that I never saw any indication that SOCOM allowed the pressure to cloud their judgment about what they actually needed and requested. The command seemed to be as assiduous in its attention to ethics and to the management of its budget authority as it was in the planning of its operations.

The congressional representatives and their staff always wrapped their proposals in patriotism, but much of it was purely political—to generate benefits for businesses in and beyond their districts. The American system is not uniquely corrupted by this kind of influence. This has been going on for thousands of years all over the globe. In many countries the process is far more egregious than in the United States. However, in the United States it takes place on a larger scale. We pour more resources into this sector and have built a larger military power than any other nation in history (so far). We are also a democracy. This has not been done by autocrats, but by and with the knowledge and support (if not the full understanding) of the people.

Throughout my career, I preferred working overseas with foreign governments to tackle problems of importance to us and to them. My two POLAD assignments were anomalies, as I was working primarily with other Americans. Nevertheless, there was a certain cultural challenge since the environments and the perspective of soldiers and diplomats can be substantially different. The skills of diplomacy are not irrelevant to promoting cooperation between the two, and that cooperation is essential. The United States cannot use just one or the other. The two must be used together, and in balance. We are still a young nation, and our political system has not yet recognized or accepted that necessity. As the pressures, the hotspots, and the multiplicity of threats in the international arena increase, it is becoming correspondingly important that our professionals in both areas ensure the health and effectiveness of that cooperation.

***

The commanding general of SOCOM travels extensively. He has a responsibility to see firsthand and on a regular basis what his people are doing, and they are spread widely. He must communicate with the special operations forces (SOF) of other governments around the world, and he must also coordinate with U.S. ambassadors in countries that might be affected by his forces or operations. After spending most of my life in the Foreign Service, I have an apparently incurable addiction to travel. So it is not surprising that for me one of the most memorable parts of my tour with SOCOM was the travel that we did. Most SOF are actually stationed within the continental United States. As a general rule, I did not travel with the general when he was only doing domestic trips. Unless there was a foreign policy component there was little justification for the expense of taking me along—or denying someone else a place on the plane.[9]

When I did travel within the United States it was usually as part of a longer trip, but in some ways the domestic trips were equally enlightening for me. We visited SOF in California, Washington (state), and Hawaii. Hawaii was interesting because on one trip we attended a conference of SOF from other nations all around the Pacific Rim. They were invited to come in and discuss multilateral cooperation in dealing with the challenge of international terrorism. It was a useful exercise getting people together to establish common ground and smooth the rough edges of cultural and political differences.

The most fascinating domestic visit for me was to a SOF winter training center. That was where the extent of SOF training was really driven home to me. The young men there were subjected to conditions that were uncomfortable even to talk about—but they seemed to love actually doing it—from survival expeditions in the mountains to night operations in frigid waters. They had the best possible equipment, but it was not always foolproof. One recruit described a midwinter exercise at night where shortly after entering the water he realized he had a leak in his suit. It was too late to go back and he could only go on with the exercise—with virtually no protection. He survived and recovered. I was impressed—and a little envious, not being able to imagine surviving something like that myself.

One thing SOCOM did for me was get me to the Middle East. Before taking this job, my only association with that region had been with Turkey when I was office director and then deputy assistant secretary for that area. I was enormously impressed by both present-day Turkey and its history as the seat of the Ottoman Empire, which dominated the Islamic world for several hundred years. I had worked with the Bureau of Near Eastern Affairs on Iraq, Syria, and Israel issues relating to Turkey, but I had never traveled to other Middle Eastern countries. That changed with SOCOM.

Special operations forces were operating in Iraq and Afghanistan, and they had cooperative relations with many of the forces in neighboring countries. The SOCOM commander made several trips a year to the region. Iraq and Afghanistan were my first visits to real war zones where U.S. forces were actively engaged. I'm not the most courageous person in the world, and I was never comfortable with it, but it was fascinating.

We first visited Iraq in 2003, not long after the invasion. On that visit we drove in convoy from the airport to Baghdad, but after that as the danger increased we relied on helicopters. In Baghdad many U.S. forces were working and living in the palaces built by Saddam Hussein. The juxtaposition of ornate marble palaces with foreign military forces and all the equipment and furniture needed for administrative control was a little bizarre. The palaces themselves were more bizarre still. They were enormous and flashy—lots of marble, pillars, impressive staircases, and oversized bathrooms with fancy fixtures. But everywhere the workmanship was shoddy. Pieces didn't fit together, the tile work was uneven, the fixtures leaked or didn't work. One evening I had left my room and gone to do some work in one of the ballrooms where computers were set up. It was quiet and still, but as I was working I noticed something move high up in my peripheral vision. When I looked up, way above me in the elaborate molding of the ceiling was a rat. He was large—about the size of a cat, and he watched me for a while before meandering casually away along the molding. I thought, "Well, that's a different take on surveillance," and wondered if I looked markedly different to the rat from the previous Iraqi residents of the palaces.

I was given my first real introduction to helicopters in Bosnia. It was beautiful flying over the endless wooded hills and valleys of Bosnia, seeing the way the small towns were nestled into them. Iraq was different. Flying over Baghdad was intriguing and mysterious. Most of the roofs were flat and apparently well used. There were a surprising number of satellite dishes, though at least in the early stages of the occupation I don't know what kind, if any, signals they were getting. I wondered what kind of things they watched, but I had no contact with Iraqis that might provide that kind of information. Flying over or driving through the cities, while interesting, was very frustrating. I wanted to walk through, stop in the stores, talk to people. I imagined there were some who might speak English, French, or even Chinese. But it wasn't possible. In the early months it might have been safe, but it was not permitted. Later it was prohibitively dangerous.

One helicopter ride made a particularly strong impact on me. We were flying from Baghdad, up the Tigris River valley. It was later in my tour, and even helicopter travel was becoming dangerous, so we were flying very low and fast to make it more difficult for hand-carried missiles to get a bead on us. Skimming over the trees with the doors wide open and dry, 100° air blowing on us, I was surprised by how rich and fertile the area was. Most of those trees were cultivated—date palms and citrus—and there were other well-tended crops around them. This was the river valley from which Western civilization started. This was the subject of those terribly boring high school lectures about Mesopotamia—but this time it was anything but boring. It wasn't just the possibility that we could get blown up at any moment—which was probably unlikely, at least statistically. It was truly awesome to contemplate the thousands of years of human existence and culture laid out below. For me, at least, it was also a little depressing that our presence there was to wage war with little appreciation for that cultural background.

My military colleagues, both those with whom I traveled and those who hosted us, were very patient and tolerant of me. Had we ever gotten into a combat situation I would have been of little help. I was unfamiliar with their procedures and needed to be watched. I didn't know when to wear my helmet, and I had difficulty putting my flak jacket on by myself. For the most part, I accompanied them wherever they went, ate what they ate, and slept where they slept—which was usually in containers or temporary buildings set aside for visitors. On one occasion, visiting a base in central Iraq, I was wakened in the middle of the night by gunfire. I wondered, and tried to ignore it, but it continued and gradually increased to quite a steady barrage. I began to think that perhaps I should find out what was going on, but I was embarrassed to bother anyone in the middle of the night. I was sharing that container with a Navy SEAL admiral, and he remained asleep, so eventually I told myself that the firing was too regular to be worrisome and dropped off to sleep again. The next day, I learned that there was a firing range just over the wall surrounding our compound, and it was just practice.

***

Travel in Iraq was impressive, but by far the most spectacular helicopter flights were in Afghanistan. There is a part of south central Afghanistan that from the air at least is the most desolate and unwelcoming territory I have ever laid eyes on. Much of the rock is black, and when we flew over there was very little visible life, either plant or animal. By contrast, the mountains in the east bordering on Pakistan have spots that are quite lush. On one trip we spent about four hours flying over them, skimming over desolate ridges and then swooping over valleys so green they looked like emeralds. Here there were people as well, working in the valleys and tending sheep or goats on the ridges. They were all viewed as potential enemies. If any congregated or showed interest in us, one of the gunships would head toward them to discourage any other kind of activity. The military serving in those areas, whether out on patrol or at any of the forward bases, were doing very difficult and very dangerous duty.

There didn't seem to be much opportunity for diplomacy in those places. I arranged meetings for the general with the ambassadors or charges in Baghdad and Kabul, and I called on some other members of the embassies myself. The general in turn took me to his meetings with the American and allied generals in those places. In Kabul, the minister of defense hosted us for lunch in his office—a lunch he said was prepared by his wife. He spoke excellent English, and we had some very interesting conversation with him. Among other things, he knew many of his opponents—Taliban and former Mujahedeen—quite well, on a first-name basis, having fought with them against the Russians. The changing circumstances and shifting alliances were part of the reality of his environment. He was quite comfortable with Western ways—but he was living in and dealing with an environment very different from our reality. He didn't appear to be uncomfortable with that. I wondered if he was consciously performing a balancing act between Western and Islamic fundamentalist concepts of right and wrong, or if it just came naturally to him.

On many of our travels in the Middle East and East Africa, we met with heads of state and senior officials in ministries other than defense. In almost all cases the resident U.S. ambassador or his or her representative would accompany us. Not a few governments see senior military officials as representing different U.S. interests than does the embassy. We always had to be careful to avoid anything that might encourage that supposition. In my experience, most U.S. military officials are very careful in that regard.

In Asia we visited special operations personnel in the Philippines, who in a strictly noncombat role had worked with the armed forces of the Philippines to fight terrorism and deliver humanitarian assistance to the people of Mindanao—classic counterinsurgency work. That area had been given a markedly higher priority by the United States when indications grew that the local insurgency had growing connections to international terrorism. The joint effort had been very successful, and some American personnel were continuing their advice and assistance to prevent a premature withdrawal of attention in the wake of that success. We also visited Korea, Indonesia, Thailand, and Australia.

In Latin America we only visited Colombia, where special operations forces were helping with training but were also proscribed from actual operations by U.S. legislation. I tried to encourage a trip to other Andean countries as well as Brazil, Argentina, and Chile, but something always came up to postpone those communications.

In Europe we traveled to Bosnia for briefings on the search for war criminals, which I hoped would also encourage the people on the ground to energize their own efforts. We visited the special operations forces of Lithuania and Poland, who had been active in Iraq, and we finally got to Paris for meetings with the French special forces. Of course, the most extensive American political and military relations are with the UK. In terms of public posture the two nations were often speaking from the same page. At the same time the British privately were also the most willing to question or criticize both policy and operations. This was true in the world of special operations as well, and it was worthwhile.

***

The assignment to SOCOM turned out to be a very positive experience for our family. When Ginger and Charles and I made the decision to proceed with the interview process for SOCOM, our situation had changed in two important ways from when I sought that one-year unaccompanied assignment to Bosnia. My father's Alzheimer's had moved into another stage, and Charles was going into his senior year of high school.

In 2002, my father had been going through what was probably the most difficult stage in the progression of his Alzheimer's disease. He was not just losing his memory. He was losing his personal orientation. He was still aware enough to recognize the pieces of his life, his children and grandchildren, our homes, his retirement home, and so forth. However, it was increasingly difficult for him to put them together. This was the period of his highest anxiety, when he was aware of how rapidly things were slipping away from him.

That was why in 2002 I first asked for a dispensation from the rule that required me to take an overseas assignment after six years in Washington. Sadly, at that time the Department of State was not prepared to grant a dispensation for personal reasons. I was disappointed but not surprised. My father would have been the first to accept such a decision. In fact, I did not tell him I was asking for the exception, because he would not have agreed with it himself. In his mind the "needs of the Service" had to come first. Nevertheless, we did need to make arrangements to care for him at that time. The "unaccompanied" assignment to Bosnia fit. I went and met those "needs of the Service," and Ginger and Charles stayed in Virginia and took care of Dad. It was very difficult for Ginger. She had to look after one eighty-eight-year-old who was going through a terrifying process of losing control over life, and one sixteen-year-old who was initiating an equally terrifying effort to take control of life. But it was the best that we could do.

One year later, my father had passed the threshold of highest anxiety. In the fall of 2002, after an incident when he wandered away and got lost for several hours, he moved into the Alzheimer's wing of Goodwin House West. He still recognized his family when we visited. However, he was less aware of the time that elapsed when we were not there. Sometimes he could not remember that a family member had visited only minutes earlier. At other times, he believed that he had visited with someone recently whom he had not seen for years. But he was far less emotionally disturbed. He was no longer disoriented. He just was not oriented.

***

Charles, our son, was another matter. Senior year is critical. It is college application time. It makes the single most important contribution to where one will spend the next four years, and that influences the rest of one's life. Ginger and I wanted the best possible assistance for Charles during this time. Senior year is also the end of high school—the end of childhood—and the last year with friends who have defined much of that childhood. Charles wanted to stay with those friends. When I called and asked whether I should proceed with the interview, Charles said yes. It sounded reasonable. A little later, when I was accepted, the idea of moving began to sound much less reasonable to him.

Since I was still in Bosnia and would not return until late June, much of the preparation for the move fell to Ginger and Charles—as is all too often the case in Foreign Service life. The first thing the two of them did was to fly down to Tampa to visit schools and find a place to live. They worked well together. In four days they looked carefully at the schools available. Charles had attended public schools since first grade, and both he and Ginger had a strong preference for public schools. However, they chose a private school for a variety of reasons and submitted an application which was accepted shortly thereafter. Helped by Ginger's sister, who had flown in from Seattle two days earlier, they also went through the Tampa real estate market with a fine-tooth comb. They boiled the choice down to two, which they presented to me over the phone. I made my choice, and they then did everything else. All I had to do was get back in time for closing in late June.

When I did get back, Charles was having serious second thoughts. He didn't want to move. He didn't want to leave his friends. He proposed finding a place to live in Arlington with a friend and staying put when we moved to Florida. We spent a long time talking about alternatives and the pros and cons—and even found two friends from our St. John's congregation who offered to adopt him for a year—but eventually he decided it would be best to move with us. We moved down in July, took some vacation, and then he moved into Berkeley Preparatory School.

As things turned out the combination of mostly public school and then senior year at a very good private school was perfect. His senior year classes were challenging, and they strengthened the interest in environmental studies that he would later carry to graduate school. He got excellent counseling on college applications and was accepted into the College of William and Mary—back to Virginia. One benefit we did not expect, however, was the boost that it gave to his music. Charles had a natural talent for the piano and had taken lessons since he was five years old. He had an excellent teacher who gave him a strong classical foundation and challenged him to take part in a variety of competitions. However, this music had little connection with friends and school. His public secondary school encouraged band, orchestra, and chorus but would not allow individual performances. There was rarely any opportunity to play the piano. He took up a whole range of percussion instruments to participate in the orchestra. In Florida we could not find a teacher who could help him as much, but Berkeley Preparatory School provided him with a stage. He played accompaniment for the school's musicals, and he recorded his first CD in its studio. Then, for the spring talent show he played the third movement (the spectacular one) of Beethoven's *Moonlight Sonata*—which he had taught himself—for the entire school and parents. The reception was very heartwarming, and it marked a big jump to maturity that would have been more difficult had he not been forced by the Foreign Service to make that move away from things more comfortable and familiar. Several years later in graduate school at Duke University he went on to start a band and produce a second CD of his own songs.

***

Ginger also made the most of our time in Tampa by becoming involved with the communities both on and off the base.

The military for the most part has a hierarchical and regimented command structure. This is necessary for battle and useful for managing an extensive organization with lots of people. The military also applies it to families. We were familiar with this at embassies, where the military attaches maintained a heavy social schedule in which the spouses were deeply involved. At SOCOM there was an active group of spouses of the general officers. It was led by the spouse of the commanding general, met regularly, and engaged in a variety of social and community support activities.

Foreign Service families are of course incorporated into missions overseas, but today this is almost entirely voluntary—in application as well as policy. In my father's time Foreign Service spouses were in many ways unpaid employees of the ambassador's spouse, or of other spouses in the hierarchy. They met regularly, and depending on the character and interests of the senior individual, they were directed in representational activities and given assignments. Until the 1960s every Foreign Service officer's efficiency report included a report on his spouse[10] (which my father claimed helped his own career enormously). Since then the trend has favored more freedom and moved inexorably away from any kind of required participation. Foreign Service spouses as a whole are very supportive of the missions to which they as family members are sent. However, it seemed to Ginger that the military spouses she knew at SOCOM were more willing to put aside their own personal freedom and ambitions to that end.

At SOCOM, Ginger chose to participate wholeheartedly in the military spouses' group. She tried to attend all the meetings and take part in the group's activities on and beyond the base. By so doing she learned a great deal about military life, and she developed a deeper understanding of what it took for the women to support their husbands and the command in spite of frequent absences—often made more difficult by the secrecy surrounding their deployments. The Special Operations community is very tightly knit, in many ways like a large family, and colleagues and families supported each other. However, Ginger still talks with some amusement about the way SOCOM would prepare plans to evacuate the command—but not the families—from the Tampa area in the face of incoming hurricanes. The rationale was to maintain the command's communications integrity rather than to protect the safety of individuals—which was rarely in danger; but the image of generals flying off to safety while their wives and children remained behind to face the storm was a little odd. She found it amusing but also poignant, because it also reminded her of the anxiety she felt during the evacuation from Burma. In that case, she and Charles were leaving while I stayed in the danger zone, but they were going to a place they didn't know. Happily, while we were in Tampa, this was never more than an image since no evacuation actually took place.

On base Ginger also volunteered at the charity thrift shop and at the elementary school that served the entire base (which included the Central Command and the Sixth Air Mobility Wing). There she tutored second-grade special-needs students in math. Working with the children also brought home to her the stresses placed on the families and communities by deployments. She was heartbroken when one of her students (not from SOCOM) told her that both his parents were being deployed, and he was going to live with a friend's family. A very young boy was going to be deprived of both of his parents for months—at least.

The fact that this was being done in the name of national security and patriotism did not justify it in her eyes. In Rangoon and in Chengdu, she had spent a good deal of time visiting and helping orphanages to which children had been abandoned because they were physically or mentally handicapped and their families could not afford to care for them. She recognized that societies throughout history have sacrificed the well-being of their children when economic conditions forced them to. However, after returning from Burma and China, which were truly struggling economically, to America, the wealthiest country on earth, it was particularly distressing for her to watch many families still consign their children—of all ages—to the daily care of others. In America it was much harder to see this as economic necessity instead of personal choice.

Off the base, Ginger also got involved with our neighborhood garden club and community groups. In particular she signed up for the Life Path Hospice and Palliative Care training given by the local chapter of hospice, the nation-wide movement that helps relieve the suffering of those affected by life-limiting illnesses and end-of-life issues. After her training she became a hospice volunteer, and she has continued that work since we returned to Virginia.

***

From Tampa we were able to visit my father every other week, but even that was not quite enough.

When my mother died in 1996, I was representing the United States at a meeting with the European Union (EU) in Brussels to discuss and coordinate policy toward Eastern Europe. When word came through, I returned to Florida to handle funeral arrangements and begin moving my father up to our house in Virginia.

When my father died, I was in South Africa. Before I left Tampa, I knew he was ailing, but he had previously defied repeated predictions of his demise. I thought I needed to do my job accompanying SOCOM commander General Brown on a trip to a number of sensitive countries in Africa and the Middle East. I was awakened at 2 a.m. on the day we arrived in Cape Town and told to call home. It had taken Ginger four hours to get that message through to me. When I could not get through to her, I called back to my father's room and the nurse put the telephone up to his ear. He could not talk, but he listened. I explained where I was, and I told him all his family were well taken care of, that we loved him, and that he could go with no regrets or worries about us. He died peacefully ten minutes later.

The Foreign Service was his life. He understood, accepted, and even valued the personal sacrifice—including family hardship—which it required. He could always put the "needs of the Service" and the needs of the country above any personal suffering. If he was concerned or confused about our inability to be with him at any time, the one thing that would restore his equanimity was to be told that I was away on assignment. That was clear and sufficient and would put him at ease.

The next morning, General Brown agreed that I needed to return. I split off from his party, which was continuing on to East Africa and the Middle East. The consulate helped me get a ticket back to Washington, and I returned to say good-bye to my father for the last time, meet with my sisters, and together arrange his cremation, funeral, and the burial of his ashes with our mother in Florida.

***

I hope it is clear from this account that I had and continue to have the highest regard for our special operations forces and their leadership. This does not mean, however, that I agreed with the way we as a nation addressed the terrorist threat. I was one of many who believed that it was a mistake to characterize the challenge as a war and to use the term "War on Terror." For one thing, it gave too much dignity to the terrorists—making them antagonists with equal status rather than criminals who were perpetuating crimes against humanity. That also led to problems when the status of prisoners of war was raised. The United States became the world's most obvious violator of long-established international rules on the treatment of prisoners, of basic human rights principles that it had made a primary foreign policy issue, and of its own laws and Constitution. We set up a prison camp (Guantanamo) on a corner of another country's territory (Cuba), and for a while we even denied access to the International Red Cross.

The most powerful nation in the world, instead of setting an example and leading the world in support of collective security and principles of civilized behavior, declared in essence that its very existence was at stake and justified the use of unrestrained unilateral power in violation of whatever principles it considered necessary.

Was that really necessary? It was declared necessary because the United States had zero tolerance for any more casualties on its own soil. It could not accept the slightest possibility of another successful attack like that of 9/11. On the one hand it seemed a necessary attitude on the part of elected leaders responsible for the protection of the nation's citizens. It was entirely possible that another airline might be commandeered for such an attack. It was also possible that the attack could be made with a weapon of mass destruction— nuclear, biological, chemical, and so on. On the other hand, it committed the nation to act in ways that undermined its moral integrity. It weakened the country in the eyes of governments and peoples around the world whose goodwill we will need in the future. It weakened the country in the eyes of its own population, by undermining values that are essential to national consensus in the face of adversity.

It was a terrible dilemma. No one knew precisely what the threat was— not the White House, not the State Department, the CIA, or the Defense Department. They only knew what the threats might be, and the president chose the most extreme form of reply: a declaration of war. Besides elevating the status of the terrorists and compromising our own principles and laws, this decision also pushed the Department of Defense and the nation's military-industrial interests to the forefront of the nation's foreign and domestic policy–making process. The Department of State was elbowed aside—even though the president had placed it under the leadership of the nation's most highly respected military leader. All of this was aggravated by a political system that in time of crisis tends to reward demagoguery, posturing, and extremism and to discourage careful deliberation and consideration of the consequences of different courses of action. This will not serve us well in the future.

NOTES

1. When SOCOM was initially created, the Marine Corps resisted inclusion. As the War on Terror progressed, however, the Marine Corps reconsidered and began posting a one-star general to SOCOM. In 2006 the Marine Corps created its own special operations unit, Marine Corps Forces Special Operations Command (MARSOC), directed by SOCOM.
2. At that time these area commanders were called commanders in chief (CINCs).
3. Also known as the MLN (Movimiento de Liberación Nacional).
4. I'm not sure if that included Vietnam.
5. An AID employee, Dan Mitrione, was kidnapped and executed in 1970. The embassy's agricultural attaché, Claude Fly, was kidnapped and released only after he suffered a heart attack. A junior FSO, Gordon Jones, actually escaped from his captors.
6. Ambassador Jackson wrote several books about his experience, including *Surviving the Long Night*.
7. The Clinton administration created a new position of national coordinator for security, infrastructure protection, and counterterrorism and included it in the National Security Council's "Principal's Committee," a cabinet-level body. Richard Clarke was the first coordinator.
8. The American Foreign Service Association is a professional association directed at maintaining the standards of professional diplomacy in the United States. It is also the exclusive representative of Foreign Service personnel in the departments of State, Agriculture, Commerce, and USAID to the management of those agencies.
9. In fact, there are relatively few opportunities for American diplomats—who represent their country to governments and peoples around the world—to travel in their own country, other than on vacation at their own expense. There was one exception for a while in the form of a seminar provided to some FSOs reaching the senior policy-making levels of the Service. The Senior Seminar was created to "reintroduce" senior American diplomats, who had spent most of their time overseas, to their own nation. They spent a year—with colleagues from the military and other foreign affairs agencies—studying American political, economic, and cultural issues, and traveling to meet with political, community, and business leaders around the country. It functioned for several decades but was abolished recently due to lack of funds.
10. The spouses were only females. By the time married women were accepted into the Foreign Service, the practice of including spouses in efficiency reports had been abolished.

Coda

Out to Pasture

Six months after my father died my tour with SOCOM ended, and Ginger and I returned to Arlington. I took a job with the Office of the Inspector General managing inspections of our overseas posts, but I did no more traveling myself. A year later I retired from the Foreign Service with exactly the same years of service as my father.

He would have been pleased by that. He might have been disappointed that I was never appointed ambassador myself. Most Foreign Service officers would like to serve as ambassador. It is a symbol of having reached the top of the diplomatic profession, it is one of the premier opportunities to serve one's country, and it is fascinating work. Actually receiving such an appointment is a combination of one's performance, politics, luck, and the path one chooses for oneself (not necessarily in that order). When I completed my assignment as deputy assistant secretary for European affairs in the late 1990s, I was offered the possibility of two separate ambassadorial assignments. However, neither place had a school for my son, and I asked that my name be withdrawn from consideration.

My father believed that Foreign Service officers should always accept their assignments with no questions asked, and adapt. I believed that too, with important exceptions. The first was if I believed what we were doing in a particular place was wrong and I would not be able to change it. The second was if it would cause my family undue hardship. My decision not to pursue the possibility of an ambassadorial appointment when I had the chance in the late 1990s was not a difficult one for me. My father might not have agreed with that decision, but during his last assignment, he did tell my sister Carol that he regretted not having spent more time with his family. I believed Charles's education was more important than any opportunity to serve as an ambassador, and I also thought he was too young at that time to send to boarding school. Although Charles himself at one point urged me to take one of the assignments, saying I could tutor him, I had seen from my father's experience that ambassadorial responsibilities were extensive and unpredictable. I was proud of my father's position and his accomplishments. However, when he became an ambassador I was already in high school and did not need—or seek—much attention from him. When it was time to make my decision, Charles was just going into sixth grade. I knew there was a very good chance that I would not be able to spend the extra time necessary to tutor him, and it was not worth taking that risk.

When I was a young boy, I was uncomfortable with many aspects of Foreign Service life. There are many things that we can adapt to; and the process of doing so is educational and good for us. The sometimes unavoidable shortage of parental attention resulting from the demands of work or social obligation, however, is more difficult to turn to the good. I initially vowed that I would never choose that life. When I eventually did choose it, I vowed to do it differently, at least in that regard. I tried to keep that vow. Later, I found some vindication reading the words of Confucius—written some twenty-five hundred years earlier:

> The ancients who wished to illustrate virtue to all those under heaven, first ordered their own states; wishing to order well their states, *they first regulated (completed) their families.* [1]

***

Three generations of my family spent a great deal of time and effort overseas trying to make the world a better place. Each generation worked on different things and sacrificed in different ways. Did those efforts make a difference? Were they worth whatever sacrifices were made by the individuals or the families?

My grandfather, Hugh Marshall, played a role in one of the most formative peace conferences of all time, the Paris Peace Conference after World War I. He was sent by the Department of State to work on financial issues related to China. The most important issue to China at that conference was the status of Germany's Shandong concession in China. China hoped that the Allied Powers would return that concession to China. It was devastated when the conference gave Germany's holdings to Japan, reinforcing the position of what was becoming the most aggressive foreign power in the region. [2] I don't know exactly what my grandfather's role there was. He was a professional banker, but he had been doing his wartime service in Washington, first helping to organize the War Savings Stamps program and then working in the

State Department's Division of Far Eastern Affairs. In addition to the political issue of Shandong, there were important debt-financing issues considered in and around the Paris Peace Conference—and there was a division of opinion in American policy circles about how to address them. The large American banks were making a big push to break into the international banking consortium that controlled lending to China. To do that they had to pressure or win over the Europeans and Japanese who controlled the consortium. They were often at odds with President Wilson and his Department of State, who wanted to promote Chinese development and American influence in China. In the end, the large banking interests seem to have prevailed, and Japan came away from the conference with both political and economic benefits. My grandfather was a banker, but having been sent by State's Far Eastern Division, I assume he was working for the government's position. I like to think that even if he and his colleagues did not fully succeed, they at least mitigated the result. Perhaps their efforts helped make possible the Washington Naval Treaty three years later, which finally did return Shandong to China. His future wife's contribution was perhaps more obvious. The hospital ward established and managed by Adelaide Porter in Europe helped a lot of wounded American soldiers cope with their physical and psychological wounds. That contributed to them, to their families, and to the communities which welcomed those soldiers back at the end of World War I.

My father's contribution is easier to assess. He played a role in the construction of the General Agreement on Tariffs and Trade (GATT), which is now the World Trade Organization (WTO). Its rules and dispute management mechanisms seem to have served the world well over the last half century. He was instrumental in establishing a major role for the United States in the Organisation for Economic Co-operation and Development (OECD), which has successfully promoted market economics and democracy throughout Europe and beyond. He initiated the negotiations that restored sovereignty over the Panama Canal to the Panamanians. The canal seems to be operating at least as well now as before, and Panama has benefited economically. He held the embassy community in Montevideo together during very difficult times. He held the line on the U.S. government's policy of not negotiating with terrorists, but I think he also moderated some of the more extreme voices in the U.S. government who advocated more pressure on the Uruguayan government or even unilateral measures. I have seen no evidence for some of the allegations that the embassy advocated or trained Uruguayan police in the use of torture, and I don't believe we did it. I am confident that my father would have opposed that approach.

The results of my contributions will have to be judged in the future. I chose a diplomatic career for the opportunity to learn from other cultures, and because I believed that diplomacy was one of the best ways to promote commerce and cooperation between people—without war. In Africa, I did some useful reporting and learned things that later made me a more effective mediator between ambassadors and generals working to counter international terrorism in that region. In China, I played a small role in helping to build a constructive relationship between the two countries that are now likely to determine the course of the twenty-first century. After I left Chengdu I received a communication sharing with me a message from a very senior official in Beijing that expressed appreciation that my time in Chengdu had contributed to a more peaceful period in Tibet and in Chinese-American relations. In Washington (not covered in this book), I did my part to promote stability in the eastern Mediterranean and reform in Eastern European countries, and as president of the American Foreign Service Association I at least tried to generate more support for the Foreign Service and professional diplomacy. Who knows, perhaps someday that proposal on removal of land mines in Bosnia may even take root.

Throughout my career, I usually avoided engaging with issues that were already the center of attention. I tried to look for what was not being done—what was missing—and tried to fill the gap or correct the course. That can be helpful or dangerous. It can be helpful because if everybody just heads down the same road together at once without looking to the side or assessing the consequences, at a minimum we will miss a lot of other things that could create obstacles later on. It can be problematic for one's career, because being at odds with conventional wisdom can be irritating to others. It can be dangerous because rarely are we individuals well informed and wise enough to understand the future impact of our actions. If my frustrated comments about the situation in Bosnia to a senior U.S. government official in 2003 had even the slightest influence on the course we took in Iraq, then I may face a serious reckoning in the future.

Were the sacrifices that we made worth it for my family? If I had been more astute and discerning, I might have managed to be with my parents when they died. Although I made some obvious choices in favor of my family, I also know that I shortchanged both my wife and son in terms of time and attention. Those things are hard to repair. However, not long after my son Charles finished graduate school and got his first job managing an environmental organization in North Carolina, he telephoned to talk about the changes in his life and the challenges of his new job. We talked for almost two hours. After I hung up, I realized that was not something that ever happened between me and my father, and I was grateful. He is strong, balanced, and has a dependable moral compass. The fourth generation will certainly make a contribution, and Ginger and I have fulfilled the family obligation part of Confucius's social cosmology. Ginger too has made the most of our experiences together and applied it here at home. Since our retirement, she has added a four-year study of Christian theology with the Episcopal Church to what she learned from her Buddhist studies in China and is using both in her volunteer work with hospice and Arlington County's programs for seniors. It's also an interesting coincidence that she did it through the University of the South at Sewanee, Tennessee, where one of my favorite teachers in high school had tried to convince me to apply.

If I had it all to do over again, with the knowledge I have now, I would certainly do a number of things differently in the Foreign Service—but I don't think I would do something different than the Foreign Service.

***

We do the best we can, and individuals can make a noticeable difference. I saw that in both Hong Kong and Bosnia. We have to exercise whatever influence or power that we have to do good—but, of course, it is so difficult to know at any given time what course will ultimately turn out to be "good." It is not always as obvious as we may think.

There is a wonderful Chinese story about how confusing fortune may be. It is called "an old man from the border loses a horse" (塞翁失馬) – sai weng shi ma. It goes something like this:

> A peasant lived in a village with his wife and son. Their one possession was an old horse that helped them work their fields. One day the horse died suddenly. The other villagers came and expressed condolences for their terrible misfortune, but the peasant replied, "Who knows—maybe bad, maybe good." A few days later, the peasant, went into the forest to chop wood. To his surprise, he came upon a beautiful large horse that was lost, and he led the horse back to his house. The villagers came again, this time to celebrate the peasant's incredible good fortune. The peasant replied, "Who knows—maybe good, maybe bad." A week later, the peasant's son fell off the horse and broke his leg badly. The villagers came to express their condolences, and the peasant made the same reply, "Who knows—maybe bad, maybe good." Shortly thereafter, the army arrived in the village and conscripted every able-bodied young man for service in the war then raging on the frontier. The peasant's son was not taken, because he was crippled with a broken leg. The villagers came again, and . . .

Most of us cannot predict our future or judge our fortune. Similarly, most of us cannot be sure that the work we do today—for whatever cause—will benefit or harm those who come after us. We can only do our best, and who knows—maybe good, maybe bad. We shall see.

***

At my graduation from Middlebury College in 1970, the commencement speaker, Senator George Aiken, finished his address by saying that he had devoted most of his life to the service of his country, and now he planned to retire and tend his garden. My father went up to him afterward, thanked him for his wisdom, and declared that was what he intended to do too. Senator Aiken retired in Vermont. My parents went to Florida—where their garden was regularly visited by alligators and manatees.

Ginger and I began spending more time in New Hampshire, where our visitors are moose, bear, and fox. The seasons come and go here with a reliability and reassurance that is less noticeable when one is living in the city or jetting regularly between different climate zones. The lives and patterns of the animals are pretty predictable, except when they are disrupted by us humans. When we returned several months early last spring we received a severe scolding for several days from a fox whose den was a few yards from our back door. She knew us, but she was not expecting us at that time of year, and she had a new family. She adjusted to our return, and for the next several months we watched her feed and train her six kits. One evening in October we watched her take them all out on patrol, but only she came back, leaving her carefully trained offspring to begin lives on their own. This year she started all over again, just a few yards farther down the hill. It seems like things don't change very much.

One evening Ginger and I were sitting on our front porch looking out over the Presidential range of the White Mountains. "How many presidents did you work for?" she asked. I calculated a minute, and then replied, "Seven: Nixon, Ford, Carter, Reagan, Bush 1, Clinton, and Bush 2." She then asked, "That's the presidential range out there, right? How many presidents do you see?" "Well, there's Lincoln, Garfield, Monroe, Washington, Jefferson, Adams, and Madison—seven." "Hmm, you came all this way thinking that you could get away, and you're still under seven presidents. It seems like not much has changed."

Well, perhaps not very much. Not only are we still looking up at all those presidents, but maybe the ones we are now living under and the ones we were working under aren't so different, either. Most of them had at least one war during their respective terms of office. They fought similar domestic political battles and were respected and reviled by different parts of the electorate. They struggled to protect their nations from internal and external dangers. They tried to promote prosperity for their nation and its people—immigrants then and immigrants now. In those ways, between the end of the eighteenth century and the beginning of the twenty-first century, it seems like not much has changed.

We have, however, become more populous, more wealthy, and more powerful. We have used our power to reach out and touch virtually every part of the planet, affecting the lives of people, the stability of nations, and the health of the environment—to the depths of the oceans and the highest reaches of the stratosphere. We would all like to think that the impact of our culture and our nation has been benevolent, and some of it has been. The

American people have often been generous. But power is dangerous, and the influence we have exercised, the wars we have waged, the economic activity we have stimulated and the inventions we have created have also hurt many people, undermined cultures, and damaged the planet itself. Shortly before his death in 1826, John Adams, the second president of the United States, issued a statement in which he said the United States was "destined in future history to form *the brightest or the blackest page*, according to the use or the abuse of those political institutions by which they shall, in time to come, be shaped by the human mind." We need to be more mindful of the potential of that "blackest page."

I have spent my career and my life watching other cultures "from horseback." By virtue of having spent my whole life in this peripatetic diplomatic continuum, I have also watched my own culture "from horseback." It seems that we have paid far less attention than we should to that shaping of the human mind to which John Adams referred. Our educational system is confused, inconsistent, and persistently underfunded. Our intellectual traditions and standards are often inadequate, and our cultural and moral foundations are shaky.

This American culture is young and still undeveloped. The nation looks proudly back to the Declaration of Independence for the core of our political philosophy: "We hold these truths to be self-evident, that all men are created equal, that they are endowed by their Creator with certain unalienable Rights, that among these are Life, Liberty and the pursuit of Happiness." It mentions nothing of mankind's mutual responsibilities and obligations to each other and to the place in which we live. In a way this seems to leap right out of the story of the Garden of Eden, where man and woman were given both freedom and responsibility. They chose the first and disregarded the latter with rather terrible consequences. The French Revolution, slightly later than ours, rather nastier and grafted on to older root stock, adopted "Liberty, equality, fraternity," which at least nominally recognizes that element of responsibility.

The word choice of those who declared independence from Great Britain in 1776, while wonderfully inspiring, perhaps set our nation on a narrower and less sustainable track. Among those three inalienable rights, Liberty has taken first place, and most schoolchildren are familiar with Thomas Paine's famous challenge, "Give me liberty or give me death." The pursuit of Happiness is a very close second place. It's a wonderful concept, much better than Thomas Jefferson's original phrase, "Life, Liberty and Property,"[3] though in practice Happiness seems increasingly to be defined by how much Property one is able to accumulate. The emphasis on freedom has stimulated tremendous energy to develop new ideas and technologies, which have in turn driven remarkable economic expansion. But those ideas and technologies often have terrible dangers as well, damaging our environment and threatening our very existence.

China historically produced some of the world's most significant scientific discoveries and inventions, such as silk, paper, the printing press, gunpowder, and so on. Joseph Needham, a British scientist, wrote a multivolume history of those accomplishments—and he wondered what had caused Chinese civilization to stop those discoveries and fall behind the West. A Chinese philosopher and historian once told me that successive Chinese emperors made the conscious decision to discourage technological development, because they believed that it tempted the population to become more materialistic and selfish and undermined the moral foundations of personal, social, and political life.

At the very beginning of the *Works of Mencius* (who was the most influential Confucian teacher after Confucius), written in the third or fourth century BC, there is a dialogue between Mencius and King Hûi of Liang. In it the King asks Mencius for counsel that may profit his kingdom. Mencius turns his question and replies that if a kingdom focuses primarily on profit it will establish a dynamic wherein the state will be endangered by the greed of some of its own citizens. Those with less will be driven to seize power and riches from those with more, and until they have taken all they will not be satisfied.[4] This dialogue from twenty-five hundred years ago makes a lot of sense to me. Our country recently went through a period of rather phenomenal growth in wealth. At first, it seemed that everyone was profiting—"a rising tide raises all boats"—but we got carried away by greed. Wall Street was leading the charge. It was sanctioned by the desire of the general populace to share in the spoils, and the philosophy that by giving those doing business as much freedom and as little regulation as possible all will benefit. That turned out to be wrong. A few people benefited enormously—they succeeded in snatching at least most of it (and are still not satisfied)—while others suffered significantly. The nation has been seriously weakened financially and economically, it seems almost dysfunctional politically, and the international consequences have yet to make themselves clear.

The United States of America is now less than 250 years old. That is not very long compared to many European nations. It is about comparable to the average length of an individual Chinese dynasty, of which there have been close to twenty, and it is barely recognizable in cultural terms. If this nation is not to become a flash in the pan of history, we will need to temper our idolization of freedom with individual and social responsibility. We will need to give serious and extended attention to the moral foundations of the relationship between individuals and society. Because we are a nation of immigrants coming from different cultures and different spiritual traditions, we will need to do so in a way that draws upon those cultures and traditions without being driven by their emotions or restrained by their dogma. It is a challenge far more difficult than just the preservation of Liberty. The rewards would be far greater than the accumulation of property, and might even help realize that elusive pursuit of Happiness.

NOTES

1. From *The Great Learning*: 故之欲明明德於天下者，先治其國，欲治其國者，先齊其家.

2. The conference's decision led directly to the May Fourth movement, a series of spontaneous demonstrations that politicized and strengthened the challenge to traditional Chinese cultural values which had been gaining steam since the collapse of the Qing Dynasty. It has since become a prominent historical example of Chinese nationalism and a popular reminder of China's humiliation at the hands of foreigners.

3. The change was suggested by Benjamin Franklin.

4. *Works of Mencius*, book I, chapter 1, verse 4: "If righteousness is put last and profit is put first, until they seize it (all) they will not be satisfied." (苟為後義而先利,不奪不饜)

Index

About the Author

Marshall P. Adair is an independent consultant on international relations, specializing in China and Europe. He retired as a Minister-Counselor in the Senior Foreign Service in September 2007. He lives in Arlington, VA, and Sugar Hill, NH.